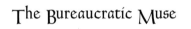

The Bureaucratic Muse

the
pennsylvania
state
university
press

university
park,
pennsylvania

The Bureaucratic Muse

THOMAS HOCCLEVE

AND THE

LITERATURE

OF

LATE MEDIEVAL

ENGLAND

ethan Knapp

PR1992.H47 Z68 2001

Library of Congress Cataloging-in-Publication Data

Knapp, Ethan, 1966–
    The bureaucratic muse : Thomas Hoccleve and the literature of late medieval
England / Ethan Knapp.
        p.   cm.
    Includes bibliographical references and index.
    ISBN 0-271-02135-7 (alk. paper)
        1. Hoccleve, Thomas, 1370?–1450?—Criticism and interpretation.   2. Literature
and society—England—History—To 1500.   3. Great Britain, Privy Council—
History—To 1500.   4. Bureaucracy—Great Britain—History—To 1500.
5. Scriptoria—England— History—To 1500.   6. Civilization, Medieval, in literature.
I. Title.

PR1992.H47 Z68   2001
821'.2—dc21   2001021460

To my parents,
Hugh and Elinor Knapp

Contents

Acknowledgments

It is a great pleasure to be able to thank publicly all those who have supported this project. First, I would like to thank David Aers, Sarah Beckwith, Fredric Jameson, Leigh DeNeef, and Lee Patterson, generous readers, good friends, and intellectual models for many years now; it has been a delight to renew conversations with each of them so many times over the past years. At Ohio State University, I have had the good fortune to work among a group of dedicated and skilled medievalists. Nick Howe, Lisa Kiser, Karen Winstead, and Chris Zacher have been ideal intellectual comrades; each has unstintingly volunteered careful readings of this manuscript, and each has added a measure of their own insight and expertise to this book. My students at Ohio State have also been a constant source of new questions and new ideas, and I thank them here for their energetic engagement with our common work.

For invitations to present parts of this book, I am grateful to Tony Hasler, Fiona Somerset, Jennifer Summit, Maura Nolan, Kellie Robertson, and Catherine Batt. I appreciate also the many insightful questions and comments offered at these occasions, most especially a lively afternoon session at the Notre Dame Medieval Institute. Charles Blyth, Jacqueline Brown, Chris Chism, Roger Ellis, Judith Ferster, James Phelan, Malcolm Richardson, Larry Scanlon, Paul Strohm, Jennifer Summit, and Nicholas Watson have all given palpable aid to this book—sharing work in progress, reading portions of the manuscript, and offering comments that helped shape the book in important ways. David Lawton and Derek Pearsall read the manuscript for Penn State University Press, and both took the time to offer gracious and challenging readings, saving me from many errors in the process. Patricia DeMarco has helped me through every idea and read every word in this text; she is my chief collaborator. Finally, though we have never met, I would also like to thank John Burrow, whose groundbreaking essays on Hoccleve encouraged me to believe that he was a poet worth spending time with.

My research was supported by several grants from the Ohio State University. A Seed Grant from the Office of Research provided for a quarter release from teaching in fall 1998. A Grant-in-Aid from the College of Humanities funded travel to British libraries and archives in the summer of 2000, and a special research assignment and probationary faculty development quarter allowed me to devote the winter of 1997 and fall of 1999 to research and writing. A grant from the Center for Medieval and Renaissance Studies at Ohio State helped defray additional costs associated with the research for this volume. I am grateful also to the staff at the Ohio State University Libraries, whom I have not yet been able to stump with any request.

I have been exceptionally lucky in the support of friends and family throughout this labor. My parents, Hugh and Elinor Knapp, are the foundations of this work, and it is dedicated to them.

Earlier versions of Chapters 1 and 4 appeared in *Speculum* 74 (1999): 357–76 and in *Studies in the Age of Chaucer* 21 (1999): 247–74. Revised versions appear here by kind permission of the editors. Last, I would like to thank Peter Potter and the editorial staff at Penn State University Press for encouraging and skillfully fostering this text.

The search for descent is not the erecting of foundations: on the contrary, it disturbs what was previously considered immobile; it fragments what was thought unified; it shows the heterogeneity of what was imagined consistent with itself.
—Michel Foucault, "Nietzsche, Genealogy, History," 1977

Introduction

This book explores the writing of the poet Thomas Hoccleve and the early fifteenth-century bureaucratic culture that shaped that writing. The past decade has produced a stunning shift in the relative importance granted to the political and religious developments of the early fifteenth century. Once generally dismissed as an age of plodding didacticism and Chaucerian mimicry, the fifteenth century now appears as a period of momentous cultural development. In a critical climate suspicious of any hint of a teleological historicism, it may seem foolhardy to suggest a privileged relation between this moment and our own modernity. Nevertheless, much current scholarship is marked by a sense of urgent connection to various topoi of the period—vernacularity, the centrifugal force of state power, textual dissemination—in short, an almost neo-Tudor sense that it is not the glories of the Ricardian court but the existential trials of the Lancastrians that most speak to our present.

The bulk of this reevaluation has come about through the study of two related topics: Lollardy and the Lancastrian regime itself. Recent work on Wycliffite theology has been ex-

2

The Bureaucratic Muse

emplary in its ability to rewrite the shifting boundaries and potentialities of vernacular literary expression in response to the pressures of a concrete social movement.[1] It should now be impossible to see the growth of English vernacular literature as a triumphant, even if delayed, ascent from Ricardian experiment to Elizabethan Renaissance. Rather, it is a history marked by radical discontinuities and by the contrary pressures created by an association between vernacular textuality and religious heterodoxy. The history of state power and of its representations in literary culture has been similarly transformed. Older treatments of the connections between the literature and politics of the early fifteenth century had tended to emphasize either the reflection of political reality in the poetry of the period or the Lancastrian use of history and chronicle as tools of propaganda.[2] More recent work, however, has attempted to trace out the complex mutual penetration of text and history in Lancastrian statecraft, suggesting that the Lancastrians were not only innovators in their use of literary propaganda but were also powerfully aware of the textual basis of power and authority itself.[3]

To these twin avenues of interpretation, Lollardy and the Lancastrians, I would add a crucial third term: bureaucracy.[4] It is the argument of this book that substantial portions of the literary culture of the early fifteenth century, including many of those most important to our own cultural preoccupations, cannot be adequately understood except as products of an emerging lay bu-

1. Among others, see David Aers and Lynn Staley, *The Powers of the Holy: Religion, Politics, and Gender in Late Medieval English Culture* (University Park: Penn State University Press, 1996); Sarah Beckwith, *Christ's Body: Identity, Culture, and Society in Late Medieval Writings* (London: Routledge, 1993); Fiona Somerset, *Clerical Discourse and Lay Audience in Late Medieval England* (Cambridge: Cambridge University Press, 1998); and Nicholas Watson, "Censorship and Cultural Change in Late-Medieval England: Vernacular Theology, the Oxford Translation Debate, and Arundel's Constitution of 1409," *Speculum* 70 (1995): 822–64.

2. For example, see C. J. Kingsford, *Prejudice and Promise in the Fifteenth Century* (1925; reprint, Oxford: Oxford University Press, 1962); and V. J. Scattergood, *Politics and Poetry in the Fifteenth Century* (London: Blandford Press, 1971).

3. Paul Strohm, *England's Empty Throne: Usurpation and the Language of Legitimation, 1399–1422* (New Haven: Yale University Press, 1998). See also Lee Patterson, "Making Identities in Fifteenth-Century England: Henry V and Lydgate," in *New Historical Literary Study*, ed. Jeffrey N. Cox and Larry J. Reynolds (Princeton: Princeton University Press, 1993), 69–107; and on textuality in the fifteenth century, Seth Lerer, *Chaucer and His Readers: Imagining the Author in Late-Medieval England* (Princeton: Princeton University Press, 1993).

4. Since the word *bureaucracy* has such unavoidably modern connotations, it is perhaps worth pointing out that the term derives from medieval French *burel*, the name of the official cloths that covered the tables where the work of administration took place, such as the green cloths at Westminster. The history of this term is discussed in R. A. Griffiths, "Public and Private Bureaucracies in England and Wales in the Fifteenth Century," *Transactions of the Royal Historical Society*, 5th ser., 30 (1980): 112.

reaucracy at Westminster. As an initial example of what may seem a large claim, let me briefly turn to an exemplary artifact of this culture, British Library MS Additional 24062. This large codex contains a collection of Privy Seal documents and letters dating mostly from the late fourteenth and early fifteenth centuries. It is usually referred to as Thomas Hoccleve's *Formulary*. At the top of the flyleaf, partly obscured by a stain, one can read an inscription giving both the name of the compiler and a period for the volume: "Tho. Hacclyf, clerk . . . pryve seal . . . temps Sir . . . Chaucer."[5] On the first folio of the table of contents, another hand has made a similar note: "Tho. Hackliff, clerke du pryve . . . en la temps Seignur Geoffray Chaucer." These inscriptions are in some ways obscure. First, they are difficult to date. The two are similar in style, both later than Hoccleve's period, and might be associated with the date 1558 found on the flyleaf. On the other hand, both the pragmatic content of later notations made by the first hand and the fact that these later notations are in French suggest that the first inscription, at least, may have been made by a reader with some practical rather than antiquarian interest in the volume and so may have been added at a relatively early date, when the volume was still in use as a formulary.[6] In addition to the problem of dating, it is also unclear whether the two inscriptions refer to the same Chaucer. The first is badly marred, but both the few remaining characters and the honorific "Sir" may suggest that this is a reference not to Geoffrey but to *Thomas* Chaucer. Such a possibility is tantalizing, as it would provide potential support for John Fisher's suggestion that a Lancastrian cabal made up of Hoccleve, Thomas Chaucer, and others was organized for the purpose of promoting Geoffrey Chaucer as a laureate poet.[7]

At whatever date these inscriptions were made, however, and whichever Chaucer is meant to be invoked, the inscriptions bear eloquent testimony to a system of cultural categorization very different from the schemes of classification within which a volume such as the *Formulary* is usually considered by modern scholars. We are so thoroughly conditioned to think of the late fourteenth and early fifteenth centuries as "Chaucerian" that it may at first seem unsurprising that this collection of bureaucratic documents is labeled and allotted a period not by the reign of a monarch but by the time of a poet

5. Elna-Jean Young Bentley, "The Formulary of Thomas Hoccleve" (Ph.D. diss., Emory University, 1965), xiv.

6. For these annotations, see Bentley, 13, 17, 20, 29, 40, 56, 61, 67, 87, 89, 104.

7. John Fisher, "A Language Policy for Lancastrian England," *PMLA* 107 (1992): 1168–80; reprinted in his collection, *The Emergence of Standard English* (Lexington: University of Kentucky Press, 1996).

(or of his influential son). But the collapse of these two cultural categories presents a challenge to our usual understanding of the distance between poetic genealogies and the bureaucratic archive.

Why should the name of a late fourteenth-century poet be used to date an early fifteenth-century collection of bureaucratic documents? Conceptually, "the time of Geoffrey Chaucer" has done good service in marking out introductory chapters of literary surveys, but it is hard to imagine the name being helpful for Privy Seal clerks trying to track down a proper model for addressing the Vatican. It is also peculiar in itself that the name of the compiler, Hoccleve, should be attached to such a collection of documents; the presence of the proper name here is an assertion of authorial identity out of place in a bureaucratic formulary, one more appropriate if the collection had been one of poetic material.[8] This distinctive use of both names, Chaucer and Hoccleve, must be read as testimony to a heretofore unrecognized degree of continuity between the bureaucratic labors and personnel in the central writing offices at Westminster and the cultural project of "Chaucerian poetry." Bureaucracy and literature are types of textual production that we have come to think of as utterly different. Literature, on the one hand, is the textual embodiment of aesthetic arrangement and interpretive activity; bureaucracy, on the other hand, is the home of the document, a zero-degree writing, denuded entirely of affect and subjectivity. But as these inscriptions suggest, such cultural worlds were not always imagined to be so distinct.

Literature and the Secular Clerk

The early fifteenth century was an important moment in the histories of both vernacular literature and bureaucratic institutions. In the literary field, these are the decades in which Chaucer's experiments in courtly English poetry were consolidated in the work of figures like Lydgate and the Scottish Chaucerians and turned into what we can now look back on as the self-conscious construction of a continuous tradition of English poetry.[9] In the history of bureaucratic structures, these same years witness three crucial developments: first, the continued separation of the central writing offices at

8. I discuss issues relating to the importance of the signature as a marker of authorial identity in Chapter 1.

9. For a standard literary historical account of this period, see Derek Pearsall, *Old English and Middle English Poetry* (London: Routledge and Kegan Paul, 1977).

Westminster away from the king's household (the transition usually thought to mark their emergence from the shadows of personal regal government into the full-blown modernity of an independent civil service); second, the linguistic transition from the use of French and Latin as the chief languages of governmental business to the adoption of English as an official language of state; and third, a growing degree of laicization among the staff of the central writing offices.[10] Part of my aim in this book is to bring these two histories together, to demonstrate that their historical confluence is not a coincidence but a reflection of the importance of lay bureaucrats, such as Hoccleve, in establishing not only the retrospective centrality of Chaucer's example but also many of our central categories of literary activity.

The expansion of bureaucratic institutions has always been a stimulus to the growth of literacy, and it must be one of the tasks of historical understanding to reweave the connection between bureaucratic and literary production. The paleographer Armando Petrucci has evoked this project in his call for an analysis of "the relationship between the scripts and culture of documentary production and the scripts and culture of books."[11] Like Petrucci, I would suggest that the connection between literature and bureaucracy is, at root, a technical one; documentary and poetic cultures must be considered jointly because for centuries they were construed as supplemental to each other, as two implicit alternatives within the techniques of literary culture. (One might think here of the durable opposition between book-hands and more cursive forms.) Unlike Petrucci, however, I emphasize not documentary culture but rather bureaucratic identity and practice as a way of calling attention to not only the technical but also the social dimensions of the relation between literature and bureaucracy.

There is, of course, a long history of bureaucratic involvement in the production of self-consciously literary texts. In the English tradition, the earliest literary bureaucrats tended to be ecclesiastical figures, such as the group Richard Firth Green has identified around the court of Henry II, which included Walter Map, Giraldus Cambrensis, Peter of Blois, Roger of Hoveden, and Richard of Ely. These figures differ from later bureaucrats, such as Hoccleve, in their comparative political importance and in that both the language—predominantly Latin—and the subject matter of their literary

---

10. A. L. Brown provides a very clear narrative of these developments in the relevant sections of his *The Governance of Late Medieval England, 1272–1461* (London: Edward Arnold, 1989).

11. "Literacy of Early Medieval Scribes," in Armando Petrucci, *Writers and Readers in Medieval Italy: Studies in the History of Written Culture*, trans. Charles M. Radding (New Haven: Yale University Press, 1995), 102.

efforts tie them more directly to the tradition of ecclesiastical learning than to the nascent vernacular. However, as Green suggests, even their use of Latin may testify to some degree of self-identification not just as courtiers or churchmen but also as members of a specifically bureaucratic cadre, a sense that they "wrote not for the amusement of a close-knit aristocratic circle surrounding the king, but for their own peers—the ecclesiastical aristocracy, as it were, that was attracted to the civil service."[12] Richard of Ely, also known as Richard FitzNeal, Henry II's treasurer for forty years, is an exemplary figure here. A close contemporary of John of Salisbury, he took as his literary subject none of the political or theological intricacies that so fascinated John and others at this moment but described instead the daily workings of his office, the Exchequer, in the *Dialogus de Scaccario*.

In the later Middle Ages we find numerous examples of literary figures who were deeply connected with the burgeoning administrative institutions of the time. As is consistent with a general laicization of administrative positions during this period, such figures tended to be either lay or in minor orders, and their literary language was most often vernacular. Indeed, the joint development of lay administrations and literary vernaculars seems to have been a widespread phenomenon in late fourteenth- and early fifteenth-century Europe. In England, we find Hoccleve, Thomas Usk, George Ashby, and Chaucer working in the central administrative bodies; numerous other figures, such as William Worcester, Stephen Scrope, John Trevisa, and John Walton, all held secretarial or administrative positions in provincial households. In France, Guillaume de Machaut, Christine de Pizan, and Alain Chartier all made use of techniques borrowed from documentary culture.[13] And in the Netherlands we see the rise of men like Dirk Potter, part of a group whom Frits Van Oostrom has described as "administrative technocrats" or, more specifically, "lay clerks who became increasingly indispensable as political advisors" and who reinforced this new importance through their literary efforts.[14]

The Dutch example is, in fact, particularly illuminating, because the brief flourishing of the Bavarian court at the Hague under Duke Albert and his son William VI (c. 1358–1433) offers a discrete example of the importance

12. Richard Firth Green, *Poets and Princepleasers: Literature and the English Court in the Later Middle Ages* (Toronto: University of Toronto, 1980), 102.

13. On Chartier's bureaucratic labors, see the introduction to J. C. Laidlaw, ed., *The Poetical Works of Alain Chartier* (Cambridge: Cambridge University Press, 1974), 6, 21.

14. Frits Pieter Van Oostrom, *Court and Culture: Dutch Literature, 1350–1450*, trans. Arnold J. Pomerans (Berkeley and Los Angeles: University of California Press, 1992), 275, 262.

of a bureaucratic class in the growth of centers of courtly culture. In Van Oostrom's account, the development of a vernacular literature particular to this court was made possible by three interconnected "political-administrative developments": (1) a large, stationary court, which provided a reliable audience and patronage for literary works and professional writers; (2) this court's requirement for a large staff of lettered clerks, which created a supply of scribes competent to produce manuscripts of these works; and (3) a nobility defining themselves through the German language and thus constituting themselves as a market for new work in that language. Unlike the idealizing self-representations of older courts, the rapid florescence of Duke Albert's court makes it clear that one of the most important stimuli to the development of a vernacular literature was the symbiotic relationship between an aristocratic community at court and the bureaucrats whose primary duty lay in the production of administrative documents but whose textual skills might easily be adapted to literary use. And this Dutch example was in no way isolated from other European courts. Jacqueline of Hainault became the wife of Humphrey of Gloucester, himself the patron of many literary endeavors and the object of at least the hopeful prospects of both Hoccleve and Ashby.[15] Across Europe, these were years crucial to the development of what we now look back on as the varied traditions of vernacular literature, years in which much of this literature "emerged in the shadow of a chancellor."[16]

The history of these bureaucratic writers extends also into the early modern period. Tudor history has been marked for the past forty years by debate circulating around G. R. Elton's thesis that the central innovation of Tudor government had been a revolution in the techniques of administration, a bureaucratic sea change in which the household government of the Yorkists was finally cast off and replaced by a modern depersonalized bureaucracy. These claims have, of course, been much modified since Elton's original work. The current picture of this chapter of bureaucratic history is closer to a view originally advanced by G. L. Harriss in response to Elton, namely that Tudor governmental practices displayed a certain affinity with the government of the late fourteenth and early fifteenth centuries.[17] In this account,

15. Lydgate wrote verses celebrating the marriage between Humphrey and "Jaque," on which see Strohm, *England's Empty Throne*, 192–95. A convenient account of this marriage can be found in H. S. Bennett, *Six Medieval Men and Women* (Cambridge: Cambridge University Press, 1955), 1–29.

16. Van Oostrom, *Court and Culture*, 9.

17. G. L. Harriss, "Medieval Government and Statecraft," *Past and Present* 25 (1963): 8–39. See also Christopher Coleman and David Starkey, eds., *Revolution Reassessed: Revisions in the History of Tudor Government and Administration* (Oxford: Oxford University Press, 1986).

the ambitious bureaucratic apparatus of the Lancastrian state had yielded to a brief restoration of household government under Edward IV and Henry VII, a backsliding against Weberian rationalization that in turn allowed Wolsey to reinvent systematized bureaucracy as an apparent innovation. Among Tudor poets it has traditionally been the figures of Skelton and Hawes whose reception has been most strongly marked by the context of this administrative history.[18] Recent work, however, has turned to bureaucratic contexts in considering even later figures such as Spenser. Richard Rambuss, for example, has articulated persistent connections between the thematization of the "secret" in Spenser's poetry and the social and rhetorical background of "the secretary," arguing that secrecy must be understood not just as a poetic device but also as a professionalized strategy for self-promotion, that "even as a poet, Spenser writes as a secretary."[19]

In arguing for a new emphasis on the bureaucratic culture of the early fifteenth century, this book is meant to be aligned with the work of a number of scholars who have begun piecing together this alternate scene of literary production. Steven Justice and Kathryn Kerby-Fulton have drawn attention to the significance of documentary culture and medieval bureaucrats both in Justice's important study of the Rising of 1381, *Writing and Rebellion*, and in a series of coauthored articles contributing much to a demonstration that "bureaucratic service in the English fourteenth and fifteenth centuries was a first home of the vernacular literary culture of Langland's and Chaucer's generation."[20] Similarly, Sheila Lindenbaum has argued that one of the most revealing dramas in the literary culture of late medieval London was a conflict between many Londoners, including the city's mercantile elite, and London's population of professional clerks, whose activities fell under the shadow first of a general suspicion of documentary culture around 1376 and

18. Lerer, *Chaucer and His Readers*, 176–208. On Skelton's position in court, see also Greg Walker, *John Skelton and the Politics of the 1520s* (Cambridge: Cambridge University Press, 1988), esp. 35–52.

19. Richard Rambuss, *Spenser's Secret Career* (Cambridge: Cambridge University Press, 1993), 28.

20. Steven Justice, *Writing and Rebellion: England in 1381* (Berkeley and Los Angeles: University of California Press, 1994); Kathryn Kerby-Fulton, "Langland and the Bibliographical Ego," in *Written Work: Langland, Labor, and Authorship*, ed. Steven Justice and Kathryn Kerby-Fulton (Philadelphia: University of Pennsylvania Press, 1997), 67–143; Kathryn Kerby-Fulton and Steven Justice, "Langlandian Reading Circles and the Civil Service in London and Dublin, 1380–1427," *New Medieval Literatures* 1 (1997): 59–83; Kathryn Kerby-Fulton and Steven Justice, "Reformist Intellectual Culture in the English and Irish Civil Service: The *Modus Tenendi Parliamentum* and Its Literary Relations," *Traditio* 53 (1998): 149–202; "Reading Circles," 59.

then the more active vendettas associated with 1381 itself.[21] In company with these arguments, this book aims to demonstrate the importance of bureaucratic identity and of the habits of scribal labor to at least one segment of the nascent vernacular literature of the Lancastrian period. I make this argument through a case study of the poet and Privy Seal clerk Thomas Hoccleve.

The Case of Thomas Hoccleve

This study of Hoccleve has two goals. The first is to establish a historical framework for thinking about Hoccleve as neither simply a "Chaucerian" figure nor as just the garrulous eccentric he is often thought to have been. The last book-length study of Hoccleve, Jerome Mitchell's *Thomas Hoccleve: A Study in Fifteenth-Century Poetic*, provided an argument for Hoccleve's quality as a poet (of both stylistic virtue and thematic interest) and deserves substantial credit for rescuing him from a long critical silence.[22] Mitchell's book, however, is also marked by the methodology of a particular kind of literary history, a genealogical account in which a writer like Hoccleve is explained by what we might think of as a *genetic*, or vertical, sort of argument.[23] Hoccleve's verse is examined for its relation to sources, stylistic or thematic, and then interpreted by its variance from these sources and from his fifteenth-century contemporaries' use of the same sources. Practically speaking, this usually comes down to questions of Hoccleve's relation to Chaucer. This sort of genealogical project has severe limitations in accounting for the historical significance of a poet like Hoccleve.

When speaking of "Chaucerian" poetry, the most frequently cited exemplars have been Hoccleve and his prolific contemporary, the monk John Lyd-

21. Sheila Lindenbaum, "London Texts and Literate Practice," in *The Cambridge History of Medieval English Literature*, ed. David Wallace (Cambridge: Cambridge University Press, 1999): 284–309.

22. Jerome Mitchell, *Thomas Hoccleve: A Study in Early Fifteenth-Century Poetic* (Urbana: University of Illinois Press, 1968). There is also a German study, which is somewhat dated and has had little impact on Anglo-American scholarship. See Günter Hagel, *Thomas Hoccleve: Leben und Werk eines Schriftstellers im England des Spätmittelalters* (New York: P. Lang, 1984).

23. My use of the term genealogy here may require some explanation, given my invocation of Foucault at the opening of this introduction. As I discuss in Chapter 4, metaphors of genealogy and paternity have long been central to the representation of fifteenth-century literary history. Consequently, the term genealogical seems most apt for describing this vision of literary progression, despite the risks of confusion with Foucault's more disruptive use of this terminology.

gate. In constructing a model of fifteenth-century "Chaucerian" literature, however, the differences between these authors are probably more instructive than are their similarities. Lydgate is an ideal poet for the application of genealogical schemes of explanation. His references to Chaucer are frequent and insistent, and he is himself a link in a carefully forged chain of literary allusions and influences passing from Chaucer to Tudor and early Renaissance writers. He has, consequently, often been treated as *the* representational voice of the early fifteenth century, particularly in accounts that emphasize the continuity of courtly traditions. Denton Fox, for instance, in an early attempt to fill in "the great *terra incognita*" of the fifteenth century, insisted that "Lydgate is certainly the crucial figure," because it was Lydgate's reading of Chaucer that influenced later poets.[24] Similarly, Lois Ebin's *Illuminator, Makar, Vates* puts Lydgate forward as the stylistic theorist who enabled the transition from Chaucerian verse to the work of the early Renaissance. In her reading, it was the terms of Lydgate's aureate poetry, derived from Chaucer's own terminology, that provided a receptive climate for the importation of Italian classicism via Wyatt's Petrarchan translations.[25] And Richard Firth Green, in his rich and influential study *Poets and Princepleasers*, draws out a similar genealogy in suggesting that "Puttenham is surely right to include in his 'company of courtly makers' both Chaucer and Sir Philip Sidney, for the line between them (through Lydgate, Skelton, and Wyatt) is, as he recognized, unbroken."[26]

Hoccleve, in contrast, has generally been treated in isolation from other cultural production of the fifteenth century. Studies of his poetry often either tacitly assume or quite explicitly declare his status as an anomaly, in literary-historical terms—and, as such, a poet whose works may be stimulating in themselves but may not be taken as the initial point from which to ask questions concerning larger cultural and social histories.[27] Admittedly, there

24. Denton Fox, "Chaucer's Influence on Fifteenth-Century Poetry," in *Companion to Chaucer Studies*, ed. B. Rowland (Toronto: Oxford University Press, 1968), 385–402.

25. Lois Ebin, *Illuminator, Makar, Vates: Visions of Poetry in the Fifteenth Century* (Lincoln: University of Nebraska Press, 1988), 20. Although her remarks are helpful for Lydgate's work, one only to contrast her emphasis on Lydgate's belief in "the inherent truthfulness of poetry and the poet's intention" (19) with Hoccleve's slippery metafictional conceits in the *Series*, or contrast her characterization of the importance of Lydgate's high style with Hoccleve's colloquial language and direct dialogue to realize how inappropriate her generalizations would be to Hoccleve, Usk, Ashby, or any of a number of non-aureate writers of the period.

26. Green, *Poets and Princepleasers*, 12.

27. For example, two of the more ambitious attempts to write literary-historical accounts of the early fifteenth century, Ebin's *Illuminator, Makar, Vates* and Lerer's *Chaucer and His Readers*, are both quite sparse in their references to Hoccleve. Conversely, most of the critical material on Hoccleve places him only vis-à-vis Chaucer, with few connections made to his contemporaries.

are good reasons for this characterization of Hoccleve. It is very hard to place Hoccleve within a diachronic account of literary history because, unlike Lydgate, he has no progeny; it has been difficult to discover encomia or allusions to Hoccleve of the sort that subsequent generations addressed to Chaucer, Lydgate, and even Gower.[28] Moreover, this sense of historical isolation has been implicitly reinforced by the almost mythic outlines of Hoccleve's life, with its perfectly Boethian trajectory from the public aspirations of early poems like the *Regement of Princes* to the solitary isolation and ruin described in the *Series*.[29]

Chroniclers of "Chaucerian" verse have thus always had a loaded choice to make between Hoccleve and Lydgate. When the gaze of diachronic history is trained on Lydgate, the result is an unbroken chain of courtly makers. When the same gaze turns to Hoccleve, however, there can be only one of two possible results. The first is the genealogical image drawn by Jerome Mitchell, in which the consideration of Hoccleve within the "Chaucerian" rubric limits the case either to a presentation of Hoccleve as a feeble echo of Chaucer or an attempt to praise Hoccleve by citing some post-Chaucerian innovation.[30] The second possibility is a fate very like that once suffered by Margery Kempe: the displacement of historical analysis by the celebration or castigation of personal eccentricity.[31] The problem, in short, is that within the limited cate-

28. The sole explicit late medieval allusion to Hoccleve of which I am aware is an anonymous recommendation of his work for the edification of children. See Charles Blyth, *Thomas Hoccleve: The Regiment of Princes* (Kalamazoo: TEAMS/Medieval Institute Publications, Western Michigan University, 1999), 1. Hoccleve was also peculiarly ignored by early printers. As D. C. Greetham has pointed out, Hoccleve was "a 'popular' medieval writer who was promptly ignored by Caxton and the other fifteenth–sixteenth-century printers who fixed the canon of vernacular literature." See his "Challenges of Theory and Practice in the Editing of Hoccleve's *Regement of Princes*," in *Manuscripts and Texts*, ed. Derek Pearsall (Cambridge: D. S. Brewer, 1987), 69 n. 23. Greetham exaggerates slightly, however, in suggesting that it took more than three centuries for Hoccleve to appear in print. William Browne inserted a modified version of the "Tale of Jonathas" into his set of eclogues called the *Shepheard's Pipe* in 1614, adding a commentary in which he attributes the poem quite explicitly to "Thomas Occleeve, one of the priuy Seale"; praises him (despite a "homely stile") as one who "did quench his thirst,/Deeply as did euer one/ In the Muses Helicon"; and suggests that he might publish the rest of Hoccleve's works. See *The Whole Works of William Browne*, ed. William Hazlitt (Roxburghe Library, 1868; reprint, Hildesheim: Georg Olms Verlag, 1970).

29. The tendency of Hoccleve's life nearly to displace the interest of his poetry goes back at least as far as the commentary of his first modern editor, F. J. Furnivall. Furnivall sketched Hoccleve's life out as a sort of tragic exemplum, and the temptation to make sense out of the trajectory of Hoccleve's works in this way still shapes many modern responses, particular to the complaints of the *Series*.

30. This is the technique used, for example, in Albrecht Classen's essay, "Hoccleve's Independence from Chaucer: A Study in Poetic Emancipation," *Fifteenth Century Studies* 15 (1990): 59–81.

31. See the criticism of this tendency in Sarah Beckwith's "Problems of Authority in Late Medieval English Mysticism: Language, Agency, and Authority in *The Book of Margery Kempe*," *Exemplaria* 4 (1992): 173–79.

gory of genealogical literary history per se Hoccleve is a dead end. It is partly for this reason that I turn in this book to the social and textual world of the Privy Seal to make sense of Hoccleve and to argue for his importance not as an eccentric but as a representative of a significant alternative to the aureate predecessors confirmed as a lineage by Philip Sidney.

This study also argues for a reading of Hoccleve not just as an imitation of Chaucer but as a specific and at times antagonistic revision, particularly striking in his rejection of the Boethian stoicism and courtly finesse of the Ricardians. The cultural energy for this revision stems from Hoccleve's partisan membership in a new, emergent class of secularized bureaucrats. It stems also from the world of textual production they inhabited, not the court of love but the court of chancery, where the isolation and lyric intensity of the poetry of *fin amor* is replaced by the *document*, texts that are neither initially the product nor, in the end, the responsibility of any one author. The second goal of this study is thus to use Hoccleve as a figure with which to pry open the literary category of the "Chaucerian." I argue for a post-Chaucerian reading of Hoccleve, one emphasizing not the similarities but the differences in their poetical projects. Consequently, the several chapters of this book will examine each of the major sections of Hoccleve's work as a way of revising received narratives about the shape of "Chaucerian" literature.

My first target is the understanding of the origins of autobiographical narrative. In the context of late medieval literature, autobiography is usually traced back either to origins in questions of gender (as in some treatments of Margery Kempe) or to an argument derived from Foucault about the importance of confessional practices in establishing modern discursive subjects.[32] Although both of these analyses have been productive, neither of

---

32. As an example of this sort of argument about Kempe, see the introduction to Elizabeth Petroff's *Medieval Women's Visionary Literature* (Oxford: Oxford University Press, 1986). Foucault's influence in treating the formation of subjectivity via the confessional is widespread. For a treatment of medieval autobiographical narratives in this context, see Jerry Root, *"Space to speke": The Confessional Subject in Medieval Literature* (New York: Peter Lang, 1997). A third tradition of treating medieval autobiography is that stemming from a more textual/deconstructive model of the paradoxes involved in any literary utterance that offers an embodiment of a speaking self. This approach has been particularly influential in the study of French literature, such as the *dits*. For representative examples, see Jacqueline Cerquiglini, "Le clerc et l'écriture: Le voir dit de Guillaume de Machaut et la définition du dit," in *Literatur in der Gesellschaft des Spätmittelalters*, ed. Hans Ulrich Gumbrecht, *Grundriss der romanischen Literaturen des Mittelalters*, vol. 1 (Heidelberg: Carl Winter Universitätsverlag, 1980), 151–68; Laurence de Looze, *Pseudo-Autobiography in the Fourteenth Century: Juan Ruiz, Guillaume de Machaut, Jean Froissart, and Geoffrey Chaucer* (Gainesville: University of Florida Press, 1997); Michel Zink, *The Invention of Literary Subjectivity*, trans. David Sices (Baltimore: The Johns Hopkins University Press, 1999); and Paul Zumthor, "Autobiography in the Middle Ages," *Genre* 3 (1973): 29–48.

them can account well for the currency of autobiography in Hoccleve's work. In the opening chapter of this book, I suggest a new source and read Hoccleve's autobiographical verse side by side with his bureaucratic production to show that Hoccleve's autobiography is actually born out of that most impersonal of textual traditions, the bureaucratic exchange of petition and response. As we will see, it is the imperative to rid the bureaucratic text of subjectivity itself that makes subjectivity into a recognizable and separable literary topos. Thus, bureaucracy and autobiography appear not as opposites but as two sides of the same coin.

After establishing the importance of this bureaucratic context, I outline a series of literary problems through which Hoccleve crafts his distinct poetic persona. My second chapter takes up the question of gender, not as a spur to autobiography but rather as an issue to which Hoccleve is led because of his marginal status in relation to the authority of ecclesiastical latinity. Here, I look at Hoccleve's translation of Christine de Pizan's *Epistre au Dieu d'Amours*, the first translation of this protofeminist work. The *Epistre* is founded on the ventriloquization of gender, as Christine writes a defense of women against the slanders of courtly lovers but places her complaint in the mouth of the god Cupid. Hoccleve, I claim, replicates Christine's ventriloquistic gambit while reversing the direction of the cross-gendered voicing. Whereas Christine writes as a woman through the voice of a male deity, Hoccleve writes as a man through the mouth of a female *auctrice*. He is driven to this very unusual feminized construction of his own authority by his position among the increasingly laicized clerks of the Privy Seal, whose liminal identity fit neither of the available authorial categories of chivalric or clerkly masculinity.

In the third chapter, I turn to the first of Hoccleve's major works, his *Regement of Princes*. Here I take up two issues: the emphasis on bodily vulnerability in the text's prologue; and the inherited Boethian philosophy that underlies the consolatory logic of the text. The evocation of physical vulnerability in texts of these periods is usually attached to penitential practices and the categories of Boethian philosophy. I use a passage from the prologue to the *Liber Albus*, a documentary record of customary tradition in the city of London, to suggest a different connection, one between physical vulnerability and the act of writing itself. Writing, particularly the documentary machinery of bureaucratic culture, works to supplement the temporal limitations of human life; it is necessitated by the fact of death. Hoccleve's *Regement* is a poem about this fact, a poem that consistently connects physical vulnerability to scribal labors and that rejects the lures of Boethian consolation in favor of the deferral of both consolation and endings.

In the fourth chapter, also devoted to the *Regement of Princes,* I look at the very important topic of Hoccleve's relationship with Chaucer. Despite the widespread evocations of Chaucer as the "father of English poetry" (a phrase made popular by Dryden's influence), Hoccleve was the only poet in the generation immediately following Chaucer to have used this paternal metaphor. I reexamine the consequences of this metaphor through the encomia to Chaucer in the *Regement,* passages that have always been read as the earliest appreciations of Chaucer's genius and of Hoccleve's modesty in the face of the Chaucerian example. My contention is that these passages represent less a rhetoric of submission than a strategy for poetic usurpation. In the *Regement,* we see Hoccleve lay claim to an inherited poetic authority and also interrogate the notions of origins and authority that underwrite the idea of generational succession.

The fifth chapter examines Hoccleve's religious poetry. In the religious conflicts of the early fifteenth century, Hoccleve is usually read as a voice of committed orthodoxy. The strong division between orthodox and Wycliffite positions, however, is not so static a division in Hoccleve's case as it is sometimes assumed to be. What we see in his religious work is a poetry committed to orthodox theological tenets, as well as a poetry that displays a set of skeptical positions on identity and authority usually associated by polemicists of the day with Lollardy. His well-known poem, the "Address to Sir John Oldcastle" works with choice irony to turn the Wycliffite attack on images on its head and produce Oldcastle as a sort of antisaint, an exemplary and cautionary image; at the same time, this treatment of Oldcastle is undercut by a persistent skeptical meditation on the power of images to effectively instantiate either sanctity or perfidy. Similarly, an examination of Hoccleve's short Marian lyrics reveals not only a due reverence for the theology of intercession but also a destablizing connection forged between this theology and Hoccleve's recurrent concerns with the economic problems of patronage in the Privy Seal.

The final chapter concerns Hoccleve's most complex work, the *Series.* This sequence of linked poems and their framing narrative may perhaps best be read as a *Canterbury Tales* for the schizophrenic subject. Written after Hoccleve suffered some sort of mental breakdown, and beginning with a complex lamentation for the social ostracization he suffered as a result, the *Series* contains both several narrative poems and an elaborate fictional frame linking their composition to his own social rejuvenation. Here, I have two linked concerns. First, I draw out the connections between madness and literary production, as madness is presented as the impetus for the composition of the poem and, at the same time, a threatened consequence of the act of writing. Second, I return to the Privy Seal and the urban fabric of London, using a model derived from the compositional procedures of the medieval writing offices, a model of the document as a collaborative and multilayered collage, to describe the distinctive process of accretion through which Hoccleve builds up the linked tales of the *Series*.

Hoccleve has long been thought of as a garrulous eccentric on the fringes of late medieval literature. I hope that this book offers an analytic and historical framework that makes Hoccleve not just an intriguing eccentric, but a recognizable symbol for the importance of bureaucratic culture in the formation of the literary field. At a certain level of abstraction, this book is thus conceived as an intervention in our notion of literary production. "Chaucerian" literature, usually thought of as a courtly form, was actually produced to a very great extent by writers associated with the court, but at some distance, by writers best thought of as bureaucrats. There is no going back to old theses about the "rise of the middle class" in the production and consumption of late medieval literature; nevertheless, Hoccleve stands as a symbol of the internal heterogeneity of the category of the "courtly" itself. As Walter Map said, echoing Augustine's evocation of temporality, "In the court I exist and of the court I speak, but what the court is I know not." Reading Hoccleve with an ear tuned to the bureaucratic muse gives us a new and valuable commentary on this essential mystery of late medieval literary culture.

Bureaucratic Identity
and the
Construction
of the Self
in
Hoccleve's *Formulary*
and
"La Male Regle"

In 1915, in a talk entitled "The English Civil Service in the Fourteenth Century," T. F. Tout drew the following contrast between Geoffrey Chaucer and his poetic disciple, Hoccleve:

Thomas Hoccleve was a friend and in a humble fashion a poetic follower of Chaucer, but while the broad sweep of the great poet's vision disregarded personal reminiscence and *anecdotic triviality* the lowly muse of Hoccleve found its most congenial inspiration in the details of his private and official life. In all the great gallery of the Canterbury Pilgrims there was no public servant whose adventures and personality Chaucer deigned to sketch. On a different plane to his master as an artist, Hoccleve is *immensely more useful* to the historian of administration by reason of his habit of talking about himself.[1]

In its suggestion that his verse is material better suited to the social historian than to the literary scholar, this statement typifies much of

1. T. F. Tout, "The English Civil Service in the Fourteenth Century," *Collected Papers*, 3 vols. (Manchester: Manchester University Press, 1934), 3: 217–18 (emphasis added).

the existing commentary on Hoccleve. What I would like to underline, how-
ever, is Tout's characterization of the anecdotal elements of Hoccleve's verse
as simultaneously "trivial" and "immensely useful." To a certain extent, this
near paradox is a result of Tout's adoption of two different evaluative perso-
nas: on the one hand, echoes of T. S. Eliot and an aesthetic scorn for mere
personality, and on the other, a dedicated archivist on the lookout for pictur-
esque details that might add color to the sometimes dry annals of administra-
tive history.

I cite Tout's description here, however, because his unusual linkage of the
trivial with the functional reproduces a central feature of Hoccleve's verse:
his tendency to disparage his autobiographical ramblings while, at the same
time, deploying this material at the formal and thematic centers of many of
his poems. For instance, in his earliest autobiographical work, "La Male
Regle," Hoccleve effects a transition from a list of past sins to the present
needs of his purse with the self-censuring comment, "Ey, what is me that to
myself thus longe / Clappid have I? I trowe that I rave" (lines 393–94)—
"rave" drawing attention to the excess of his anecdotal disclosure and the
"what is me?" serving to question the value of the self produced thereby.[2]
But Hoccleve is not raving here; he has just written an intricate and highly
self-conscious variation on the begging poem, and he knew very well that it
was the autobiographical detail within the poem that would make it a strik-
ing and, with luck, a *lucrative* piece of verse.

H. S. Bennett made a point similar to that of Tout when he suggested
that the most important fact about Hoccleve was his "constant gossiping
about himself."[3] Hoccleve's dominant mode of self-representation is as the
iangler, one whose speech is caught midway between restraint and release,
between triviality and institutional *gravitas*, between sexual identity and in-
determinacy.[4] His work occupies a curious middle ground between gossip and
autobiography. He adopts the voice of the gossip, a voice of informal and
scandalous revelation, but instead of using this voice to expose another, Hoc-

2. M. C. Seymour, *Selections from Hoccleve* (Oxford: Clarendon Press, 1981). Further references
to "La Male Regle" are drawn from this edition and cited by line number within the text.

3. H. S. Bennett, *Chaucer and the Fifteenth Century* (New York: Oxford University Press, 1954),
147.

4. Karma Lochrie's work on the complex gendering of gossip and its place in the deauthorization
of women's secrets provides an important context for understanding the fluidity of Hoccleve's repre-
sentations of gender (see Chapter 2). Lochrie, *Covert Operations: The Medieval Uses of Secrecy* (Phila-
delphia: University of Pennsylvania Press, 1999). On gossip, see also the stimulating reflections in
Patricia Meyer Spacks, *Gossip* (New York: Knopf, 1985).

cleve insistently prods at himself. Considered historically, this gossiping habit raises a difficult question. Why should such gossip, which might also claim to be the dramatic first stirrings of vernacular autobiography, come from a clerk at Westminster, one of those whose professional responsibilities had less to do with self-expression than with the endless reduplication of a language of grave bureaucratic anonymity? As many critics have pointed out, the basic elements of Hoccleve's poetic persona (a man anxiously peering in from the edge of the social order, obsessively confessing his inadequacies in love, knowledge, skill, and finance) were provided by the example of Chaucer's experiments in self-portraiture.[5] But what were the historical and sociological causes that led to the perpetuation and intensification of this figure in the post-Chaucerian poetry of the fifteenth century? It will be my contention that Hoccleve's interest in the trivia of subjectivity can only be fully understood once we appreciate the cultural impact of an emergent class of secularized bureaucrats. Indeed, Hoccleve's role in the consolidation of the tradition of Chaucerian poetic identity was itself underwritten by the unstable economic terrain the clerks of the central bureaucracy inhabited and by the influence of extrapoetical forms of literary practice in the period, in other words, by the very labor and objects of bureaucratic textual practice.

Hoccleve has benefited in recent times from commentary by two distinct scholarly communities. He served as a star witness in the last volumes of Tout's *Chapters in the Administrative History of England,* and ever since, administrative historians have been aware of Hoccleve's verse as one of the most useful sources for the details of daily life of the clerks of that period.[6] The other community is that of literary critics, whose work on Hoccleve has

---

5. On Hoccleve's relationship with Chaucer, see D. C. Greetham, "Self-Referential Artifacts: Hoccleve's Persona as a Literary Device," *Modern Philology* 86 (1989): 242–44; David Lawton, *Chaucer's Narrators* (Cambridge: Cambridge University Press, 1985), 13–16; Jerome Mitchell, "Hoccleve's Tribute to Chaucer," in *Chaucer und seine Zeit: Symposion für Walter F. Schirmer,* ed. Arno Esch (Tübingen: Max Niemeyer, 1968), 275–83; and Seymour, *Selections from Hoccleve,* xxv. As William Calin has demonstrated, an additional source for these techniques of self-representation may also be found in French texts, such as Machaut's *Voir Dit* and Froissart's *Paradis d'Amour.* See Calin, *The French Tradition and the Literature of Medieval England* (Toronto: University of Toronto Press, 1994), 399–418.

6. See especially A. L. Brown, "The Privy Seal Clerks in the Early Fifteenth Century," in *The Study of Medieval Records: Essays in Honour of Kathleen Major,* ed. D. A. Bullough and R. L. Storey (Oxford: Oxford University Press, 1971), 260–81; A. Compton Reeves, "The World of Thomas Hoccleve," *Fifteenth Century Studies* 2 (1979): 187–99; Malcolm Richardson, "Hoccleve in His Social Context," *Chaucer Review* 20 (1986): 313–22; and Tout, "The English Civil Service in the Fourteenth Century," 191–221.

focused mainly on the autobiographical nature of Hoccleve's poetry and on Hoccleve's relation to Chaucer.[7] This chapter brings these areas of research together through a consideration of the influence of bureaucratic identity on Hoccleve's literary production. First, I discuss the institutional background of Hoccleve's life and writing in order to delineate a corporate social identity that was crucial to the production of a specifically post-Chaucerian verse. Second, I offer an analysis of the construction of selfhood in Hoccleve's *Formulary*, the massive collection of writs and letters that he compiled toward the end of his life for the use of junior clerks in the Office of the Privy Seal. I conclude with an examination of Hoccleve's early comic self-portrait, "La Male Regle," in order to substantiate the connections between bureaucratic identity and the place of autobiography in Hoccleve's poetic work.[8]

Lancastrian Bureaucracy and the Secular Clerk

Thomas Hoccleve was a poet and clerk of the Privy Seal active in the late fourteenth and early fifteenth centuries. It is possible to speak of his life in more detail than is the case with most writers of this period because of the autobiographical nature of much of his verse and because his name can be

7. For useful bibliographies of scholarship on Hoccleve see the appendix to Mitchell, *Thomas Hoccleve*; and Jerome Mitchell, "Hoccleve Studies, 1965–1981," in *Fifteenth-Century Studies: Recent Essays*, ed. R. F. Yeager (Hamden: Archon Books, 1984), 49–63. Long overdue attention has also begun to be paid to his more public and political poetry, including three recent important essays: Judith Ferster, "A Mirror for the Prince of Wales: Hoccleve's *Regement of Princes*," in her *Fictions of Advice: The Literature and Politics of Counsel in Late Medieval England* (Philadelphia: University of Pennsylvania Press, 1996), 137–59; Derek Pearsall, "Hoccleve's *Regement of Princes*: The Poetics of Royal Self-Representation," *Speculum* 69 (1994): 386–410; and Larry Scanlon, "The King's Two Voices: Narrative and Power in Hoccleve's *Regement of Princes*," in *Literary Practice and Social Change in Britain, 1380–1530*, ed. Lee Patterson (Berkeley and Los Angeles: University of California Press, 1990), 216–47, material that is reworked in Scanlon's *Narrative, Authority, and Power: The Medieval Exemplum and the Chaucerian Tradition* (Cambridge: Cambridge University Press, 1994), 299–322.

8. For a fundamental account of the importance of bureaucratic administration in establishing the habits of textuality in earlier centuries, see M. T. Clanchy, *From Memory to Written Record: England, 1066–1307*, 2d ed. (Cambridge, Mass.: Harvard University Press, 1993). For an account of the intellectual history underlying the emergence of this textual culture, see Brian Stock, *The Implications of Literacy: Written Language and Models of Interpretation in the Eleventh and Twelfth Centuries* (Princeton: Princeton University Press, 1983). Anne Middleton has offered a groundbreaking treatment of the connections between late medieval literature and this emergent bureaucratic class in "Chaucer's 'New Men' and the Good of Literature in the *Canterbury Tales*," in *Literature and Society*, ed. Edward Said (Baltimore: The Johns Hopkins University Press, 1980), 15–56.

found in many surviving administrative documents.[9] Hoccleve was born about 1367 and entered the Privy Seal near Easter of 1387. He would no doubt have entered the office as an apprentice clerk, and we know that he served as underclerk to Guy de Roucliff.[10] Some time before the year 1408 he had progressed in seniority to the point at which he merited his own assistant clerk, John Welde. As was not unusual, he worked at the Privy Seal for the rest of his life, retiring quite close to his death in 1426.[11]

The other facts of his life that have come down to us are largely financial, and these are very useful in gaining a sense of the economic imperatives in the lives of these clerks. Hoccleve's most consistent form of income, despite his complaints of their perennial delay, was a succession of annuities granted by the king. On November 12, 1399, he was granted an annuity of £10, an award made provisionally until an ecclesiastical benefice could be found for permanent support.[12] This was raised in 1409 to 20 marks (or £13

9. The bulk of the relevant documents were first collected by R. E. G. Kirk for Furnivall's EETS edition of Hoccleve's writings. Frederick J. Furnivall and I. Gollancz, eds., *Hoccleve's Works: The Minor Poems*, EETS, ES, 61 and 73 (London, 1892; rev. A. I. Doyle and Jerome Mitchell, 1970). John Burrow gives an exceptionally helpful biographical treatment and collection of documentary evidence in *Thomas Hoccleve* (Aldershot: Variorum, 1994).

10. Roucliff was a senior member of the Office of the Privy Seal whose career was much more successful than that of Hoccleve, as he served both as intermediary between the king and his council and later as Master of the Mint. On his death he left Hoccleve five marks (a more substantial bequest than that left to Roucliff's other Privy Seal colleagues) and a copy of *De bello Troie*. Roucliff has himself received attention from literary scholars because in 1382 he sold two manor houses to John Gower. Hoccleve had offered *mainprise* for Roucliff in 1392, guaranteeing his appearance as defendant in court. For the details of Roucliff's will, see Elizabeth Ingram, "Thomas Hoccleve and Guy de Rouclif," *Notes and Queries* 218 (1973): 42–43. For Hoccleve's service as *mainpernour*, see John Fisher, *John Gower: Moral Philosopher and Friend of Chaucer* (New York: New York University Press, 1964), 39, 62; and Jerome Mitchell, "Thomas Hoccleve: His Traditionalism and His Individuality" (Ph.D. diss., Duke University, 1965), 335.

11. Hoccleve's date of death has been determined from the last known payment of his annuity, recorded on February 11, 1426, and from a posthumous reference to him in a document dated May 8, 1426, a letter conferring his corody onto a new beneficiary; see Brown, "Privy Seal Clerks," 270 n. 1. We can surmise that he worked at the Privy Seal in some capacity until quite near to his death because the *Formulary* was assembled between 1423 and 1425 out of materials that would have been available only through the records of that office; see Bentley, "Formulary," vii–viii.

12. The Crown preferred to support its clerks through grants of ecclesiastical positions rather than annuities, which had to be paid out of the Exchequer. However, the growing number of married clerks and the perennial shortage of benefices necessitated more and more direct support in the form of annuities. J. R. Lander has suggested that this laicization of the bureaucratic corps led in time to long-term changes in the clerks' power over their own labor. "In government departments clerics generally held office at the king's pleasure, sometimes during good behavior. The king could dismiss them easily, as they could fall back on their benefices for support or they could be granted others at no cost to the king. Laymen proved more recalcitrant. They possessed no benefices to soften the blow of dismissal and they had families dependent upon them. For greater security they soon began

6s. 8d.).[13] These annuities were sometimes supplemented by special grants.[14] The clerks also received gratuities for the production of some petitions. Clerks would expect a small payment for writing the document, and since the clerks themselves had the juridical function of introducing petitions to the Council and the courts, they were sometimes paid an additional small consideration to encourage an enthusiastic presentation.[15] A final source of income available to these clerks was the scribal piecework very much in demand in the London book trade.[16] Due to the lack of any surviving records of payment, it is impossible to gauge accurately the relative importance of these sources of income. What is clear, however, is that clerks like Hoccleve were dependent for their living on a number of overlapping and individually unreliable systems of payment.

It is not difficult to posit an explanation for this irregular livelihood. Hoccleve's place of employment, the Office of the Privy Seal, was at this time one of the three writing offices (in company with Chancery and the Signet office) that formed the administrative center of government at Westminster. Clerks working at these offices were holders of some of the most secure positions available in late medieval society. Most held tenure for life, and even after retirement the average clerk seems to have been granted some form of

to demand life tenure in their offices, and reversionary interests and the appointment of poorly paid deputies to do the work followed closely upon the life interest. All this, though only beginning in the fifteenth century, led before its end to the concept of royal offices as marketable items, as a form of investment." Lander, *Conflict and Stability in Fifteenth-Century England* (London: Hutchinson University Library, 1969), 168.

13. Michael Seymour has suggested that this raise may well have been the result of Hoccleve's marriage and the loss of the potential for ecclesiastical support (Seymour, *Selections*, xiii). The question of which event was cause and which effect, however, seems an open one. Hoccleve may have been disqualified from a benefice because of his decision to marry, or he may have decided to marry because his prospects for ecclesiastical preferment seemed poor.

14. On September 3, 1398, Hoccleve is recorded as one of four clerks to share a £40 forfeiture of property. In 1401 he shared with seven clerks a special grant, requested from the new king, Henry IV, as recompense for unusually arduous work. And on July 4, 1424, he was granted a corody, theoretically room and board in a monastery upon his retirement, but most likely an award easily converted into ready cash.

15. In 1423, for example, Hoccleve was paid two marks for writing to the Council on behalf of the Earl Marshall and for handling the course of the warrant thus produced; see J. L. Kirby, "An Account of Robert Southwell, Receiver-General of John Mowbray, Earl Marshall, 1422–23," *Bulletin of the Institute of Historical Research* 27 (1954): 196–97. Brown also discusses the sale of this sort of influence in *Governance*, 59.

16. A. I. Doyle and M. B. Parkes have demonstrated that Hoccleve worked as a copyist with some limited supervisory role in the production of a deluxe manuscript of Gower's *Confessio Amantis*. Doyle and Parkes, "The Production of Copies of the *Canterbury Tales* and the *Confessio Amantis* in the Early Fifteenth Century," in *Medieval Scribes, Manuscripts, and Libraries: Essays Presented to N. R. Ker*, ed. M. B. Parkes and A. G. Watson (London: Scolar Press, 1978), 163–203.

a corody, or the cash equivalent, as security against old age.[17] However, during the time of Hoccleve's tenure, the widespread social instabilities of late fourteenth- and early fifteenth-century England combined with problems in payment specific to the central bureaucracy to create a profound sense of anxiety in Hoccleve and his colleagues. The old structures that had given security to both the identity and the finances of these clerks, namely, their ecclesiastical status and membership in the king's household, were giving way as the administration became increasingly laicized and increasingly distant from the household of the king.

To make this point properly, it is first necessary to establish its prehistory, a story chronicled authoritatively by Tout in his *Chapters in the Administrative History of England*.[18] Tout constructed the history of bureaucracy in England as a narrative in which the holders of first the great seal, then the privy seal, and in time the signet went, one by one, "out of the household." In the early days of minimal bureaucratic saturation, the central bureaucracy was limited to a relatively small number of literate men, conveniently already trained for ecclesiastical duties but easily adapted to secular courts and correspondence. At this early stage of development, such persons would have been members of the king's household.

However, as the complexity of the administrative controls over England grew, it became less convenient for this work to be done by members of the household.[19] Speaking generally, the story of the writing offices is best understood as a story of private government yielding to depersonalized administration. The Office of the Privy Seal had first come into existence when

17. Green, *Poets and Princepleasers*, 28. For length of tenure, see Brown, "Privy Seal Clerks," 265.

18. Tout's work has been updated in important aspects, the most notable revisions for the late fourteenth and early fifteenth centuries being those made by A. L. Brown, but his general paradigm of a shift from an administration carried out by members of the king's household to an administration enacted via independent bureaucratic machinery remains quite valid. Nevertheless, as Brown comments, "Tout's work was concerned with the offices of the royal Household and only incidentally with the Westminster offices, and this has led to an imbalance and a theory of 'Household government' which has only recently been righted." *Governance*, 43n.

19. The increasing professionalization and political independence of these administrators are vividly represented in A. L. Brown's depiction of Henry IV's search for loyal manpower after his usurpation of the throne. By investigating who retained their positions after the change of government and especially by examining records of attendance at Parliament and meetings of the Council, Brown is able to support conclusively Tout's earlier suggestion that the most remarkable thing about this usurpation was the lack of significant change in personnel. "The Reign of Henry IV: The Establishment of the Lancastrian Regime," in *Fifteenth-Century England, 1399–1509: Studies in Politics and Society*, ed. C. D. Ross, S. B. Chrimes, and R. A. Griffiths (Manchester: Manchester University Press, 1972), 21.

the small privy (private) seal, which had been used by King John before his accession, began to be used regularly as an official supplement to the great seal.[20] And within a year of the date that the privy seal was first assigned a keeper with the assent of Parliament and the baronage (Roger of Northburgh in 1313), the signet was established as a new private device.[21] Edward III used it at first for private correspondence, but the usage expanded to include official state transactions. By the 1370s the signet, too, had its own independent keeper.[22] In Hoccleve's time, Richard II attempted to turn back the clock and use the signet as a channel of personal autocratic authority, independent of review by the Council.[23] But political pressures made it easier for a seal to go out of the household than to be brought back within, and Richard was, to say the least, unsuccessful.

The central point here is that the process of "going out of the household" is crucial in understanding Hoccleve's verse because the slow movement away from the king's household had made previously simple forms of payment increasingly complex. The clerks of the Privy Seal lived in the difficult position of being largely dependent on the occasional gifts and rewards of patronage that had supplied the needs of their fellows in the days when they had been part of the king's household but that had become less dependable as wages took the place of gratuities.[24] Indeed, so drastic and yet unassimilated was this transition that, as A. L. Brown puts it, the Exchequer maintained "the fiction that the keeper's wages of £1 a day were paid only until arrangements were made for the continuous residence of himself and his clerks in the royal Household," and this arrangement was perpetuated until 1409, or "at least three generations after it had ceased to have any meaning."[25] In other words, Hoccleve and his fellows were caught up in the insecurities

20. Pierre Chaplais, *English Royal Documents: King John-Henry VI, 1199–1461* (Oxford: Clarendon Press, 1971), 24–25.

21. Chaplais, *English Royal Documents*, 34. See also Brown, *Governance*, 46.

22. Brown, *Governance*, 47.

23. S. B. Chrimes suggests that "the practice of using letters *sub signeto* for the initiation of action was greatly extended in the years 1383–86, but inevitably receded during the years of the ascendancy of the Lords Appellant, when the exercise of the king's personal initiative was under restraint." Chrimes, *An Introduction to the Administrative History of Mediaeval England* (Oxford: Basil Blackwell, 1966), 215. See also T. F. Tout, *Chapters in the Administrative History of England* (Manchester: Manchester University Press, 1920–33), 3:404–5; and the criticisms of Tout in Nigel Saul, *Richard II* (New Haven: Yale University Press, 1997), 109–12, 127–29.

24. Tout records examples of clerical stipends falling as far as six years in arrears. Tout, *Chapters*, 5:87.

25. Brown, *Governance*, 46 n. 5. The keeper's £1 a day probably went to maintain the hostel where many of the unmarried Privy Seal clerks lived.

attendant upon the long and uneven transition from household government to salaried administration.[26] As they were no longer exactly members of the king's household, they were not exactly "king's clerks" in the sense that had applied in earlier centuries. But what exactly they were, or were becoming, was a harder question to answer.

A first clue to this emergent identity can be found in one of the surprising but highly effective measures adopted within the machinery of the Privy Seal to forestall the starvation of its clerks. Put quite simply, it became the universal practice to produce redundant paperwork in correspondence moving between departments at Westminster. A. L. Brown has described standard protocol within the Privy Seal:

> In the fifteenth century it was common, though not necessary, for a grant of grace made by the King to lead to a signet letter to the chancellor ordering a letter under the great seal. Sometimes distance did make this round-about system necessary but it was also used to give the clerks an income. It was a restrictive practice, given statutory authority in 1536, which continued for centuries for the benefit of the clerks.[27]

Clerks working in this system were thus paid on what we would now call a piecework basis. The more documents necessary, the better their wages, a situation that may have contributed to the rising tide of documents produced in this period.

The second point to register is that however effective this system of redundancy may have been, it obviously lacked the reassuring predictability of royal annuities and gifts. Operating outside the security of the king's household, clerks in Hoccleve's position had no power to assure that even the fees due them would ever be paid. Hoccleve himself gives us a striking image of the vulnerability of these clerks in a passage from the *Regement of Princes*. Here he complains that the clerks of the Privy Seal are abused by the very men who owe them gratitude, those who needed their assistance in present-

26. From a modern perspective the shift from a gift economy to the regular use of wages is a clear secular trend, but in Hoccleve's time these were competing and overlapping systems, neither one completely predominating. For example, in the mid-fourteenth century, clerks received regular daily wages, but this practice had ceased by August 1399, replaced by annuities, a form of support that was neither exactly a gift nor a wage. After Henry IV's death in 1412 few annuities were given, and the new clerks had to rely wholly on fees for individual documents and on extraordinary petitions to the king. Brown, "Privy Seal Clerks," 267–68.

27. Brown, *Governance*, 49.

ing petitions. The clerks do their job well and honestly assist petitioners, but when it comes time for their reward, the servants of these men pocket the gratuities meant for the clerks, putting them off with vague promises of favors to come their way in the future. Moreover, the clerks are powerless to complain when cheated, for fear of worse happening: "Ne we nat dar lete him of it to knowe,/Lest our conpleynte ourselven overthrowe" (lines 1525–26).[28]

One of the results of this financial insecurity was a tendency for these clerks to act in collective economic units. The Chancery rolls contain numerous examples of attempts by small groups to band together into temporary alliances for mutual financial gain. Such clerks frequently formed "syndicates" in which they might pool their minimal resources and jointly act as moneylenders. Alternatively, they might work together to profit through real-estate speculation. One clerk might spot a bit of land newly forfeit to the Crown that another could then snap up before anyone outside the office knew about the bargain. A clerk might also profit, or work with other clerks to do so, by acting as bondsman in offering *mainprise* (at interest, of course) for any accused on criminal charges. These clerks also testified for one another in court and acted as executors of one another's wills.[29]

Moreover, the clerks would have needed to look no further than France for an enviable model of corporate clerical power. The clerks of the Crown in Paris were the beneficiaries of a much more rapid process of secularization and perhaps also of a weaker central monarchy. Tout describes a confraternity established by the royal secretaries and notaries in 1352. In addition to the usual panoply of religious services, banquets, and guidelines for the "sobriety of dress and gravity of deportment," these French clerks bound themselves together in order to act as a collective negotiating body and to gain control over both their wages and their labor. As Tout describes them:

> So powerful did the college become that the king handed over to its two proctors the arrangement of the rotation in which its members discharged some of its official functions. . . . When the secretaries and notaries complained that they could not get their wages, either

28. Blyth, ed., *The Regiment of Princes.* Subsequent references are drawn from this edition and cited by line number within the text.

29. Malcolm Richardson discusses such joint activities as moneylending, real estate speculation, and service as *mainpernor* in his essay "Hoccleve in His Social Context." I thank Professor Richardson for allowing me access to his unpublished manuscript, *The Chancery Under Henry V,* which thoroughly documents the economic activities of the Chancery clerks of this period. See also Griffiths, "Public and Private Bureaucracies in England and Wales in the Fifteenth Century," 126.

from the household *Chambre de Deniers* or from the national *Chambre des Compts*, they were allowed to appoint one or two receivers from among themselves, empowered to lay hands upon the fines and other dues levied in parliament and to pay their colleagues from this source.[30]

Although the clerks of the privy seal never attained this degree of collective activity, their business syndicates hint at a strong esprit de corps. Political and cultural links between England and France in this period were extensive and included the institutional hybrid of the "French secretaries," an administrative cadre who administered French territories for the English crown using largely French techniques and customs. Given this close cultural proximity, especially in the realm of bureaucratic organizations, the English clerks must have been aware of the benefits enjoyed by their French colleagues and must have envied them.[31]

But this is not to say that it was a fool's bargain to become a clerk at Westminster in this period. The very same moment that had witnessed a crisis of financial insecurity on the part of these clerks also seems to have witnessed an elevation in their social position. As Robin Storey has made clear in his study of the "gentleman-bureaucrat," it was in the era immediately following Hoccleve's death that many of the king's clerks, particularly those who had married, began to refer to themselves as "gentlemen."[32] Although the frequent use of the term gentleman seems to be chiefly a phenomenon of the 1420s, the immediate causes of this lexical shift find their roots in two trends of the earlier part of the century: the growing importance of laymen in the bureaucratic service; and, under the Statute of Additions of

30. Tout attributed the greater prestige of the French clerks to the fact that the French secretariat had remained a single institution and had retained its close link to the king and his household. "The comparative lateness with which the French *curia regis* split up into distinct offices of state resulted in the chancery remaining in complete association with the royal household until 1321, and even then being only partially separated from it. This persistence of household control led to a strong group of royal notaries growing up in France with interests and traditions of their own. As time went on . . . whether they wrote at the Chambre des Comptes or at the Chatelet, they continued to take their pay and their allowances from the chancellor himself, or from the household." Tout, *Chapters*, 5: 146.

31. On the French secretaries, see J. Otway-Ruthven, *The King's Secretary and the Signet Office in the Fifteenth Century* (Cambridge: Cambridge University Press, 1939), 89–91.

32. Robin L. Storey, "Gentleman-Bureaucrats," in *Profession, Vocation, and Culture in Later Medieval England*, ed. C. H. Clough (Liverpool: Liverpool University Press, 1982), 90–129. Storey gives one example that is particularly close to Hoccleve in the story of the Exchequer clerk Simon Yerll, who was granted a farm in 1419 under the name of Simon Yerll of Cornwall, "gentilman." See also Brown, *Governance*, 148–49.

1413, the required identification of all defendants in court by their estate or degree, which encouraged the increasing use of the term gentleman. Any doubt that the first inklings of Storey's trend are already to be found in the early years of the century should be laid to rest by Hoccleve's own "La Male Regle" (1405), in which he describes the temptation to succumb to the flattery of those boatmen who would call him "maister":

> Othir than maistir callid was I neuere
> Among this meynee in myn audience.
> Me thoghte I was ymaad a man foreuere.
> So tikelid me Þat nyce reverence
> Þat it me made largere of despense
> Than Þat I thoghte han been.
> (lines 201–6)[33]

The king's clerks were flattered because of their connections to the house-hold of the king and because of their comparative wealth. But as Hoccleve's irony suggests, the very moment of their honor was a moment of some vulnerability. For, although he is called "maistir," his acceptance of the title only leads him more quickly and foolishly toward real poverty.[34]

Finally, we should note that this combination of financial vulnerability and social aggrandizement becomes particularly potent when we reflect on the centrality of the petition in the administration of the time. The petition was the "key to governmental action," the form through which every suppli-cant was expected to approach the king or any of his mediating agents.[35] And for no one in England was the petition more central than for these

33. While such a use of master occurred most typically in the case of university graduates, Christopher Cheney also cites the use of the term as a pure honorific used for senior bureaucrats. "When a man was appointed notary public he seems to have enjoyed the honorific title of *magister*. . . . The mastership is so commonly credited to those notaries public who have left no trace in a university that it probably came into use here as in certain offices and crafts in the later Middle Ages to signify a certain status, without an academic connotation. In support of this conjecture one may note that the chief clerks of the English royal chancery were styled *magistri*." Cheney, *Notaries Public in England in the Thirteenth and Fourteenth Centuries* (Oxford: Clarendon Press, 1972), 89.

34. This sense of social dislocation might also be related broadly to the "Male Regle" itself in that the term *misrule* was often used to complain of ruptures in social hierarchy, specifically those ruptures in which the commons adopted the manners of the magnatial class. Saul, *Richard II*, 200.

35. Brown, "The Authorization of Letters Under the Great Seal," *Bulletin of the Institute of Historical Research* 37 (1964): 148. Brown estimates that Henry IV received "over 2,000 and perhaps 3,000 or 4,000" petitions just in the year running from September 30, 1404, until September 29, 1405. Ibid., 154.

clerks. The annuities and special grants gained by Hoccleve would most likely all have been the results of petitions to the king.[36] Most of their working hours were spent in the drafting and copying of endless series of petitions and responses to such petitions. Given the ubiquity of the petition in the life of these clerks, it is not surprising that it was the bureaucratic instrument of the petition that gave a specific shape to their financial anxiety.

In a social order in which advancement was based on the petition, financial security for any servant of the court must have been based on the willingness and ability to speak out and request rewards from the king. However, such requests generated their own anxieties because, as the whole system was theoretically grounded on the independent largesse of the king, to ask for a reward was already to imply that the reward was past due. Such petitions could only too easily make their authors seem presumptuous. Hence we see in Hoccleve's *Regement of Princes* the clerks' anger at those whose social position gave them the security and the right to speak in their support but who instead stood dumb as stones, and hence the clerks' intimidated silence: "Lest our conpleynte ourselven overthrowe" (line 1526).

The experience of financial insecurity in the context of social relations determined by the act of the petition created a crucial historical background for the development of post-Chaucerian depictions of subjectivity. The class experience of financial anxiety provided the impetus and the bureaucratic instrument of the petition provided the form through which Hoccleve transformed the persona he inherited from Chaucer. This social anxiety and extrapoetic literary form came together to produce in Hoccleve an autobiographer as gossip, a clerk bent on turning all the trivia of his existence to the use of a continual, obsessive petition.[37]

Self-Revelation in the Formulary

The very existence of Hoccleve's *Formulary* is a wonderful stroke of luck for those writing the history of literary production in this period. Administrative

36. These petitions would have become all the more central during the reign of Henry V, when neither wages nor annuities were regularly granted, leaving most clerks with only fees for piecework and whatever grants they could secure via petitions to the king (see above, n. 26).

37. Hoccleve's use of the petition has, of course, been treated by John Burrow in his articles "The Poet as Petitioner," *Studies in the Age of Chaucer* 3 (1981): 61–75, and "Autobiographical Poetry in the Middle Ages: The Case of Thomas Hoccleve," *Proceedings of the British Academy* 68 (1982): 389–412. I have benefited greatly from Burrow's discussions but would hope here to throw

historians have long known of it and have drawn on it for everything from anthologies of letters illustrative of diplomatic procedure to debates concern‑ ing the exact duties of the Office of the Privy Seal in the late fourteenth and early fifteenth centuries.[38] But although Hoccleve's *Formulary* has frequently been cited as a prime source for diplomatic and administrative history, it is of even greater interest as an example of a form of literary practice that developed side by side with what we now see as the "literature" proper of the late fourteenth and early fifteenth centuries. Such bureaucratic composi‑ tions, topical and pragmatic though they may be, bear the constant marks of the cultural construction of a new urban scribal class preoccupied with the difficulties of their particular labors and with their own economic vulnerabil‑ ity. John Fisher, Malcolm Richardson, and others have argued that it was the linguistic stability and widespread circulation of Chancery documents that led to the establishment of a uniform national vernacular, or what we now call Standard English.[39] Given both the sheer volume of texts produced in the writing offices at Westminster (estimated by A. L. Brown at between thirty and forty thousand documents per year in this period) and the number of late medieval literary figures with experience in some capacity as adminis‑ trators and secretaries (Hoccleve, Thomas Usk, George Ashby, and Chaucer in the English tradition, and Guillaume de Machaut, Christine de Pizan, and Alain Chartier in France), it seems clear that literary historians need to be attentive to the relation between texts such as Hoccleve's *Formulary* and the poetry of this period.[40]

---

emphasis on the petition not as a literary form but as a site connecting Hoccleve's verse to the sociotextual world of Lancastrian bureaucracy. For a general appraisal of the importance of the petition in these decades, see J. A. Tuck, "Richard II's System of Patronage," in *The Reign of Richard II: Essays in Honor of May McKisack,* ed. F. R. H. Du Boulay and C. M. Barron (London: Athlone Press, 1971), 1–20; and the remarks in Brown, *Governance,* 19–20, 51–52, 215–17, and passim.

38. For the first usage, see Edouard Perroy, *The Diplomatic Correspondence of Richard II,* Camden Society, 3d ser., 48 (London: Royal Historical Society, 1933); and M. Dominica Legge, *Anglo‑ Norman Letters and Petitions* (Oxford: Basil Blackwell, 1941). For the latter, see Brown, "The Autho‑ rization of Letters Under the Great Seal."

39. See, for example, John H. Fisher, "Chancery and the Emergence of Standard Written En‑ glish in the Fifteenth Century," *Speculum* 52 (1977): 870–99; Fisher, "A Language Policy for Lancas‑ trian England"; and Malcolm Richardson, "Henry V, the English Chancery, and Chancery English," *Speculum* 55 (1980): 726–50. Fisher's articles are reprinted in his collection *The Emergence of Stan‑ dard English* (Lexington: University of Kentucky Press, 1996).

40. Brown, *Governance,* 52. Historians have often seemed more comfortable with such connec‑ tions than have literary scholars. Jeremy Catto, for instance, has suggested that the Office of the Privy Seal was the natural breeding ground of a poetry of national interest. "The formalization of the privy seal constituted the recognition in England of the art of diplomacy: letters to foreign princes or to English lords were the material of the privy seal clerk's art, and the same rhetorical techniques could be used for propaganda purposes in poems on current events such as Hoccleve's

I consider the *Formulary* in some detail here because Hoccleve is one of the earliest vernacular authors for whom one can construct a textual environment, a world of labor focused solely on the production of textual artifacts. Indeed, these laicized clerks might well be considered the first class one could point to whose identity was based solely on a relationship to the written word. Unlike the clerisy who had been responsible for the vast proliferation of documents in the previous centuries, these secular clerks held no claim to a special relationship to divinity.[41] The king's clerks were increasingly bound together simply by their common ability to produce, circulate, and organize the instruments of literate administration.

The *Formulary* is carefully organized, with a detailed table of contents listing both the topics of large sections and the subject matter of each individual letter for about the first half of the volume. And although the table of contents appears to have been left incomplete, there are marginal notations throughout the volume, giving a summary of every document. This apparatus testifies to the practical function for which the volume was compiled, that of offering an easily referenced collection of model documents. The table of contents and marginal summaries would allow a clerk to access any model he needed; and since these tools are almost always in French, they might even have worked as a usable crib for any clerk whose Latin was a bit shaky. However, despite the clear orientation of the volume as a whole to the function of a book of exemplars, there is a certain schizophrenia of purpose here, discernible in the inclusion of a number of letters so firmly linked to specific historical moments or voiced so clearly as letters to and from specific persons, not institutions, that it is impossible to imagine their use as simple exemplars.[42] These letters may have been included in part because, unlike the

---

verses on the Oldcastle rising." Catto, "The King's Servants," in *King Henry V: The Practice of Kingship*, ed. G. L. Harriss (Oxford: Oxford University Press, 1985), 80. For a more literary account of connections between "professional" identities and literary production, see Andrew Galloway, "Private Selves and the Intellectual Marketplace in Late Fourteenth-Century England: The Case of the Two Usks," *New Literary History* 28 (1997): 291–318.

41. For the process of laicization among the clerks of the Privy Seal in this period, see Storey, "Gentleman-Bureaucrats," and Brown, *Governance*, 60.

42. Letter 67, for example, is a letter to the dean of Hereford cathedral, complaining that the doors to the cemetery are being left open at night, allowing unbaptized children to be buried at night and allowing pigs to run amok in the cathedral grounds:

> Pur deffaute de la closure du dit cimitere, cestassavoir robberie des biens de la dite eglise ont este faites, et enfanz abortifs, nient baptisez, en dit cimiter enseveliz privement de nuyt, et aussi les corps des mortz enseveliz en mesme le cimiterre ont este traitz hors de la terre par porcs et autre bestes, et grandes occasions dincontinence et dautres mesprisions et debatz ont avenuz deinz le dimiterre susdit, a grand peril des almes et escandoille de leglise avantdite et des ministres dicelle.

Exchequer and Chancery, the Privy Seal lacked any system for the regular enrollment of its documents, and the *Formulary* may thus have taken on a secondary function as a register of documents included because of their historical importance.[43] It is also possible that these letters were meant as exemplars in their stylistic luster.[44] But whatever the reason for their inclusion, the general effect produced is that of a bifurcation in the material of this volume between two kinds of documents, the first characterizable by their anonymity and the second by their almost flamboyant concern with notable individuals, historical particularity, and stylistic eccentricity.

The significance of this split in function can best be seen through an examination of a peculiar series of letters, 159–61 in Elna-Jean Bentley's edition. These letters are of particular significance because they all concern a clerk identified by the initials "T.H." Given the context of the initials as references to one of the king's clerks, and details in a later letter specifying reimbursement to "T.H." ink and wax used at the Privy Seal, these initials clearly refer to the compiler, Hoccleve himself.[45] It is not in itself surprising to find autobiographical touches in a formulary. Thomas Sampson, an instructor in the *dictamenal* arts at Oxford, included numerous references to himself in the letters he provided to his students as models, often references to his own great oratorical prowess, the great success of his pupils, and matters of

---

Bentley, "Formulary," 61. It would be surprising if this letter had to be consulted as a model on many occasions.

43. As examples of documents enrolled for their historical importance, see letter 1096, which contains a 1376 petition of the clergy to deal with heretics, and letter 1103, which gives a lengthy and detailed list of reasons for war in France. Bentley, "Formulary," 1093, 1115.

44. This is clearly the intent of a whole section of the manuscript (letters 863–1085), entitled "Exordies and Extraits," which is written entirely in Latin and consists only of fragments, either clauses and brief passages marked by rhetorical flourish or brief proverbial sentences. A junior clerk could, no doubt, turn to this section when in need of a something ornamental for especially significant correspondence. The subheadings of this section are indicative of the tone of the whole. Letters 863–923 are labeled "Miscellaneous"; 924–25 are "Dictum Quintiliani"; 926–55 are "Dictum Liberii"; 956–1026 are "De Fortuna"; 1027–31 are "Nota de necessitate"; 1032–37 are "Nota de detractione"; 1038–84 are "Nota de lingua lubrica"; and 1085 is "Dicit Jeronimus." Bentley, "Formulary," 1023–66. These headings are also significant as evidence that Hoccleve had greater affinities than is usually imagined to an early international classicism, that culture represented by figures such as the French Boccaccians, Christine de Pizan, and the brothers Col.

45. Altogether, there are nine letters in this collection referring to "T.H." (numbers 139, 159–61, 179, 200, 219, 567, and 982—though 567 probably does not refer to Hoccleve). Number 219 is given the marginal description "Pur paier tiele somme pur parchemyn, ynke et cire etc. despenduz en loffice du prive seal." The text reads: "Roy as tresorer et chamberleins de notre eschequer saluz. Nous vous mandons que a notre ame clerc, T.H. facez paier tiele somme pur parchemyn, ynke et cire rouge par lui achatez dun tiel, haburdassher de Londres, et despenduz en loffice de notre prive seal de tiel jour, tiel an, en cea. Donne etc." Bentley too supplies Hoccleve's name for these initials in letter 219. Bentley, "Formulary," 214.

similar modesty.[46] But the use of the initials "T.H." in these letters is surpris-
ing in the context of Hoccleve's *Formulary*. Hoccleve is usually quite careful
to remove all signs of particular identity in his letters by replacing proper
names with "un tiel" or some other marker of anonymity.[47] Since his docu-
ments are meant to be easily appropriable for multiple uses, any sign of partic-
ular identity would be extraneous and even a distraction for the junior clerks.
Hoccleve makes exceptions and uses initials or, more rarely, proper names,
only when one of two conditions is met. He includes markers of specific iden-
tity in his letters when the individuals involved were of sufficient social impor-
tance—great magnates, major ecclesiastical figures, or merchants who were
owed money by the Crown or who had been granted trade privileges. He
also includes such markers in those documents, alluded to above, that are so
historically specific as to look more like exhibits than practical models.

But the striking thing about this sequence of "T.H." letters is that they
fulfill neither of these requirements. If there was ever an illusion to which
Hoccleve would not have succumbed, it would have been that he was grand
enough to merit social attention. And far from having any inescapable his-
torical particularity, these letters could claim to be the most formulaic, the
most bureaucratic, in the whole volume. Usually, Hoccleve offers one model
for each category of letter. In this sequence, however, he offers three letters
of the same genre, safe conduct, which are distinguished by only the most
minute of variations.[48] Given both the precedents for the inclusion of auto-
biographical material in letter collections and the tendency to find autobio-

46. H. G. Richardson, "Business Training in Medieval Oxford," *American Historical Review* 46
(1941): 259–80. Sampson was by no means unique. Richardson also supplies the example of William
Kingsmill, another teacher of the *ars dictaminis* who referred to himself in his sample letters by use
of his initials. Richardson, "Letters of the English Dictatores," in *Formularies Which Bear on the
History of Oxford*, ed. W. A. Pantin, H. E. Salter, and H. G. Richardson, Oxford Historical Society,
n.s. vol. 5 (Oxford: Clarendon Press, 1942), 340.

47. See, for example, the letter cited above (n. 44) ordering payment for the purchase of parch-
ment and ink in which Hoccleve is said to have purchased these items "*dun tiel,* haburdassher de
Londres" (emphasis added). Another technique of anonymity used in these documents is the re-
placement of proper names with algebraic substitutions, such as "A. de B."

48. Bentley, "Formulary," 154. The text of these letters runs as follows in Bentley's edition:

159. Fiat protectio cum clausula volumus pro T.H., qui in obsequiam nostrum sic. ad partes Francie
profecturus est ibidem in comitiva dilecti consanguinei et fideli nostri talis in eodem obsequio
nostro moraturus, per unum annum durature. Datum etc.

160. Fiat proteccio cum clausula volumus pro T.H., qui in obsequio nostro in comitiva talis in
partibus Francie moraturus per unnum annum duratura.

161. Fiat proteccio cum clausula volumus pro T.H., qui in obsequio nostro ad partes Picardie
profecturus est ibidem in comitiva talis custodis talis castri super salva custodia eiusdem castri
moraturus, per unnum etc.

graphical material erupting out of most any genre in Hoccleve's works, it is quite remarkable that Hoccleve chooses to include himself within his *Formulary* only in this exaggeratedly impersonal sequence of letters. It is as though he were gesturing at the act and theatrically turning himself into a cipher. Or, to be more precise, my point is that subjectivity in the *Formulary* is only represented through an act of signification that is simultaneously an act of assertion and one of reticence. Trained in the highly vexed generic terrain of the petition, Hoccleve comes to autobiography by way of bureaucratic hide-and-seek.[49]

To understand why Hoccleve would place such significance in mere initials, we need to consider briefly another little-studied medieval phenomenon: graffiti. As V. Pritchard has shown, graffiti were widespread in medieval England, sometimes as cartoon drawings or devotional mottoes and, as in the *Formulary*, sometimes as names or initials.[50] Moreover, the late fourteenth century was something of a watershed moment in the history of the proper name. The reign of Richard II witnessed the first use of the royal signature instead of a seal for the authentication of documents.[51] And John Bowers has suggested that Hoccleve's unprecedented concern with the collection, preservation, and proper attribution of his works is reflected concretely in the highly elaborate signature at the end of the Durham MS of the *Series*.[52]

---

49. On the "ludic" element in Hoccleve, see Classen, "Hoccleve's Independence from Chaucer." This game also has affinities to the presentation of authorial signatures through anagrams, something Hoccleve might very well have encountered in Machaut or in the acrostics of monastic writers. On these signifying games in particular, see Burt Kimmelman, *The Poetics of Authorship in the Later Middle Ages: The Emergence of the Modern Literary Persona* (New York: Peter Lang, 1996), esp. 1–35.

50. V. Pritchard, *English Medieval Graffiti* (Cambridge: Cambridge University Press, 1967). Such graffiti seems often to have been made as an accusation or admission of poor craftsmanship, such as the example Pritchard gives of a mason carving "I spit at it" into faulty stonework, or Hoccleve's apologetic note in his *Formulary*, "Heer made y leep yeer—ex negligencia etc." Ibid., 79; and Brown, "Privy Seal Clerks," 271. Of course, scribal graffiti is also sometimes notable for its complete irrelevancy, as in another note in the *Formulary*: "Item, to bie me more beddyng for shame."

51. Richard used at times a full name and at times simply initials. Chrimes, *Introduction to the Administrative History of England*, 215. Perroy also attests to this fact, in passing, and credits Maxwell Lyte as having been the first to notice it. Perroy, *Diplomatic Correspondence*, xxxi. See also Otway-Ruthven, *The King's Secretary*, 26–27. For more on the importance of the signature at this moment, see Anne Middleton, "William Langland's 'Kynd Name': Authorial Signature and Social Identity in Late Fourteenth-Century England," in *Literary Practice and Social Change in Britain* (Berkeley and Los Angeles: University of California Press, 1990), 15–82. Béatrice Fraenkel provides an ambitious history of the signature marked by structuralist meditations on the sign in *La Signature: Genèse d'un signe* (Paris: Gallimard, 1992).

52. John M. Bowers, "Hoccleve's Huntington Holographs: The First 'Collected Poems' in English," *Fifteenth-Century Studies* 15 (1989): 42. See also H. C. Schulz, "Thomas Hoccleve, Scribe,"

More broadly, however, I would suggest that graffiti can provide a very powerful model for thinking about Hoccleve's writing. Graffiti is an assertive textual marking of the self, and of the presence of the self, through a graphics that is necessarily supplemental to official textuality. To write graffiti is to place a mark where there is supposed to be no mark, or to place a mark in the margins. Graffiti cannot exist without either an official text or an official blankness to set it off. This relationship provides a very close analogy to the relationship between the representation of the self in Hoccleve and the creation of the document, the text expunged of any autobiographical particularity, in bureaucratic writing. As graffiti can only be perceived as a thing in itself once the authorized text has been expunged of any such topicality, so, for Hoccleve, autobiography begins its history in the wake of the bureaucratic document.

Any reader of Hoccleve's poetry must also be struck by the fact that the early sections of the *Formulary* contain a number of letters pertaining to grants and the transference of corodies, benefices, and annuities such as would have constituted the rewards of any relatively prosperous Privy Seal clerk. These letters read like positive responses to the petitionary verse that makes up the bulk of Hoccleve's poetic output. Such documents are of interest to our investigation because they dramatically highlight the stark stylistic differences that distinguished supplication and response in a petitionary society. Instead of the witty and anxious self-dramatization of a needy clerk, these letters embody the high-toned anonymity of a regal proxy.[53] This shift in tone is even more striking when we reflect that in all probability Hoccleve wrote both. Far from being simply an interesting and probably frustrating condition of Hoccleve's job, this confluence actually expresses an important historical point. For here we come face to face with the fact that the very same Hoccleve who has been so often described as excessive, rambling, and obsessed with himself was professionally responsible for the endless reduplication of a language of grave anonymity. It is in the way that this professional

---

Speculum 12 (1937): 73. Van Oostrom points to a similar concern for an elaborate signature on the part of Dirk Potter, and connects the particular flourishes of the script to the chancery hand Potter had acquired as a clerk. Van Oostrom, *Court and Culture*, 9.

53. See, for example, letter 54, marginally annotated as "Graunt dune corrodie en une abbacie." The text reads as follows: "Roy au chanceller saluz. Combien que avant ces heures eussiens grantez a A. de B. autiele sustenance, a prendre pur terme de sa vie en labbacie de S. come L. M., qui mort est, y avoit et prist qant il vesquist du grant de notre trescher sire et aiel, le roy, que Dieux assoille, sur quoy les abbe et covent de mesme labbacie ont receu le dit A. a mesme la sustenance par lettres souz lour commun seal, selont le purport de notre dit grant, a ce que nous sumes enformez." Bentley, "Formulary," 47–48.

habitus shaped the anxiety of a petitioning class, I believe, that we can explain the ubiquity of autobiography in Hoccleve. For what is striking about the administrative game of petition and response is that if the petition relies on the expression of individual particularity, the response is predicated upon regal anonymity. Hoccleve's interest in the self as its own end is thus generated only in opposition to bureaucratic anonymity. The language of bureaucracy and that of autobiography are, in effect, mutually constitutive.

This dialectical effect provides the ideological underpinning to that most representative scene in Hoccleve's verse, a scene that is both so typical of Hoccleve and so functionally crucial to each of his major works that we might be warranted in calling it the narrative germ of his writing. Both the *Regement of Princes* and the *Series* begin with representations of Hoccleve physically alone, in some isolated Boethian chamber, brooding over his ill fates past, present, and feared. Each poem then proceeds with the extrusion of Hoccleve into the social order; more specifically, in each there is an assertive interruption by some questioner who encourages Hoccleve to cease brooding and instead to take up his pen and write for the prince. The centrality of these moments is further underlined by the transition into dialogue that arrives as both a thematic and a structural departure from the monologues out of which they had developed, thus philosophically transcending the Boethian resignation of the Hoccleve persona and formally displacing the monologic conventions of the complaint genre. In sum, if there is a systematic poetics at the heart of Hoccleve's work, its essence lies in the attempt to transmute private anxiety into public discourse, in the attempt to move beyond the solipsism of the complaint and into the social world of the petition.[54] This generic shift epitomizes the strong bifurcation between the expression of subjectivity and the anonymity of bureaucratic society; for in the petition, the lowly clerk must simultaneously assert the particularities of desire and yet, for the sake of propriety, take shelter in the bureaucratic nature of the document.

"La Male Regle" and the Education of a Supplicant

One of Hoccleve's most well-known autobiographical poems, "La Male Regle," substantiates these links between bureaucratic practices and the con-

54. James Simpson has anatomized just such a movement between isolation and public dialogue in Hoccleve's *Series*; see his "Madness and Texts: Hoccleve's *Series*," in *Chaucer and Fifteenth-Century Poetry*, ed. Julia Boffey and Janet Cowen (London: King's College London Centre for Late Antique and Medieval Studies, 1991), 15–29. I discuss these transitions in Chapter 3.

struction of autobiography in Hoccleve's verse.[55] "La Male Regle" is among Hoccleve's earliest works, written in 1405. Hoccleve presents himself in this brief work as an apostate to the god Helthe. He has for twenty years been a glutton and a fool, eating and drinking until he can't get out of bed in the morning, and spending all his little money to buy the flattering words of boatmen on the Thames and of "Venus femel lusty children deere." The poem shows Chaucer's influence in the comic presentation of Hoccleve's past misdeeds, but it is quite un-Chaucerian in its detailed imagination of clerkly life in early fifteenth-century London.[56] The generic background is twofold. As Eva Thornley has demonstrated, insofar as the poem is addressed to the figure of a deity and structured so as to first recount a detailed and repentant confession of misdeeds (the misrule) and then to beg for mercy and redemption, the poem operates as a "parody" of the conventions of penitential lyrics.[57] In addition, insofar as the poem was addressed to Thomas Neville in the hopes of eliciting an installment of Hoccleve's annuity, the poem obviously belongs to one of the largest categories in Hoccleve's oeuvre, the begging or petitionary poem.

This poem is striking, however, in that it yokes together the petitional and penitential genres in such a way that they work at cross-purposes. Part of Hoccleve's penitential confession to the god Helthe is the Boethian argument that only now that he has wasted his money and his health on tavern life, only now that he has been crushed by poverty and ill health, can he see that he was doing anything wrong before:

> But I haue herd men seye longe ago,
> Prosperitee is blynd and see ne may,
> And verifie I can wel it is so
> For I myself put haue it in assay.
> Whan I was weel, kowde I considere it? Nay.

55. Though I emphasize the autobiographical content of this poem, one should acknowledge that it was not always read as autobiography. Marian Trudgill and J. A. Burrow have discovered a balade in the Canterbury Cathedral Library that represents a version of "La Male Regle" shorn of its particular references to Hoccleve and rewritten as a general treatment of youth and moderation. See their "Hoccleve Balade," *Notes and Queries* 45 (1998): 178–80.

56. A. C. Spearing, in a fine reading of "La Male Regle," draws a series of distinctions between Chaucer's poetic technique and that of Hoccleve in this poem, including Hoccleve's more "whole-hearted" and "vulnerable" autobiographic representations and his use of a *Piers Plowman*-like technique of "small-scale personification." A. C. Spearing, *Medieval to Renaissance in English Poetry* (Cambridge: Cambridge University Press, 1985), 110–20.

57. Eva M. Thornley, "The Middle English Penitential Lyric and Hoccleve's Autobiographical Poetry," *Neuphilologische Mitteilungen* 68 (1967): 295–321.

But what, me longed aftir nouelrie
As yeeres yonge yernen day by day,
And now my smert accusith my folie.

(lines 33–40)

Only in his current poverty can he see that he had been a fool to abuse his health in the past. In other words, the opening of the poem establishes a sequential and causal link between poverty and penance: once one has experienced poverty, one is then mentally equipped to turn to penance.

This Boethian sequence, however, is rapidly complicated. As Hoccleve explores the metaphors of penitential verse, he comes upon the metaphor of the sick purse, a figure that collapses the temporal sequence of his earlier argument and treats the two illnesses as a single malady: "My body and purs been at ones seeke" (line 409). And even this identity does not last long, for Hoccleve has joined these two illnesses together through the metaphor of the sick purse only in order to rearrange their relationship. In the final stanza he begins to speak not of illness but of the prospect of cures and medicine:

By coyn I gete may swich medecyne
As may myn hurtes alle þat me greeue
Exyle cleene and voide me of pyne.

(lines 446–48)

Here we see these two elements again arrayed as a causal and sequential pair, but the line of causality has been reversed. In the schematic narrative offered by the poem's story of penance, coin had been the first element of the narrative: lack of coin had led to illness, which had then led to penance. But in this *petitional* ending, coin is not a beginning but a triumphal ending.

One might be tempted to conclude that with this ending Hoccleve has simply subordinated the penitential to the petitional and shown his real interest to be the payment of his annuity. However, such quick cynicism fails to take the Boethian element of the autobiography seriously. In fact, the conflict between penitential and petitional genres goes much deeper than a simple absorption of the penitential. By reversing the causal sequence between coin and confession, between poverty and penance, Hoccleve has come full circle and reentered the beginning of his penitential narrative. Since only poverty created the preconditions for successful penance, then the success of the petition, the securing of coin or "medicine," brings him back to the very beginning of his penitential narrative, back to his riches and presumably back to the accompanying folly.[58]

Is Hoccleve thus suggesting that a successful petition is an act requiring penance? I think that he is, as we will see by examining the role of flattery within Hoccleve's poem. Flattery is a significant thematic interest throughout "La Male Regle." Indeed, the evils of flattery are a common theme in much of Hoccleve's later poetry, and along with the metaphor of misrule, the discussion of flattery is in part an anticipation of the concerns of Hoccleve's more explicitly public verse. In the context of his more private autobiographical verse, however, flattery provides not just a moralizing theme but a specific tactic through which Hoccleve unites penitential and petitional verse. Hoccleve adopts the conventions of penitential discourse less to confess his sins than to flatter his potential patrons. He creates a poetry of implicit and witty flattery aimed at inciting the generosity of his audience; his is a strategy that is best understood as embodying something we might call aggressive self-denigration.

For an example of Hoccleve's characteristic approach, we can turn to his famous description of the Paul's Head Tavern. The point of this scene is less to present Hoccleve's conduct as some sort of sin than it is to present it as a failure:

> I dar nat telle how þat the fressh repeir
> Of Venus femel lusty children deere,
> Þat so goodly, so shaply were and feir,
> And so plesant of port and of maneere,
> And feede cowden al a world with cheere,
> And of atyr passyngly wel byseye,
> At Poules Heed me maden ofte appeere
> To talke of mirthe and to disport and pleye.
>
> Ther was sweet wyn ynow thurghout the hous
> And wafres thikke, for this conpaignie
> Þat I spak of been sumwhat likerous.
> Where as they mowe a draght of wyn espie,

---

58. David Mills has recently posited another very interesting reading of this conclusion, suggesting that Hoccleve here depicts himself as a buyer and seller of words in a world in which "money and texts are inextricably linked." David Mills, "The Voices of Thomas Hoccleve," in *Essays on Thomas Hoccleve*, ed. Catherine Batt (London: Centre for Medieval and Renaissance Studies, Queen Mary and Westfield College, University of London, 1996), 102.

Sweete and in wirkynge hoot for the maistrie
To warme a stomak with, thereof they drank.
To suffre hem paie had been no courtesie;
That charge I took to wynne loue and thank.

Of loues aart yit touchid I no deel;
I cowde nat, and eek it was no neede
Had I a kus I was content ful weel,
Bettre than I wolde han be with the deede.
Theron can I but smal, it is no dreede.
When þat men speke of it in my presence
For shame I wexe as reed as is the gleede.

(lines 137–59)

Hoccleve artfully moves the reader back and forth between the expectation of some steamy confession and the realization that there is not really anything much to confess. He begins with "I dar nat telle," extravagantly suggesting that the something to come is too awful even to speak of, but then refers to his sirens with the coyly ambiguous "Venus femel lusty children deere" and regretfully admits the innocence of the encounter. Hoccleve continues this oscillation over the course of the anecdote. He first establishes a highly charged setting by describing the women as sexual objects and by deploying throughout a language of sensual and erotic valences: they "disport," are "likerous," and drink wine to "warme a stomak." However, this rhetorical foreplay does not get very far. Far too embarrassed for "the deede" itself, Hoccleve contents himself with a kiss, blushing at the mere mention of anything further. There is even, perhaps, a suggestion of physical impotence in lines such as "I cowde nat" and "Theron can I but smal." These highly ironic stanzas are not about who has fallen into the sins of the tavern; they are about who can "be a man" in the tavern and who cannot. Hoccleve offers here a vision of comparative masculine prowess through which his self-denigration serves to flatter his audience. Insofar as his poem is autobiographic, it is a confession of failures, a confession meant to allow his readers, especially the addressee, Lord Furnivall, to feel themselves superior and thus, with a little luck, generous.

But Hoccleve being Hoccleve, even self-denigration may be something for which to apologize. Here, for example, is Hoccleve's central metaphor for flattery, his account of the story of Ulysses and the Sirens:

Whan þat Vlixes saillid to and fro
By meermaides, this was his policie:
Alle eres of men of his conpaignie
With wex he stoppe leet, for þat they noght
Hir song sholde heere, lest the armonye
Hem mighte vnto swich deedly sleep han broght;

And bond himself vnto the shippes mast.
Lo, thus hem alle saued his prudence.
The wys man is of peril sore agast.
O flaterie! O lurkyng pestilence!
If sum man dide his cure and diligence
To stoppe his eres fro thy poesie,
And nat wolde herkne a word of thy sentence,
Vnto his greef it were a remedie.

(lines 251–64)[59]

Hoccleve's deployment of this anecdote resembles nothing so much as the rhetoric of Chaucer's Pardoner. Hoccleve, the inveterate flatterer, warns his readers to beware flattery. The irony is heightened by Hoccleve's persistent metaphoric connection between himself and the Sirens in alluding to their "harmony" as "poesie." By creating this metaphoric link Hoccleve casts himself as a Siren and acknowledges the flattering intent of his petitional verse. These stanzas thus offer a preemptive defense against the charge of flattery by first recognizing the possible accusation and then refusing it by denouncing the vice in others.

Hoccleve concludes this poem with three stanzas that both provide a more elaborate defense of his flattery and connect it with the more specific concerns of the petitioning subject:

I kepte nat to be seen inportune
In my pursuyte; I am therto ful looth.
And yit þat gyse ryf is and commune
Among the peple now withouten ooth;
As the shamelees crauour wole, it gooth,
For estaat real can nat al day werne.

---

59. This passage is drawn from Holcot (see Chapter 5).

But poore shamefast man ofte is wroth;
Wherfore for to craue moot I lerne.

The prouerbe is, the doumb man no lond getith.
Who so nat spekith and with neede is bete
And thurgh arghnesse his owne self forgetith,
No wondir thogh anothir him forgete.
Neede hath no lawe, as þat the clerkes trete,
And thus to craue artith me my neede,
And right wole eek þat I me entremete,
For þat I axe is due, as God me speede.

And þat that due is, thy magnificence
Shameth to werne as þat I byleeue.
As I seide, reewe on myn impotence,
þat likly am to sterue yit or eeue
But if thow in this wyse me releeue.
By coyn I gete may swich medecyne
As may myn hurtes alle þat me greeue
Exyle cleene and voide me of pyne.
(lines 425–48)

There could be no better illustration of the social anxieties attendant on the
form of the petition than these stanzas. The only way to answer need in this
economy of grants and annuities was to petition, and the only hope of suc‐
cess lay in speaking up in its support. However, as Hoccleve here acknowl‐
edges, reminding one's social betters of outstanding debts is at best awkward,
at worst disastrously presumptuous. The result is the formation of a social
identity labeled here as the "crauour." The "craver" is, quite simply, the man
who has learned that the successful petition is best achieved through the
strategy of insistent self‐denigration. The very opposite of the "doumb man,"
the craver speaks of himself continually but always with great humility; he
does not demand but asks only that "magnificence" should "reewe on myn
impotence."

Nevertheless, as with Chaucer's Pardoner, it is often in the most appar‐
ently abject moments that we discover an aggressive and even acerbic tone
in Hoccleve.[60] In this discussion of himself as craver, Hoccleve is first careful

60. For an example of a moment of similarly surprising assertiveness in Hoccleve's more political
poetry, see Charles Blyth on Hoccleve's "elaborately nervy wit." "Thomas Hoccleve's Other Mas‐
ter," *Mediaevalia* 16 (1993): 349–59.

to differentiate himself from the mass of common supplicants; indeed, the slippery "wherfore" of line 433 implies that any blame for his present actions lies with those who have preceded him and made it a custom. Moreover, he explains his resort to the petition through a progressive trio of causes, moving from the growth of custom, to proverbial wisdom, and then to the doctrine of clerks—a progression surely meant to remind the audience of his own dignity and intellectual status as a clerk even at the moment at which he seems to be accepting the humble role of the craver. Finally, there is even something biting in Hoccleve's reference to that magnificence which would shame to refuse his just request. Magnificence is written as the mirror image to Hoccleve's "impotence"; but as Hoccleve's rhetorical ploys have underlined the extent to which he exaggerates his powerlessness, so we might wonder whether "magnificence" is itself meant to be read as an exaggeration, as a word that acts less to describe than to throw into question. In short, it is in these stanzas nominally written to explain his acceptance of the humble role of the petitioner that Hoccleve appears at his most insistent and self-aggrandizing.

In its depiction of the education of a "craver," "La Male Regle," demonstrates the way in which the bureaucratic form of the petition mediated the financial anxiety of these secular clerks. It also demonstrates how such anxiety could form the raw material of a poetics of self-representation. In "La Male Regle" Hoccleve writes a poem that attempts to balance his anxiety over seeming to be "importune" with an argument that "need" dictates that he speak. This seesaw effect, which is reflected in the larger structural synthesis of penitential and petitionary verse, is an exact corollary to the effect of the placement of the "T.H." letters in his *Formulary*. What we see in each instance is the representation of selfhood via an act of almost simultaneous assertion and apology. Driven by the irreconcilable demands of need and propriety, Hoccleve turned the textual gambits of the petition into a poetry of intense self-examination, a poetry that both enacts autobiography and meditates upon the difficulties of the genre. It should come as no surprise that autobiography was born in Westminster; in a sense, it was a game played by every clerk in town.

The

Letter of Cupid

Gender

and the

Foundations

of

Poetic

Authority

The parameters, both material and textual, within which the autobiographical component so central to Hoccleve's work was constructed, also frame one of his early compositions, the *Letter of Cupid* (1402).[1] The literary culture of fifteenth-century England suffered a protracted crisis in authority, a recurrent doubt about the grounding and merit of vernacular poetic composition. As Seth Lerer has argued, Chaucer's overpowering precedent led many fifteenth-century poets into incessant admissions of inadequacy and attempts to reground their authority by crafting authorial personae in the footsteps of Chaucer or even of Chaucer's fictional characters.[2] Others attempted to create a place of authority as vernacular authors through strategic alliances with patrons such as the Lancastrian monarchs and Humphrey of Gloucester.[3] One must always beware of attributing too quickly a depth of psychological reality to this crisis, but whether the poets of the

1. I refer to Hoccleve's poem by this English title for the sake of consistency with current critical practice, though the title is editorial. Manuscript evidence tends toward the French title, *Lepistre de Cupide*. Thelma A. Fenster and Mary Carpenter Erler, *Poems of Cupid, God of Love* (Leiden: E. J. Brill, 1990), 174.

2. Lerer, *Chaucer and His Readers*; see also Jocelyn Wogan-Browne, Nicholas Watson, Andrew Taylor, and Ruth Evans, eds., *The Idea of the Vernacular: An Anthology of Middle English Literary Theory, 1280–1520* (University Park: Penn State University Press, 1999), esp. 3–4, 16–17, 320–21.

3. On these points, see David Lawton, "Dullness and the Fifteenth Century," *English Literary History* 54 (1987): 761–99; Strohm, *England's Empty Throne*.

early fifteenth century labored under a collective neurosis or whether these justifications were made in the spirit of a literary exercise, the poetry of this period is frequently marked by complicated negotiations of poetic personae and literary authority. In the *Letter of Cupid*, as we will see, Hoccleve sets out a specific case for his authority as a vernacular poet by building on the example of Christine de Pizan.

Hoccleve's *Letter of Cupid* is a translation of Christine's *L'Epistre au Dieu d'Amours*, a poem that voices the complaints of women wronged by men through the device of a letter written by Cupid, the God of Love. Like many similar mythographic exercises, such as Alain de Lille's *De Planctu Naturae*, the poem speaks through an allegorical persona borrowed from classical mythology and uses this frame to offer an ethical satire of contemporary mores. Here Cupid offers a defense of women against the clerkly slanders of Jean de Meun and the Ovidian love tradition with which he was associated. Cupid, presented as the divine arbitrator of the court of love, receives a petition from the women of France in which they lament the abuse suffered at the hands of men, especially the false lovers who are traitors in Cupid's court. Cupid lists the many misdeeds of these men, the corresponding virtues of the women, and concludes by banishing all slanderers and false seducers from his court.

Christine's original poem is famous, in part, as a precursor to the *Querelle de la Rose*, the early fifteenth-century exchange of letters among leading members of the French literati that pitted Christine and her ally, Jean Gerson (chancellor of the University of Paris), against three opponents, the brothers Gontier and Pierre Col, and Jean de Montreuil (the provost of Lille).[4] The topic of the debate was a disagreement over the representation

4. The literature on the *Querelle* is substantial. For a convenient account, see Charity Cannon Willard, *Christine de Pizan: Her Life and Works* (New York: Persea, 1984), 78–79. For the principal texts in this exchange, see Eric Hicks, *Le Débat sur la "Roman de la Rose"* (Paris: Champion, 1977), and the translations in Joseph L. Baird and John R. Kane, *La Querelle de la Rose: Letters and Documents* (Chapel Hill: University of North Carolina, 1978). For other texts and commentaries, see Barbara K. Altman, *The Love Debate Poems of Christine de Pizan* (Gainesville: University of Florida Press, 1998); Pierre Yves Badel, *Le Roman de la Rose au XIVe siècle* (Geneva: Librairie Droz, 1980); Joseph L. Baird, "Pierre Col and the Querelle de la Rose," *Philological Quarterly* 60 (1981): 273–86; Kevin Brownlee, "Discourses of the Self: Christine de Pizan and the *Romance of the Rose*," in *Rethinking the Romance of the Rose*, ed. Kevin Brownlee and Sylvia Huot (Philadelphia: University of Pennsylvania Press, 1992), 234–61; Jacqueline Cerquiglini, "Trials of Eros," in *A New History of French Literature*, ed. D. Hollier (Cambridge, Mass.: Harvard University Press, 1989), 114–18; Helen Solterer, "Christine's Way: The *Querelle du Roman de la rose* and the Ethics of a Political Response," in *The Master and Minerva: Disputing Women in French Medieval Culture* (Berkeley and Los Angeles: University of California Press, 1995), 151–75; Helen Solterer, "Flaming Words: Verbal Violence and Gender in Premodern Paris," *Romanic Review* 86 (1995): 355–78; Karen Sullivan, "At the Limit of

of women and virtue in Jean de Meun's continuation of the *Roman de la Rose*, with Christine arguing that a foolish veneration for Jean de Meun served to mask his underlying vulgarity and misogyny. This exchange survives as a dossier of letters collected by Christine and sent to Isabeau of Bavaria with the request that Isabeau might judge the debate, a courtly gesture that locates the dossier within the generic terrain of the *demande d'amour*. Christine's *Epistre* predates the exchange of letters that made up the dossier of the *Querelle* proper, but the *Epistre*'s attack on Jean de Meun and its assertion of female experience as a valuable source of authority closely anticipate the concerns and arguments of the later *Querelle*.

Christine de Pizan's poem is thus one of the earliest examples of the brilliant and highly important raids she was to make on the masculine preserve of medieval literate culture. Her work in the *Epistre* is of great significance as an early example of a woman taking up public letters and asserting not only that she could engage in debate over the shape of intellectual culture but, even more important, that she was uniquely qualified, *as a woman*, to comment on the alliance of theological misogyny and *fin amor* so central to the cultural imagination of gender at this moment. Indeed, in her debate with the defenders of the *Roman de la Rose*, Christine comes near to making the assertion that the arguments of the clerks were suspect purely because of their gender and that her own gender gave her arguments a contrasting reliability.[5] This strong insistence on the importance of gender in the con-

---

Feminist Theory: An Architectonics of the *Querelle de la Rose*," *Exemplaria: A Journal of Theory in Medieval and Renaissance Studies* 3 (1991): 435–66; and Charity Cannon Willard, "A New Look at Christine de Pizan's 'Epistre an Dieu d'Amours,' " in *Seconda miscellanea di studi e ricerche sul Quattrocento francese*, ed. Jonathan Beck and Gianni Mombello (Chambéry: Centre d'études franco-italien, 1981), 73–92.

5. It is this elevation of specifically female experience as a valuable source of textual authority that has inspired many of the claims for Christine as a protofeminist writer. For extensive discussions of Christine's efforts to fashion a specifically feminine poetic authority, see Maureen Quilligan, *The Allegory of Female Authority: Christine de Pizan's "Cité des Dames"* (Ithaca: Cornell University Press, 1991); and her later essay "The Name of the Author: Self-Representation in Christine de Pizan's *Livre de la Cité des Dames*," *Exemplaria* 4 (1992): 201–28. For additional treatments, see Sandra Hindman, "With Ink and Mortar: Christine de Pizan's *Cité des Dames*: An Art Essay," *Feminist Studies* 10 (1984): 457–84; the essays gathered in Marilyn Desmond, ed., *Christine de Pizan and the Categories of Difference* (Minneapolis: University of Minnesota Press, 1998); Mary McKinley, "The Subversive 'Seulette,' " in *Politics, Gender and Genre: The Political Thought of Christine de Pizan*, ed. Margaret Brabant and Jean-Bethke Elshtain (Boulder, Colo.: Westview, 1992), 157–69; Patricia Phillippy, "Establishing Authority: Boccaccio's *De Claris Mulieribus* and Christine de Pizan's *Le Livre de la Cité des Dames*," *Romanic Review* 77 (1986): 167–93; and Lori Walters, "Fathers and Daughters: Christine de Pizan as Reader of the Male Tradition of *Clergie* in the *Dit de la Rose*," in *Reinterpreting Christine de Pizan*, ed. E. J. Richards (Athens: University of Georgia Press, 1992), 63–76.

struction of authorship and authority gave her arguments a historical impor-
tance and also led to her influence on Hoccleve.

Hoccleve's translation of the *Epistre* has had a spotty past. The poem
seems to have been relatively popular early on, surviving in ten manuscripts
and several early printed editions, though some of its early popularity in print
may have been the result of its mistaken attribution to Chaucer.[6] Modern
scholarship has been mostly concerned with two issues: the question of
whether the work should be thought of as a translation proper or as an
adaptation; and the related matter of the extent to which Hoccleve's version
honors the anti-misogynistic intent of Christine's original. This first question
is perhaps not possible to answer in the terms in which it is usually asked, as
any hard and fast distinction between translation and adaptation misrepre-
sents the extent to which it was an expected practice of translators in the late
medieval period to contract, add to, or alter the material of their originals,
particularly when translation was from one vernacular language to another.

The second question, of whether Hoccleve's poem is an elaboration of
Christine's antimisogynist original or a mocking parody, is central to this
chapter. In a debate that has reproduced the divisions of its historical object,
scholarship has divided mostly over the question of tone in Hoccleve's poem
(mirroring the *Querelle*'s argument over the propriety and function of satire).
The modern dossier of what we might call the *Querelle de L'Epistre* begins
with the comments of Jerome Mitchell and John Fleming on the one side
and those of Diane Bornstein on the other. Fleming and Mitchell both sug-
gest that Hoccleve's poem is meant to be consistent with the antimisogynis-
tic arguments of Christine's original (though Fleming does admit that
Hoccleve was motivated by the aim of "teaching" Christine how to read Jean
de Meun's poetry); Mitchell goes so far as to suggest that "the *Letter of Cupid*,
viewed as a whole, is at least as feminist in its outlook as its French source."[7]
Bornstein, on the other hand, argues that Hoccleve reversed the sympathies

6. See Fenster and Erler, *Poems of Cupid, God of Love*, 172; John Burrow, "Hoccleve and Chau-
cer," in *Chaucer Traditions: Studies in Honour of Derek Brewer*, ed. Ruth Morse and Barry Windeatt
(Cambridge: Cambridge University Press, 1990), 55; and Burrow, *Thomas Hoccleve*, 13–14. The
poem was printed in 1532 in William Thynne's collection of Chaucer's works and in subsequent
printings of this edition. The correct attribution was made in Thomas Speght's 1598 edition of
Chaucer, but Chaucer's authorship was still maintained as late as George Sewell's 1718 translation.

7. John V. Fleming, "Hoccleve's 'Letter of Cupid' and the 'Quarrel' over the *Roman de la Rose*,"
Medium Aevum 40 (1971): 21–40; and Mitchell, *Thomas Hoccleve*, 53, 77–84. For similar views, see
also the comments in Derek Pearsall, "English Chaucerians," in *Chaucer and Chaucerians*, ed. D. S.
Brewer (Alabama: University of Alabama Press, 1966), 201–39; Calin, *The French Tradition*, 402–3;
and William Quinn, "Hoccleve's 'Epistle of Cupid,' " *Explicator* 45 (1986): 7–10.

of Christine's original—that he removed several of Christine's exempla and turned a serious poem into farce, making the poem a joke at Christine's expense.[8]

Recent discussion has continued to revolve inconclusively around these questions of tone, asking, in essence, whether Hoccleve took Christine de Pizan (and her poem) seriously or whether he made of it grist for the mill of antifeminist satire. Karen Winstead and Anna Torti have both attempted to pin down the *Letter*'s slippery tone by comparing it to the treatment of women in others of Hoccleve's works, especially the paired tales of "Jereslaus's Wife" and "Jonathas" from Hoccleve's last poetic work, the *Series*. It is a sign of Hoccleve's serious and persistent interest in gender that the *Series* uses these two tales drawn from the *Gesta Romanorum* to return to his discussion of women's virtue begun some twenty years earlier in the *Letter of Cupid*. The tales of "Jereslaus's Wife" and "Jonathas" present, respectively: (1) a tale of female virtue explicitly meant to atone for any offense taken by earlier readers of the *Letter of Cupid* (in obvious imitation of Chaucer's *Legend of Good Women*); and (2) the story of Felicula, a deceitful woman who ends as the victim of apparently righteous and horrific vengeance at the hands of a man whom she had deceived. Winstead and Torti are in agreement that this symmetrical pairing of the third and fifth poems of the *Series* is meant to create a metatextual conundrum about a poet's duty to represent women's virtue; Hoccleve himself raises the point by commenting that a movement from apology back to a tale about a deceitful women is at best a questionable strategy for reconciling himself with his female audience.[9]

Winstead and Torti disagree, however, on what this pair of tales suggests about Hoccleve's final sympathies. For Winstead, the apparent ambiguities of this abrupt switch from virtue to villainy are actually a sign of Hoccleve's tactic of "baiting" his female readers. Hoccleve mocks women like Christine de Pizan by seeming to apologize for maligning women while presenting a

8. Diane Bornstein, "Anti-Feminism in Thomas Hoccleve's Translation of Christine de Pizan's *Epistre au dieu d'amours*," *English Language Notes* 19 (1981): 7–14.

9. This pattern of apologies, which seems designed to create further suspicion of their authors, is so common that we should perhaps read many of them as attempts to initiate *querelles* over their works. As Richard Green comments of Chaucer's elaborately awkward apology in the *Legend of Good Women*, such moments often seem "less an attempt to forestall possible criticism than to provoke it." Green, "The *Familia Regis* and the *Familia Cupidinis*," in *English Court Culture in the Later Middle Ages*, ed. V. J. Scattergood and J. W. Sherborne (London: Gerald Duckworth, 1983), 106. For a similar suggestion, see A. J. Minnis, "The Author's Two Bodies? Authority and Fallibility in Late Medieval Textual Theory," in *Of the Making of Books: Medieval Manuscripts, Their Scribes and Readers: Essays Presented to M. B. Parkes*, ed. P. R. Robinson and Rivkah Zim (Aldershot: Scolar, 1997), 278.

series of buffoons, from Cupid to the "Thomas" persona, whose incompetence undermines all attempts at praise and implicitly lampoons the pretensions to authority of women like Christine.[10] In contrast, Torti argues that Hoccleve strikes a careful balance between the tales of "Jereslaus's Wife" and "Jonathas" in order to turn the reader away from considerations of women's vice and virtue and toward Hoccleve's interest in the experience of suffering itself. This balance is meant not to scuttle the defense of women but to lead the serious reader past the clichéd depictions of good and bad women in the tales and out to the framing narrative, out to another level of reality that then offers positive treatments of Hoccleve's mother, wife, and potential patron, Lady Westmoreland.[11]

As this critical history should suggest, it has proven difficult to arrive at a consensus concerning Hoccleve's depictions of women. In a slippery body of work, perhaps it is in the treatment of gender where Hoccleve's work is most "notable for its doubleness."[12] Christine de Pizan's radical critique of the prevailing connections between gender and authority were, however, fundamental to Hoccleve's sense of such authority. In the *Letter of Cupid*, Hoccleve works to carve out a space from which to speak that would be identical to neither of the dominant types of masculine literary identity, the competing models of *chevalerie* and *clergie*.[13] In his evasion of these models, Hoccleve is indebted both to the general example of Christine's feminized authorial voice and also to specific tactics she uses in her *Epistre*. Indeed, much of the difficulty in demonstrating whether Hoccleve was recapitulating Christine

---

10. Karen Winstead, " 'I am al othir to yow than yee weene': Hoccleve, Women, and the *Series*," *Philological Quarterly* 72 (1993): 143–55. She cites also Hoccleve's skepticism about women reading the Bible, in *Virgin Martyrs: Legends of Sainthood in Late Medieval England* (Ithaca: Cornell University Press, 1997), 139.

11. Anna Torti, "Hoccleve's Attitude Towards Women: 'I shoop me do my peyne and diligence/ To wynne hir loue by obedience,' " in *A Wyf Ther Was: Essays in Honour of Paule Mertens-Fonck*, ed. Juliette Dor (Liège: Université de Liège, 1992), 264–74. For other commentaries on the relationship between these poems, see Roger Ellis, "Chaucer, Christine de Pizan, and *The Letter of Cupid*," in *Essays on Thomas Hoccleve*, ed. Catherine Batt (London: Centre for Medieval and Renaissance Studies, Queen Mary and Westfield College, University of London, 1996), 29–54; and Glenda K. McLeod, "A Case of *faux semblans*: 'L'Epistre au dieu d'amours' and 'The Letter of Cupid,' " in *The Reception of Christine de Pizan from the Fifteenth Through the Nineteenth Centuries: Visitors to the City*, ed. G. K. McLeod (Lewiston, N.Y.: Mellen, 1991), 11–24.

12. Fenster and Erler, *Poems of Cupid, God of Love*, 167.

13. For an account of these cultural identities stressing their derivation from the medieval sex/ gender system, see Simon Gaunt, *Gender and Genre in Medieval French Literature* (Cambridge: Cambridge University Press, 1995). See also Jennifer Summit's trenchant discussion of Christine's challenge to these identities in *Lost Property: The Woman Writer and English Literary History, 1380–1589* (Chicago: University of Chicago Press, 2000), esp. 66–68.

or differing from her is a product of what is an essentially supplemental relationship between Christine's original and Hoccleve's translation. Hoccleve's relation to Christine here may be understood first through the dynamics of late medieval translation and, second, through a much more extended set of intertextual relations than just those between Hoccleve's poem and Christine's original.

Translation and Vernacular Authority

It is a well-known fact that English vernacular literature of the late fourteenth and early fifteenth centuries derived its subject material far less from invention than from translation. In the early fifteenth century, France provided much of the raw material for English poetry. Lydgate's major works, for instance, were largely either translations from French material or from Latin with the aid of French intermediaries.[14] Within the context of Lancastrian sponsorship of the English vernacular, it is also possible to suggest a conscious political strategy behind this interest in translation. As John Fisher and others have argued, the Lancastrian kings presented themselves as the patrons of an English national culture (in implicit contrast to the francophile Ricardian court) as part of a strategy for consolidating their reign.[15] The Lancastrians made a conscious policy out of the promotion of the English language in the business of state and may even have sponsored the creation of Chaucer as a national poet through the financing of some of the many lavish manuscripts of his works, which began to appear early in their reign.

The vast output of translations from Latin and French into English needs to be read in the context of this "state-generated linguistic nationalism."[16] Indeed, particularly in the case of French literature, we might go so far as to suggest that in making their translations, English poets were aggressively reconstructing, even stealing, the chief ornaments of a rival court. After all, literary works were often understood in this period to be both aesthetic ob-

---

14. Calin, *The French Tradition*, 14.
15. Fisher, "A Language Policy for Lancastrian England." The other major impetus for the pace of translation in these years came from the Wycliffite labors at Biblical translation and vernacular theology. On this topic, see especially Margaret Aston, "Wyclif and the Vernacular," in *From Ockham to Wyclif*, ed. Anne Hudson and Michael Wilks (Oxford: Basil Blackwell, 1987), 281–330.
16. The phrase is borrowed from Patterson, "Making Identities in Fifteenth-Century England," 82.

jects and also, quite straightforwardly, valuable commodities, like plate or jewelry, that testified to the grandeur of their owners and patrons.[17] Thus, translation at this moment was, at least in part, a series of competitive exercises meant to redistribute the prestige of national languages and cultures. The exact sense in which a translator in this period could have imagined their work as a sort of aggressive importation can be specified with the help of Rita Copeland's work on the theory behind what she calls "translation as rhetorical invention."[18] She makes two points relevant to Hoccleve's translation of Christine's *Epistre*. First, Copeland describes the transformations in rhetorical theory that led to translation being considered "a form of aggressive rivalry":

> Medieval vernacular translation of the classical *auctores* emerges from this historical intersection of rhetoric and hermeneutics, and carries the chief features of the academic practice from which it arises. It takes over the function of commentary on the *auctores*, and in so doing replicates the characteristic move of academic exegesis, that of displacing the very text that it proposes to serve. Like commentary, translation tends to represent itself as "service" to an authoritative source; but also like commentary, translation actually displaces the originary force of its models.[19]

Late medieval translators worked in a context that all but assured the centrality of the sorts of questions concerning tone marking the reception of Hoccleve's *Letter*, a context determined by an unstable balance of deference and assertion. The essence of medieval translation was a form of the transfer of authority, a *translatio auctoritatis*. Just as the kings of England had always found reference to their mythological descent from Troy both flattering and politically expedient, so vernacular poets could justify claims to poetic authority through the construction of prestigious literary genealogies.

The competitive rivalry depicted here may also be understood through the changing relationship between translation and the rhetorical category of invention. In classical rhetoric, "invention" had referred quite simply to the initial conception of raw material from which to manufacture finished discourse such as a speech or poem. Since the defining element of translation

17. For numerous examples, see especially Green, *Poets and Princepleasers*, 64 and passim.

18. Rita Copeland, *Rhetoric, Hermeneutics, and Translation in the Middle Ages* (Cambridge: Cambridge University Press, 1991).

19. Ibid., 4

as a distinct form of composition was the fact that this initial material was always already there, it is not surprising that the two rhetorical categories tended to blur into one another. As Copeland describes the transition, "Translation comes to be perceived as a form of rhetorical *inventio*, which has in turn been redefined as exegetical performance on a text or textual *topos*."[20] This blurring of rhetorical categories contributed to the lingering sense of competitive rivalry surrounding so many medieval translations. Certainly, the illustrious poems of the past were often approached through a language of reverence; but since the older poem was frequently represented as raw material in need of the refining labor of a later poet, the very expenditure of this labor might easily imply some lack, something in the original that called out for a supplement.

This essentially agonistic trope of translation as invention would have been quite familiar to any English poet of the early fifteenth century. Lydgate, for example, follows Boccaccio's *De Genealogia deorum* in much of his poetic theory but departs from it radically when, in his section "On Poets" in the *Fall of Princes*, he leaves aside any treatment of invention and concentrates instead on the poet's use of pre-existing material.[21] Similarly, when the conversation in Hoccleve's *Series* turns to a search for possible poetic topics, the consideration of options is presented not only through a search for topics but also for works that might fittingly be translated, with Hoccleve first suggesting that "For him I thoghte han translated Vegece" ("Dialogue," line 561), but then deciding that "A tale eek/which I in the Romayn Deedis // Now late sy . . . // Wole I translate . . ." ("Dialogue," lines 820–21, 825).[22]

Translation thus held out at least two advantages for the post-Chaucerian poet. As translation replaced invention, it became less and less a name for a specialized form of composition and more a synonym for poetic composition itself. In addition, translation offered a high road to poetic authority. Through this relation of "aggressive rivalry" an apprentice poet might be enabled to make an instant claim to poetic authority. Given this understanding of translation, Hoccleve's decision to translate Christine de Pizan's *Epis-*

---

20. Ibid., 7.
21. Ebin, *Illuminator, Makar, Vates*, 39.
22. John Burrow, ed., *Thomas Hoccleve's Complaint and Dialogue* EETS, o.s. 313 (Oxford: Oxford University Press, 1999). The lack of a complete modern edition of the *Series* necessitates a reliance on two editions. Citations from the sections of *Series* known as the "Complaint" and "Dialogue" are drawn from Burrow's new edition and cited by line number within the text. Citations from later sections of the *Series* are from Furnivall's edition.

tre appears in many ways to be a very practical choice as an initial foray into the world of courtly poetry. After a likely early apprenticeship spent with brief religious lyrics, the choice of this poem enabled Hoccleve to announce his intention to take part in the far more prestigious games of *fin amor*. Christine had already acquired a significant reputation in England, so by offering a translation of one of her works Hoccleve associated himself with the latest fashion from Parisian literary circles.[23] Moreover, in announcing his poetic career with a translation, Hoccleve was replicating the steps of his mentor, Chaucer, who had himself translated Guillaume de Lorris's *Roman de la Rose* early in his career.[24] Hoccleve's translation, like Chaucer's, allowed him rapid access to the prestige of the French tradition, which meant both the privileged models for the poetry of courtly love and, Dante excepted, the most proximate sources of contact with the clerkly treasures of the classical past.[25] Hoccleve's translation was not nearly so ambitious as Chaucer's, neither in the scale of the project nor in the prestige of the original text, but it is recognizable as an attempt to stake a claim to a lineage of poetic authority.

Nevertheless, despite these benefits, this translation is also in many ways a very surprising thing. First of all, the speed of the translation is striking. Christine's *Epistre* is internally dated to 1399, and Hoccleve's text similarly establishes its own date as 1402. It has been plausibly suggested that Christine's early works, such as the *Epistre au Dieu d'Amours*, reached England with her son, who was a page in the household of the Earl of Salisbury after 1397, but even with an easily available source, a mere three years between original and translation is quite unprecedented.[26] The lists compiled by P. G. C. Campbell and Jane Chance for fifteenth-century translations of

23. P. G. C. Campbell, "Christine de Pizan en Angleterre," *Revue de littérature comparée* 5 (1925): 659–70; and Jane Chance, "Christine de Pizan as Literary Mother: Women's Authority and Subjectivity in 'The Floure and the Leafe' and 'The Assembly of Ladies,'" in *The City of Scholars: New Approaches to Christine de Pizan*, ed. Margaret Zimmerman and Dina de Rentiis (Berlin: Walter de Gruyter, 1994), 245–59.

24. John Burrow points out that the poem also invokes Chaucer as a predecessor in its reference to "our legende of martirs" (line 316) and in its use of the Chaucerian rhyme-royal. Burrow, *Thomas Hoccleve*, 13.

25. John Fleming suggests that Jean cited only Latinate authorities and studiously avoided citing other vernacular poets in order to insist that his own work had more in common with the classical past than with previous vernacular efforts. Fleming, "Jean de Meun and the Ancient Poets," in *Rethinking the Romance of the Rose*, ed. Kevin Brownlee and Sylvia Huot (Philadelphia: University of Pennsylvania Press, 1992), 81–100.

26. For the connections between Christine, her son, and Jean Montague, the Earl of Salisbury, see Chance, "Christine de Pizan as Literary Mother," 246; and J. C. Laidlaw, "Christine de Pizan, The Earl of Salisbury and Henry IV," *French Studies* 36 (1982): 129–43. Salisbury was beheaded in 1400 for resisting Henry IV, and Christine's son had to seek the king's protection.

Christine's work into English are lengthy, but even so, the next earliest trans-
lation of one of her works was Scrope's translation of the *Epistre Othea*, dated
by its most recent editor between 1440 and 1459, at least forty years after
the composition of the French original.[27] It is possible that the unusual speed
of Hoccleve's work was due to a specific request for such a translation. Henry
IV had come into possession of Salisbury's copies of Christine's work upon
the Earl's death in 1400 and had subsequently invited Christine to England;
a quick translation may have been Hoccleve's way of offering himself as a
substitute when Christine declined Henry's offer.[28] Alternatively, this speed
might suggest the existence of a bureaucratic equivalent to the close cultural
links between English, French, and Italian aristocracies that Gervase Ma-
thew outlined under the rubric of "international court culture," some bu-
reaucratic coterie crossing national boundaries.[29] Christine and the various
participants in the *Querelle* all were in contact with the French civil service,
and it is quite likely that the esprit de corps among English clerks outlined
in Chapter 1 extended internationally and had a significant component of
shared cultural interests, even extending to common literary debates.

The speed of the translation aside, another perplexing element of Hoc-
cleve's translation of the *Epistre* lies in the fact that, although this poem
carried all the prestige of the French poetry of love, the *Epistre* was also a
poem explicitly dedicated to an attack on one of the chief poems of that
tradition, the *Roman de la Rose*. In the act that provided Hoccleve with a

27. Curt Bühler, *The Epistle of Othea* (London: Oxford University Press, 1970), xxi. Jane Chance
sums up the proliferation of Christine's other works as follows: "In addition to the paraphrase of
Christine's early poem by Thomas Hoccleve, there are several translations into Middle English of
her *Epistre Othea*, by Stephen Scrope, 1440–59, stepson of Sir John Fastolf; Anthony Babyngton;
and Robert Wyer, 1540. Sir John Fastolf was believed to have brought back from France some French
original of the *Epistre* which his stepson Stephen Scrope used as a model for his various copies of his
translation, perhaps from war campaigns, between 1440 and 1459, probably begun, however, during
the first decade of the century. That there was continuing royal interest in Christine's work is
attested by the dedications of the translations: one copy of Scrope's translation was dedicated to
Fastolf and one to Duke Humphrey of Gloucester, patron of the library at Oxford's Bodleian."
Chance, "Christine de Pizan as Literary Mother," 247–48.

28. On these manuscripts, see Laidlaw, "Christine de Pizan, The Earl of Salisbury, and Henry
IV."

29. Gervase Mathew, *The Court of Richard II* (London: John Murray, 1968). On the interna-
tional nature of this culture, see also Elizabeth Salter, "Chaucer and Internationalism," *Studies in the
Age of Chaucer* 2 (1980): 71–79, reprinted in *English and International: Studies in the Literature, Art,
and Patronage of Medieval England*, ed. Derek Pearsall and Nicolette Zeeman (Cambridge: Cambridge
University Press, 1988): 239–44. On the civil service and coterie audiences, see Paul Strohm,
"Chaucer's Fifteenth Century Audience and the Narrowing of the 'Chaucer Tradition,' " *Studies in
the Age of Chaucer* 4 (1982): 3–32; and Kerby-Fulton and Justice, "Langlandian Reading Circles."

model, Chaucer's initiation of a poetic career through translation, Chaucer had himself chosen the *Roman* as the foundation stone of his authority. Thus, if Hoccleve's act of translating courtly French verse seems consistent with Chaucer's example, it does seem peculiar that Hoccleve should translate a poem which sets itself in opposition to Chaucer's model.[30] The explanation for this decision lies in the relation between translation and fidelity. Translation is often seen as a sort of genealogical link, in which a poet constructs a lineage by birthing him or herself out of a predecessor's own words. But along with such genealogical claims, translation always contains the potential for infidelities. Hoccleve's translation of Christine de Pizan's *Epistre* places him as an heir to Christine and Chaucer but also acts as a declaration of infidelity to the Ovidian line of love poetry, which led from Jean de Meun to Chaucer and, finally, to Christine's own vision of the defense of women.

Gender in the *Letter of Cupid*

One of the most striking features of the literary debates over the merits of the Ovidian tradition and its continuations in works like the *Roman de la Rose* was the centrality in these discussions of categories of gender and authority. There are numerous occasions in the *Querelle*, for example, at which Christine anticipates and attempts to preempt the response that her arguments against the *Roman* were motivated by her gender. As she writes to Jean de Montreuil:

> And do not believe or let anyone else think, dear Sir, that I have written this defense out of feminine bias, merely because I am a woman. For, assuredly, my motive is simply to uphold the pure truth, since I know by experience that the truth is completely contrary to those things I am denying. And it is precisely because I am a woman

30. Chaucer's translation was of the opening section of the *Roman*, the more idealized verse by de Lorris. De Lorris, of course, would not have been susceptible to many of the charges Christine had aimed at Jean de Meun (such as that of vulgarity). Nevertheless, the attack on de Meun should be understood as potentially encompassing Chaucer as well, both because Chaucer never himself makes much of a distinction between the visions of *fin amor* represented by de Lorris and de Meun and because it is de Meun who becomes central to Chaucer's later work (as in his use of de Meun in creating the Wife of Bath).

that I can speak better in this matter than one who has not had the
experience, since he speaks only by conjecture and by chance.[31]

Christine's account of the importance of her gender is complex. She does
not allow that she writes simply because she is a woman ("pour ce que femme
suis"), as such an admission would lead to easy dismissal of her motivation
through the misogynist categories of the shrewish woman. Nevertheless, she
insists that her gender is central to her claim to epistemological and interpre-
tive privilege as a reader of Jean de Meun's texts. Christine's presentation of
her own authority in this debate is bound up with a careful negotiation of
her gender as a speaker; she is to be heard as a woman in her experience but
not to be dismissed as a woman in her motivation.

In the later middle ages, such questions of gender and authority were
often made prominent formally through the manipulation of poetic voicing
and personae. This technique was so widespread that its impact can be seen
as a structuring principle even in such an apparently nondramatic format as
the dossier of literary correspondence that makes up the *Querelle de la Rose*.
Christine insists that her writing should not be received through the simple
category of female voice, but her opponents (Pierre Col, in this case) persist
in visualizing her as a speaking subject in order to make concrete and to
simplify her status as woman: "Oh excessively foolish pride! Oh opinion
uttered too quickly and through the mouth of a woman!"[32] Similarly, even
though Jean Gerson enters the debate as an ally of Christine's, he adopts a
tone of only temporary estrangement from his opponents in debate, referring
to Pierre Col as "brother" three times in the opening of one of his letters,
and so reconfirming the bond of their shared gender even as he takes issue
with Pierre's reading of the *Roman de la Rose*.[33]

As these examples may begin to suggest, by the late fourteenth century
there had arisen a fashion for playing elaborate games with a particular vari-
ety of personae that complicated and called attention to the gender of speak-

31. Baird and Kane, *La Querelle de la Rose*, 53. "Et ne croiéz, chier sire, ne aucun autre n'ait
oppinion, que je die ou mette en ordre ces dictes deffenses par excusacion favourable pour ce que
femme suis: car veritablement mon motif n'est simplement fors soustenir pure verité, si comme je la
sçay de certaine science estre au contraire des dictes choses de moy nyees; et de tant comme voire-
ment suis femme, plus puis tesmoingnier en ceste partie que cellui qui n'en a l'experience, ains parle
par devinailles et d'aventure." Hicks, *Le Débat sur la "Roman e la Rose,"* 19.

32. Christine to Pierre Col, 1402. Baird and Kane, *La Querelle de la Rose*, 103. "O tres fole
oultrecuidance! O parole trop tost yssue et sans avis de bouche de fame" Hicks, *Le Débat sur la
"Roman de la Rose,"* 100.

33. Baird and Kane, *La Querelle de la Rose*, 145. Hicks, *Le Débat sur la "Roman de la Rose,"* 162.

ing poetic subjects. Alcuin Blamires has described this fashion as "a vogue for structuring both misogynous and profeminine discourse into a dramatized situation, and for complicating its effect by problematizing the nature of the persona who utters it."[34] This vogue was not limited to the poetry of the court. The Oxford *dictamenal* instructor Thomas Sampson played an innovative change on the classical device of adopting *personae* in rhetorical exercises by requiring his students to write letters that ventriloquized female voices.[35] Hoccleve uses exactly this dramatizing technique in the *Letter of Cupid* to call attention to the construction of gendered identities in the Ovidian poetic tradition and to found for himself a position of poetic authority independent of the dominant existing masculine literary models of clerkly and courtly castes. In making this suggestion, I am assuming a very knowing audience for this poem, who would have some familiarity with Christine's work and with the literary history lying behind the *Querelle*. Such an assumption is warranted by Hoccleve's translation of Christine's poem at a moment when, given her fame and personal contacts in London, her authorship could not have been unknown to his audience. Moreover, given the literary emphasis in this period on questions of voice and gender, it would be hard to imagine that Hoccleve meant his decision to translate a woman's poetry to be an invisible one.[36] Among other implications, the slippery tone of Hoccleve's poem should be taken as a barometer of the intimacy of its audience.

A similar knowingness was clearly expected of Christine's audience. Kevin Brownlee has suggested that the *Epistre* should be read as a complex intertextual exercise meant to wrest control of the authoritative lineage of Ovidian poetry.[37] Christine speaks her poem through Cupid's mouth in order to rewrite the tradition so dear to Montreuil and the Col brothers, the line of masculine poetic descent running from the Latin classical authors, particularly Ovid, to their French and vernacular mediator, Jean de Meun himself. Specifically, Christine's target is that crucial scene at the center of the

---

34. Alcuin Blamires, *The Case for Women in Medieval Culture* (Oxford: Oxford University Press, 1997), 33. Blamires also cites Howard Bloch's controversial suggestion that in reading misogynist texts "one is to some degree always dealing with a problem of voice, the questions of who speaks and of localizing such speech." Howard Bloch, "Medieval Misogyny," *Representations* 20 (1987): 7.

35. Sheila Lindenbaum, "Plenary Address," New Chaucer Society, University of London, July 2000.

36. Blamires cites two similar cases of male poets speaking through the mouths of not just female characters but poetic personae (Deschamps and Jean Le Fevre). Blamires, *The Case for Women*, 34–37.

37. Brownlee, "Discourses of the Self," 234–61.

Roman de la Rose in which Cupid appears and delivers a speech licensing Jean as the proper continuator of Guillaume de Lorris's poem. By putting her poem in the mouth of this Cupid, Christine can implicitly claim a level of authority equal to that of Jean de Meun. Moreover, this displacement of Christine's voice into Cupid's mouth provides an ironic commentary on the relationship between male poets and female material in Ovidian poetry. Christine's Cupid complains that the books about women are all written by men and for men, and this argument is both ironized and strengthened by an awareness of the female poet standing behind the male god. In effect, Christine uses Jean de Meun's own god against him and steals Ovid away, making the old Roman authorize a pro-woman, "anti-clerkly" moral.

Lori Walters makes a related point in noting, "Christine's corrected portrait of Cupid is made possible through the creation of an androgynous narrative voice in which a female clerk speaks through the male God of Love."[38] And, although I suggested above that Hoccleve wrote the *Letter* in imitation of the shape of Chaucer's career, it would also be possible to think of Hoccleve imitating Christine in this composition. Christine's *Epistre au Dieu d'amours* and Hoccleve's *Letter* are the first datable narrative poems that survive from either author.[39] Each poet begins a career with a metacritical reflection on the poetry of *fin amor*, and each begins with an elaborate game of cross-gendered ventriloquism—a point that has not been sufficiently recognized. As Walters has suggested, Christine may have been drawn to the figure of Cupid as an object of such transgendered voicing because the identity of the God of Love was so emphatically "the 'filz de Venus' (line 4), a deity famous as his mother's son."[40] Similarly, Hoccleve may have been drawn to Christine's subversive ventriloquism because it offered an opportunity to slip between the categories of *clergie* and *chevalerie*, reversing Christine's gambit to allow himself to enter the *Querelle*, so to speak, in drag.

The questions of gender and authority that intrigued Hoccleve throughout his poetry are brought together nicely in a key passage from the *Series* that establishes the dramatic frame for the tales of Jonathas and Jereslaus's Wife. Here, in an exact parallel to the *Legend of Good Women*, Hoccleve presents a scene in which his "Friend" insists that Hoccleve needs to tell some tales of virtuous women to atone for his scandalous slanders against

38. Lori Walters, "The Woman Writer and Literary History: Christine de Pizan's Redefinition of the Poetic *Translatio* in the *Epistre au Dieu d'amours*," *French Literary Series* 16 (1989): 4.

39. Mary Carpenter Erler also points this out. Fenster and Erler, *Poems of Cupid, God of Love*, 159.

40. Walters, "The Woman Writer and Literary History," 4.

them in the past. As evidence for women's dislike of such slanders, the Friend introduces Chaucer's Wife of Bath as his "auctrice":

The Wyf of Bathe take I for auctrice
Þat wommen han no ioie ne deyntee
Þat men sholde vpon hem putte any vice;
I woot wel so / or lyk to Þat, seith shee.
By wordes writen / Thomas, yilde thee.
                    ("Dialogue," lines 694–98)

The creation of this neologism establishes a remarkably complex interplay of gender and textual authority. Simply to create this feminized form of the latinate *auctor* is to suggest nicely that *auctoritas*, the weight of Latin learning and clerkly authority, might well reside in a female speaker.[41] In addition, this passage creates a series of ironies around the familiar oppositions of male/female and speech/text. First of all, the Friend's insistence that Thomas yield to *written authority* resonates ironically in light of the fact that the Wife of Bath herself continually emphasizing her belief in the priority of personal experience over textual tradition. Moreover, the Friend's parenthetical admission that he can't quite remember his auctrice's exact words serves to further undermine the signal precondition of specifically textual authority, that difference from the spoken word which derives from the permanent and verifiable status of the written text.

And, finally, to underline the *written* word at this moment must remind the reader that the real authority being cited here is not the Wife of Bath, but Geoffrey Chaucer. With this passage, Hoccleve lays bare the way in which the construction of textual authority is so often predicated on ventriloquistic games and, in particular, the crossing of gender identities at such moments. Chaucer is the authority, but only through a process of mediation in which his written text pretends to be speech and pretends to be feminized speech. It is perhaps part of the work of this text to poke fun at the notion of the Wife of Bath as *auctor*, but it is equally the work of this passage to confess the importance of these moments of speaking as a woman to the

41. For usage of auctour, see *Middle English Dictionary*, ed. Hans Kurath and Sherman M. Kuhn (Ann Arbor: University of Michigan Press, 1956) 1:514–15. The only usage of auctrice cited here is that of Hoccleve as cited above. The editors do find two uses of the term auctrix, a near variant; the most similar usage to that of Hoccleve occurs in Capgrave's *Life of St. Katherine*. As Burrow comments, this distinctive usage seems to have puzzled the scribes of two of the *Series* manuscripts. Burrow, *Hoccleve's Complaint and Dialogue*, 105 n. D694. Hoccleve's neologism is also reminiscent of Christine's category of the *clergesce*.

construction of Chaucerian and Hocclevian vernacular authority. This is a confession which thus recapitulates the central issue in considering Hoccleve's *Letter*: Is Christine de Pizan to be understood in this poem as a powerful and authoritative precursor or as an epiphenomenon of essentially masculine authority?

Hoccleve makes two major structural revisions to Christine's *Epistre*, both of which help to sketch an answer to this problem.[42] First, he changes the sequence of Christine's argument, diminishing the sense of an orderly progression through the estates in order to foreground differences of gender. And second, he retains a more limited consideration of the estate category of the clerk and places this in the always crucial position of the poem's midpoint, thus enabling and highlighting self-referential reflections on his own status as author.[43] Christine's original poem had organized Cupid's address by moving through a hierarchy derived from the three estates (although only courtly and clerkly estates are actually described, as the peasantry are, by definition, seen as irrelevant to a discussion of love). Cupid addresses first complaints lodged against the nobility and then moves on to those directed against the clerkly caste, especially, of course, against Jean de Meun. Christine's emphasis on the different vices of different estates can be seen in her reproach against the clerkly estate:

> Si se plaignent les dessusdites dames
> De plusieurs clercs qui leur surmettent blasmes.
> Dictiez en font, rimes, proses et vers,
> En diffamant leurs meurs par moz divers.
> Si les baillent en matiere aux premiers,
> A leurs nouveaulx et jeunes escoliers,
> En maniere d'exemple et de doctrine
> Pour retenir en aage tel doctrine.
>
> En vers dient, Adam, David, Sanson,
> Et Salomon, et autres a foison

42. Within the very limited quantity of attention given to Hoccleve's *Letter*, one of the few recurrent observations has been that Hoccleve substantially rearranged Christine's original; however, criticism has been less successful at suggesting a coherent principle behind this rearrangement. On the matter of arrangement see especially Ellis, "Chaucer"; Fleming, "Hoccleve's 'Letter of Cupid' "; and Mitchell, *Thomas Hoccleve*, 77–84. Furnivall also includes an appendix listing several sections of the poem accompanied by their sources from Christine's original. Furnivall, *Hoccleve's Works*, 243–48.

43. Ellis notes that Hoccleve's work is more "class-conscious" than that of Christine. Ellis, "Chaucer," 47, 50–51.

Furent deceu par femme main et tart:
Et qui sera dont li homs qui s'en gard?

(The ladies mentioned here above complain/Of many clerks who lay much blame to them,/Composing tales in rhyme, in prose, in verse,/In which they scorn their ways with words diverse;/They give these texts out to their youngest lads,/To schoolboys, who are young and new in class,/Examples given to indoctrinate/So they'll retain such doctrine when they're grown./Thus, "Adam, David, Samson, Solomon,"/They say in verse, "a score of other men,/Were all deceived by women morn and night;/So who will be the man who can escape?")[44]

The structure of Christine's *Epistre* progresses from estate to estate, allowing her to define the social particularities of misogyny, in this case, highlighting the specific institutional ground of clerical denigrations of women: clerical appropriations of the classical literary tradition form the matter, while clerical supervision of schooling provides the vehicle for the perpetuation of misogynist stereotypes.

Hoccleve, in contrast, downplays Christine's emphasis on the particularity of each estate. His own poem progresses through a series of exempla and commentaries, in which men are dissected vice by vice, without regard to estate. For example, Hoccleve's translation of this same passage concerning clerks foregrounds differences of gender over those of estate:

Ladyes eek conpleynen hem on Clerkis
Þat they han maad bookes of hir deffame
In whiche/they lakken wommennes werkis
And speken of hem/greet repreef and shame
And causelees/ hem yeue a wikkid name
Thus they despysid been on euery syde
And sclaundred/and belowen on ful wyde

Tho wikkid bookes/maken mencion
How they betrayeden in special
Adam/Dauid/Sampson and Salomon

---

44. Fenster and Erler, *Poems of Cupid, God of Love*, lines 259–70. Further references are drawn from this edition and cited by line number within the text. The translation is by Thelma Fenster.

And many oon mo/who may rehercen al
The tresoun/ þat they haue doon and shal
Who may hire hy malice conprehende?
Nat the world/Clerkes seyn, it hath none ende
(lines 190–203, emphasis added)

The opening and closing lines frame Cupid's complaint with reference to clerks, but the framed discussion evacuates Christine's vividly detailed rendering of the specific social context of clerkly misogyny (a social specificity paralleled in Christine's depiction of the courtly social gatherings of the aristocratic estate). Hoccleve's emphasis falls on the exemplary point: "Thus they despysid been on euery syde/And sclaundred and belowen on ful wyde." The function of this modification is to clear the field for a structural examination of gender by effacing the discriminatory categories of the estates.

Hoccleve's *Letter of Cupid* does, however, follow Christine in emphasizing the categories of the estates at one moment, significantly a moment at the midpoint of the text. In French poetry of this period, the midpoint is frequently used as a moment for metafictional reflection; it is a moment at which a sophisticated audience would expect a particularly explicit form of authorial self-consciousness. Thus, it is at the midpoint of the *Roman de la Rose* that Jean de Meun brings Cupid onstage to establish his own authority. Christine structures her poem so that the central section contains a lament that there is no tradition of female authorship she could counterpose to the misogyny of Ovid and Jean de Meun:

> Et s'on me dit li livre en sont tuit plain
> (C'est le respons a maint dont je me plain!),
> Je leur respons que les livres ne firent
> Pas les femmes, ne les choses n'i mirent
> Que l'en y list contre elles et leurs meurs.
> . . . .
> Mais se femmes eussent li livre fait,
> Je sçay de vray qu'aultrement fust du fait,
> Car bien scevent qu'a tort sont encoulpees.
> (lines 407–11; 417–19)

(Should it be said that books are filled with tales/Of just such women (I deplore that charge!),/To this I say that books were not composed/By women, nor did they record the things/That we may

read against them and their ways. . . . If women, though, had
written all those books,/I know that they would read quite
differently,/For well do women know the blame is wrong.)

Whereas Christine uses this emphatic midpoint position to make clear the
lack of any alternative feminine tradition from which she might write, Hoc-
cleve structures his text so that the midpoint contains a discussion of clerkly
misogyny.[45] Hoccleve leads up to this midpoint by constructing a clerkly
genealogy: Ovid's poetry exemplifies "a clerkes custume"; "scolers lerne" his
misogynistic lore in their youth at school. This literary tradition leads clerks
to attempt "by hire outrageous tirannye/Thus vp on wommen kythen hire
maistrye," and to "rebelle ageyn" Cupid and his laws.[46] Playing off Chris-
tine's own use of the midpoint as an opportunity for self-referential reflec-
tion, Hoccleve's dark genealogy of the clerkly estate functions to launch a
criticism of the very clerical tradition of which he was a disgruntled member.

Hoccleve's structural revisions of Christine's poem, then, seem at first to
emphasize thematic points very consistent with her defense of women
against clerkly slanders. When we turn, however, to Hoccleve's depiction of
gender in this poem, the picture becomes more complex. If there is a strain
very different in spirit from Christine de Pizan in this poem, it consists not in
Hoccleve's covert attribution of vice to women or virtue to men; he follows
Christine quite exactly in his gendered apportionment of vices and virtues.
The proposition on which Hoccleve does differ markedly from Christine is
that concerning the consequences of basing one's discursive gender analyses
on categories of vice and virtue. The key to this disagreement is a sense of
what it is that Hoccleve attributes to women when he attributes virtue.

Like much of Hoccleve's work, the *Letter* can be read as a self-reflexive
meditation on its own genre, in this case the complaint. In its content, the
Letter is Cupid's confirmation and amplification of the charge that men are
unfaithful; and to say that men are unfaithful is only to say in nonliterary
language that the complaints they make to women that they are dying for
love are invalid complaints. As the God of Love, Cupid reigns over cultural
terrain powerfully shaped by the literary form of the complaint, and his job

45. As Brownlee puts the point, "Indeed, what occurs at almost the precise midpoint of the
Epistre (immediately following Cupid's negative treatment of the male, misogynistic poetic genealogy
linking Ovid and Jean de Meun) is the explicit articulation of an absence of any corresponding
genealogy of female authors." Brownlee, "Discourses of the Self," 240.
46. Hoccleve's pointed reference to clerks occupy the four stanzas leading up to the exact mid-
point of his poem, thus, respectively, lines 208, 211, 223, and 231.

here is to police standards that are at once both ethical codes of conduct and literary techniques. Hoccleve is quite clear that the charges leveled against these false men are to be understood as critiques of a certain mode of speech, a particular masculine form of complaint:

> Hir wordes spoken been so sighyngly
> And with so pitous cheere and contenance
> That euery wight þat meeneth trewely
> Deemeth / þat they in herte han swich greuance
> They seyn / so importable is hir penance
> þat but hir lady / list to shewe hem grace,
> They right anoon moot steruen in the place
> (lines 22–28)

Men are constituted by hypocrisy, by a nonidentity of gesture and intent. In the ethical frame established by Cupid's condemnation of false complaints and false lovers, this nonidentity is obviously a trait to be censured. At the same time, however, a difficulty arises in that it is just this sort of discontinuity that creates the complex subjectivity so important elsewhere in Hoccleve's work. The very structure of masculinity here is imagined as an interior voice of desire sly enough to disguise its outward reflection, a structure that is a very close analogue to the tactically adaptable interiority of "La Male Regle." Masculinity is identical to vice, but in that vice it also begins to resemble subjectivity itself.

Furthermore, what I have been calling hypocrisy has a much more precise name in the philosophy of the time and a more exact textual precedent, namely, the pitfalls of doubleness explored by Boethius in the *Consolation of Philosophy*. Hoccleve's *Letter* is, in fact, full of language borrowed from Boethian texts. Men "blynde wommen with hir doublenesse" (line 21), and his comparisons between genders are often marked with a Boethian accent:

> And therfore it may preeued be ther by
> That in womman regneth al the constaunce
> And in man is al chaunge and variaunce.
> (lines 446–48)

Hoccleve puts his structural analysis of gender into the context of Boethian philosophy, and the result is a partial evacuation of the ethical charge behind the descriptions of hypocrisy. In effect, the invocation of Boethius allows the removal of his depiction of masculinity from the realm of ethics into that of ontology. In Boethius's thought, there is no element of personal will involved in such doubleness: it is a given, an unavoidable state of being, and Hoccleve's false courtiers are, to a certain extent, microcosmic illustrations of this universal fact. Thus, although Hoccleve's comparative gender analysis charges men with being the bearers of a deeply problematic "doubleness," this charge also credits them with being the bearers of both complex subjectivity and Boethian truths.

Turning to Hoccleve's depiction of women, we find that female virtue in this poem is usually identified in relation to the key term pity. As Cupid says, if a woman is seduced, it is no shame to her, for:

> To here, nay / yit was it no repreef
> For al for pitee was it þat shee wroghte
> But he þat breewid hath al this mescheef
> þat spak so faire / and falsly inward thoghte:
> His be the shame / as it by reson oghte
> And vn to here, thank perpetuel
> þat in a neede, helpe can so wel
> (lines 71–77)

The remarkable thing about this passage is the fact that Hoccleve attributes everything in women to the single affect of pity—"al for pitee was it þat shee wroghte." In contrast to the divided and complex masculinity we saw above, woman here exists as the extrapolation of a single element. We can see how this works in more detail in a meditative passage from near the poem's end, a moment at which Cupid is summing up his argument:

> The more vertu: the lasse is the pryde
> Vertu so noble is / and worthy in kynde
> þat vice and shee / may nat in feere abyde
> Shee puttith vice / cleene out of mynde
> Shee fleeth from him / shee leueth him behynde
> O womman/ þat of vertu art hostesse
> Greet is thyn honur and thy worthynesse
> (lines 456–62)

Hoccleve's imagination of woman's relation to virtue is depicted here in a striking trope. Woman is described as the host to virtue in a relation metaphorically imagined as that of womb and fetus. Hoccleve duplicates this image elsewhere, as, for example, in an earlier description of Mary, in which she is described as being literally pregnant not only with Christ but with also virtue itself:

> Of our lady / of lyf reparatrice
> Nolde han be born / but for þat shee of vice
> Was voide / and of al vertu wel he wiste
> Endowid; of hire be born him liste
>
> (lines 403–6)

These images of pregnancy are further reinforced by a persistent contrast between women's fertile capacity for virtue and a corresponding sterility in men. Whereas Cupid says of women that "Of constance / they been nat so bareyne" (line 298), in the case of men the reverse is true: "The soile is naght / ther may no trouthe growe" (line 321).[47]

In the strong bifurcation between masculine and feminine in this poem, the feminine is distinguished as a subject with the capacity for a sort of moral pregnancy. Woman plays host to virtue, which is "born" in the acting out of pity. Biology is destiny here, but only in a fashion heavily mediated by hagiographical and Ovidian traditions, as this complex image draws on the conventional sufferings of female virtue associated with love and religious persecution. Most important for our investigation, this image of woman pregnant with virtue is one that Hoccleve did not borrow from Christine. What, then, are we to make of this strange representation of female subjectivity? This contrast between the hypocritical complexity of masculine subjectivity and the transparent simplicity of female virtue might be taken to be Hoccleve's last word on the subject were it not for the fact that his poetry displays elsewhere a sense of quite androgynous complexity. Alternatively, since all of these descriptions are put in Cupid's mouth, we might read this comparative gender analysis as an implicit commentary on the limits of gender identities available within the generic universe of courtly love.[48] Or, last, and most likely, we might read this image of moral pregnancy as the means by which

---

47. On "truth" in this context, see Richard Firth Green, "Chaucer's Victimized Women," *Studies in the Age of Chaucer* 10 (1988): 3–21.

48. The linkage of virtue and fecundity is certainly appropriate to the God of Love. Indeed, this somewhat strained analogy between the virtues appropriate to the canons of Saints' Lives and a celebration of fertility may go far toward explaining Cupid's mysterious error in briefly seeming to forget the shining virginity of St. Margaret.

Hoccleve stages a specific criticism of the discursive tactic of defending women through the ethical category of virtue.

Although Christine's *Epistre* is not the source for Hoccleve's metaphor of moral pregnancy, this image does have strong resonances with images of procreation elsewhere in her work. Images of procreation and pregnancy are central to Christine's articulation of her own poetic project, particularly in her strategic revision of Jean de Meun and his use of the conventional Chartrian analogy between poetic composition and the erotic generation of Nature. As Sylvia Huot has argued, Christine creates "an explicitly feminine form of the familiar construct," in which Nature and poetic fertility are cast as analogues of feminized generative potential.[49] Like these images of pregnancy, Hoccleve's emphasis on virtue itself should also be seen as a response to the larger terms of Christine's project. In describing the inhabitants of her ideal City of Ladies, Christine had declared that "the walls of the city will be closed to those women who lack virtue."[50] In the context of *The Book of the City of Ladies*, this stipulation is meant to be a direct rebuttal to "the book of Mathéolus" with its conventional lists of women's vices; but more broadly, partly because of the frequency of her responses to what Blamires has called "the case against women," and partly because of the centrality of ethical thinking in her work, virtue is a central category throughout Christine's work on gender.[51]

It is in its discussion of women's virtue that Hoccleve's version of the *Letter of Cupid* differs most from Christine's thinking. This virtue, for Hoccleve, is as much a danger as it is a defense:

The more vertu: the lasse is the pryde
Vertu so noble is / and worthy in kynde
Þat vice and shee / may nat in feere abyde
Shee puttith vice / cleene out of mynde
Shee fleeth from him / shee leueth him behynde

---

49. Sylvia Huot, "Seduction and Sublimation: Christine de Pizan, Jean de Meun, and Dante," *Romance Notes* 25 (1985): 367.

50. Christine de Pizan, *The Book of the City of Ladies*, trans. Earl Jeffrey Richards (New York: Persea Books, 1982), 11.

51. Christine's work is also very different from Chaucer's in this respect. As Judith Laird sums up the difference between the *Legend of Good Women* and *The Book of the City of Ladies*, "the central question of her work is not, as Chaucer's appears to be, 'Can women be faithful in love?' but rather 'Does virtue recognize gender?'" Laird, "Good Women and Bonnes Dames: Virtuous Females in Chaucer and Christine de Pizan," *Chaucer Review* 30 (1995): 58.

O womman/ þat of vertu art hostesse
Greet is thyn honur and thy worthynesse
(lines 456–62)

The element of critique here derives from the preternatural activity of this
fetal "vertu" and its relation to the larger form of female subjectivity. Al-
though this description comes at a moment in the argument at which Cupid
is summing up the attributes of each gender, this description moves quickly
from woman herself to the germ of inner "vertu" that gives woman her mean-
ing. This "vertu" is busy throughout the stanza expunging vice and altering
the very shape of its host(ess). The point of this passage is that the best that
can be claimed for virtue as a purely formal value is its effectiveness as a
policing force, exiling all that is not self-identical outside the bounds of the
self. And thus we arrive at the central difficulty in defending women through
the terms of virtue. If an understanding of gendered identity that counter-
poses hypocritical complexity to virtuous simplicity offers an obvious conde-
scension in its defense of women, Hoccleve is suggesting that the fault lies
not just in the implication of "simplicity" but also in the category of "virtue"
itself. Virtue is defined essentially here as a negation of vice and hence as a
regulatory (and simplifying) attribute. The implication is that as long as
virtue is defined through its power to eliminate the complexities we saw
defined above as hypocrisy, these images of pious simplicity risk leading in
a rhetorical circle back to the misogynist stereotypes they were meant to
oppose.[52]

It is possible to read Hoccleve's criticism of the gender politics of virtue
(and of Christine de Pizan on this point) as either a mark of final complicity
with the misogyny of courtly culture or as Hoccleve's attempt to move dia-
lectically beyond the positions represented by either de Meun or Christine.
On the one hand, in privileging complex interiority and linking this value
to masculinity and to his own poetic project, Hoccleve certainly risks falling
into the jovial complacency toward issues of gender of the sort for which

---

52. In making this criticism Hoccleve is following Chaucer. See, for example, Janet Cowen's
discussion of Hoccleve's debt to *The Legend of Good Women* in the tales of "Jereslaus's Wife" and
"Jonathas." "Hoccleve too, in the end, produces his set of good and bad examples, but I think that
the framework of discussion in which he places it shows that he realized that there was more at issue
than recruiting examples for a rhetoric of praise or blame." Cowen, "Women as Exempla in Fifteenth
Century Verse of the Chaucerian Tradition," in *Chaucer and Fifteenth Century Poetry*, ed. Julia Boffey
and Janet Cowen (London: Centre for Late Antique and Medieval Studies, King's College London,
1991), 63.

Elaine Hansen has criticized Chaucer.[53] On the other hand, one might see in Hoccleve's use of Christine as his *auctrice* an anticipation of the mixed respect and criticism called for in Sheila Delany's skeptical treatments of Christine de Pizan as a model for a feminist middle ages.[54] Hoccleve borrows from Christine all the key elements of his thinking about gender in this poem, but by criticizing the language of vice and virtue he also suggests a limitation to the polemical tactic she adopts, in part as a result of the *Querelle*, of defending women through an appeal to virtue.

Moreover, this category of virtue is not only the rhetorical basis for Christine's defense of women but also the foundation of her vision of poetic authority, a vision of a writer speaking for virtue and (unlike Jean de Meun) leading their audience into virtue. By commenting skeptically on the power of virtue, Hoccleve implies the insufficiency of the language of vice and virtue not only for the defense of women but also as a theoretical basis for poetic authority. Hoccleve followed Christine's examination of the connections between gender and authority and yet, in the end, pulled away from her sense of authorship and authority.

Authority and the Secular Clerk

Hoccleve demonstrates throughout his works a consistent interest in gendered identity.[55] Most interestingly, there is lexical evidence to suggest that in thinking about gender, Hoccleve thought in terms of systemic categories. Hoccleve used the very unusual term "wommanhode" in the tale of "Jeres-

53. Elaine Hansen, *Chaucer and the Fictions of Gender* (Berkeley and Los Angeles: University of California Press, 1992), esp. 10–15.

54. For Delany's original protest against a too easy attribution of terms such as feminist and revolutionary see Sheila Delany, " 'Mothers to Think Back Through': Who Are They? The Ambiguous Example of Christine de Pizan," in *Medieval Literary Politics* (Manchester: Manchester University Press, 1990), 88–103. For the subsequent exchanges, see Sheila Delany, "History, Politics and Christine Studies: A Polemical Reply," in *Politics, Gender, and Genre: The Political Thought of Christine de Pizan*, ed. Margaret Brabant and Jean-Bethke Elshtain (Boulder, Colo.: Westview, 1992), 193–206; Quilligan, *The Allegory of Female Authority*; Christine Reno, "Christine de Pizan: Feminism and Irony," in *Seconda miscellanea di studi e ricerche sul Quattrocento francese*, ed. Jonathan Beck and Gianni Mombello (Chambéry: Centre d'études franco-italien, 1981), 125–33; and Jane Chance, "Christine's Minerva, the Mother Valorized," in her edition of *Letter of Othea to Hector* (Newburyport, Mass.: Focus Information Group, 1990), 122.

55. For a marvelous reading of the wide resonances of gender in Hoccleve's work, see Catherine Batt, "Hoccleve and . . . Feminism? Negotiating Meaning in the Regiment of Princes," in *Essays on Thomas Hoccleve*, ed. Batt, 55–84.

laus's Wife" (lines 484–88), and the "Address to Oldcastle" is marked by frequent calls for Oldcastle to strive toward more "manly" behavior.[56] These terms are significant because, unlike words such as women or men, womman- hode and manly imply a sense of gender as an abstract category standing beyond the individual and not made up simply from the accumulation of all individuals in a given category. In other words, these terms imply a sense of gender profoundly separable from the individual, an abstracting distance allowing Hoccleve to suggest that manly may have little to do with men or womanhode with women.

As a representative of an emergent class of secularized clerks, Hoccleve had no easy route of identification with any established source of textual authority. The two distinct traditions of literary activity at the time were the twin paths of *chevalerie* and *clergie*, which, as Simon Gaunt has argued, were conceived and mutually defined as contrasting types of masculine identity.[57] As Christine's gender barred her from writing with the traditional authority of either of these roles, so Hoccleve was not situated to speak for the estab- lished cultural traditions of either courtly verse or clerkly didacticism. Al- though much of Hoccleve's work describes life in London on the margins of the court, Hoccleve did not have access to the authority of a poet like Chau- cer, who wrote from inside the court. Chaucer's position within the court was, of course, itself peripheral; he was not a member of the inner circle of the court and yet he had connections to some of the powerful knights of the chamber.[58] These connections help contextualize those moments when Chaucer allows himself to speak for *chevalerie*. The ubiquity of courtly genres, lavishly drawn aristocratic figures, and the centrality of love to the inner life of his characters created a Chaucerian corpus ripe for adoption as a semi- official court literature. In contrast, Hoccleve's writing about the court is consistently mediated by the mechanisms of patronage, going out of its way not to suggest even the tentative identification of the sort Chaucer allows but asserting instead the insurmountable distance of supplication.

In occasionally adopting the tones of *clergie*, Hoccleve is equally circum- spect, showing here an affinity with his other London contemporary, Lang- land. It is a point not frequently emphasized, but one crucial to the understanding of texts like Christine's *Epistre* and Hoccleve's subsequent

56. On wommanhode see Blamires, 168 n. 57.
57. Gaunt, *Gender and Genre in Medieval French Literature*.
58. Paul Strohm, "Chaucer's Fifteenth-Century Audience and the Narrowing of the 'Chaucer Tradition,' " *Studies in the Age of Chaucer* 4 (1982): 3–32; and Patterson, *Chaucer and the Subject of History*, 32–39.

translation, that at a certain level, the *Querelle* was a debate simply about what it was to be a clerk. Christine's opponents found a convenient response to all her criticisms of the *Roman* in the simple fact that she was a woman and so not qualified to take part in a debate concerning the proper role of didactic poetry.[59] Although Christine argued that her gender gave her a privileged position from which to discuss Jean de Meun's text, her opponents spoke for the more orthodox position that her gender barred her from membership in the only group eligible even to enter such discussion, the literate masculine clergy. In response, Christine crafted a new hybrid identity of a "female clerk," an identity that led her to become an important (though often uncredited) source in the development of fifteenth- and sixteenth-century English literary culture.[60] Indeed, the adoption of the language of virtue is an important part of Christine's claim to the occupation of a clerkly position, a claim strengthened by her argument in the *Querelle* that her opponents have abandoned the serious aims of ethical literature.

Hoccleve, too, creates a poetic voice in relation to traditional clerkly authority, but he is distanced from this role by two distinct historical trends. First, Hoccleve was a member of an emergent class of men whose distinct identity lay in their growing tendency toward laicization.[61] Someone in Hoccleve's position in the Privy Seal would have been unproblematically considered a clerk in previous generations, but the growing differences between these bureaucrats and their ecclesiastical brethren made such identification increasingly problematic. In addition, there was a second bar to Hoccleve's assumption of the authority of *clergie*—the fact that Hoccleve was married. Hoccleve's depictions of his own marriage are unusual enough to have led some critics to treat him as a commentator on marriage and on the alleged genesis at this moment of the Western version of romantic or protobourgeois love.[62] Indeed, there is something about Hoccleve's marriage that smacks of modernity. He is the first English poet to use this autobiographical fact to

59. Fenster and Erler, *Poems of Cupid, God of Love*, 5.
60. The complex history of the usage of Christine's work in the late medieval and early modern period by gentleman-bureaucrats such as William Worcester and Stephen Scrope is presented incisively by Jennifer Summit in *Lost Property*. For Scrope, see also my "Bought and Sold Like a Beast: Stephen Scrope's Translation of *The Letter of Othea to Hector*" (forthcoming).
61. For the process of laicization among the clerks of the Privy Seal in this period, see Storey, "Gentleman-Bureaucrats"; Brown, *Governance*, 60; and my discussion in Chapter 1.
62. Albrecht Classen, "Love and Marriage in Late Medieval Verse: Oswald von Wolkenstein, Thomas Hoccleve, and Michel Beheim," *Studia Neophilologica* 62 (1990): 163–88. Hoccleve's depiction of marriage is one of many elements in which he might be more profitably compared to Langland than Chaucer.

sever public space from a private and domestic sphere. And in being married, Hoccleve was at the forefront of a new trend, new even among the increasingly laicized clerks of the central bureaucracy. Maurice Keen lays out the chronology of marriage among these bureaucrats as follows:

> At the beginning of the fifteenth century, all the major clerical posts in the Exchequer were held by beneficed clergy (a position incompatible with marriage): by 1430, these were the exceptions rather than the rule. In Chancery the process was slower. In 1388 a royal ordinance affirmed the traditional rule that the clerks of Chancery should not be married; but by the middle of Henry V's reign there were at least eleven married clerks. The proportion increased steadily and at last, in 1523, even the six senior masters were permitted to marry.[63]

Hoccleve alludes to his marriage in the *Regement of Princes* and so was married at some point in the first decade of the fifteenth century—not unprecedented, but still an early date among his peers. As a married clerk, Hoccleve was faced with a problem similar to that of Christine's in the *Querelle*. Debarred from the priesthood and from the authority of ecclesiastical identity, Hoccleve was ill at home in the progression of celibate *auctors*.

Hoccleve thus translates Christine's *Epistre au Dieu d'Amours* as a space in which to negotiate the distance between the dominant masculine literary traditions of the moment and the emerging identity of the married lay clerk. In writing clerkly arguments against Jean de Meun, Christine needed to invoke the tradition of clerkly *auctoritas* while at the same time struggling against its implicit limitations for a woman; the result for Christine is the hybrid role of the *clergesce*. For his part, Hoccleve used Christine's *Epistre* to explore the technical possibilities of layering the voice of one gender over another, not creating a stable hybrid as Christine does, but rather creating an authorial voice that strives for a skeptical distance from all such categories of authorial identity, whether textual traditions such as the Ovidian, or categories of gender such as womanhode and the manly. Vernacular authority in Hoccleve's *Letter* is thus a paradoxical exercise in which authority lies less in the triumphant assumption of a given position than in the assertion of a valid skepticism in relation to such positions.

63. Maurice Keen, *English Society in the Later Middle Ages, 1348–1500* (London: Penguin Books, 1990), 236. Keen's chronology is roughly accurate for the other writing offices as well. In the Signet, for example, we find the example of William Hugoun, a married clerk who served from 1399 to 1415. See Otway-Ruthven, *The King's Secretary*, 127.

Here is a concrete example of this paradoxical stance. In one of the more infamous episodes of this poem, Hoccleve allows his Cupid to become momentarily confused, so thoroughly caught up in his praise of Saint Margaret that he briefly forgets his opposition to virginity and has to interrupt his effusive praise to remind his audience that virginity is not a good thing:

> But undirstondith / We commende hir noght
> By encheson of hir virginitee
> Trustith right wel / it cam nat in our thoght
> For ay We werreie ageyn chastitee
> And euere shal / but this leeueth wel yee
> Hir louyng herte / and constant to hir lay
> Dryue out of [our] remembrance we nat may
> (lines 428–34)

Like the drama of virtue arranging and rearranging woman, the real battle here is not Cupid's external war against chastity but an impossible internal struggle to erase a thought that has already entered his mind. Cupid's assertion that Margaret's virginity had had no place in his thought is belied both by his language of struggle and, more significantly, by the substitution of the active "Dryve out of our remembrance" for the earlier passive "it cam nat in our thoght." In effect, Cupid is here saying that blessed virginity had never entered his mind and that, anyway, it is love that is *particularly* hard to drive out, with the sudden switch to a comparative mode implicitly reneging on his earlier denial. This brilliant expression of internal double-think (or Freudian "kettle-logic") is not presented here simply as a depiction of comedic forgetfulness. The strains on the language of desire here register the fact that this Cupid is an impossible hybrid caught between the demands of two incommensurate cultural traditions. This Cupid is half a sophisticated courtier admiring a glorious lady and half the parody of a religious icon insisting on the points of his doctrine (fecundity). Hoccleve's tactic is not to join these elements into some synthesis but rather to show the seam between them by allowing Cupid to speak first as courtier and then to reverse himself in self-censorship as the divinity regains control.

The depiction of Cupid here gives us a concrete figure for the authority of the poet in Hoccleve's *Letter*. Unable or unwilling to create a textual home for himself in either of the dominant masculine modes of *chevalerie* or *clergie*, Hoccleve follows the example of Christine de Pizan's subversive ventriloquism and situates himself as a clerk writing through the precedent of his *auctrice*. Distancing himself, however, both from Christine's reliance on the literature of virtue and from even this modified clerkliness, Hoccleve creates images of authority emphasizing the fragmented and contradictory nature of the models of textuality and gender that were being brought together to form new vernacular traditions. His Cupid, the grand rhetorician, is the very image of the triumphant poet, speaking with unquestionable authority as the arbiter of virtue and love. He is also, just as much as the false courtiers, a hypocritical thing, smoothing the clashing lineages of his speech into an authority fragmented at its core.

"Wrytynge no
travaille is"

Scribal Labor

in the

Regement of Princes

It has been the aim of the first two chapters of this study to trace out the implications of an early bureaucratic culture as an important source of Hoccleve's poetic persona, to argue on the one hand that the contemporary financial anxieties in those offices were a shaping influence on his experiment in autobiography and, on the other hand, to argue that the growing laicization of clerkly bureaucrats led him into an interest in the more liminal definitions of gendered identity and an attempt to find a source of authority independent of masculine positions within the court and ecclesiastical structures. In this chapter, I will turn to the more public poetry of Hoccleve's *Regement of Princes*.

The *Regement of Princes* was the centerpiece of the most successful phase of Hoccleve's poetic career. After the composition of the *Letter of Cupid* in 1402, there followed a relatively productive, and public, period in which he wrote "La Male Regle" (1405), numerous short balades addressed to significant men in London government such as Henry Somer, the Keeper of the Wardrobe, and John Carpenter, the town clerk of London.[1] Hoccleve's next

1. For brief discussions of these men and the works addressed to them, see Seymour, *Selections*, 111.

datable poem was the *Regement*, a long and ambitious text that survives in more than forty copies, at least two of which were presentation copies made under Hoccleve's close supervision.[2] The political events of the early fifteenth century help explain why this poem might have found such popularity or at least such widespread and well-funded distribution. The period between 1410 and late 1412, the years during which the *Regement* was written, have long been famous as the years in which the ailing Henry IV, still trying to consolidate the rule gained by the usurpation of Richard II's throne, was faced by a strong challenge for power from his eldest son, the future Henry V.[3] The exact maneuverings of these years are obscure in the contemporary chronicles, perhaps because of a need to keep the future king's name spotless, but what facts we do know indicate that the prince was perceived to be encroaching on his father's prerogative.[4] Indeed, the prince was so active in these years that many histo-

2. Seymour, *Selections*, 114. The forty-three surviving manuscripts of this poem, compared to fifty-seven of the *Canterbury Tales*, forty of Gower's *Confessio Amantis*, and only thirty of Lydgate's *Fall of Princes*, indicate that the *Regement* was one of the most widely distributed poems of the fifteenth century. For data on these manuscripts, see A. S. G. Edwards and Derek Pearsall, "The Manuscripts of the Major English Poetical Texts," in *Book Production and Publishing in Britain, 1375–1475*, ed. Jeremy Griffiths and Derek Pearsall (Cambridge: Cambridge University Press, 1989), 257–78. The literature on the manuscript tradition of the *Regement* is enormous, partly because of the number of the manuscripts and partly because of the issues of patronage involved in the production of the presentation copies. The fundamental treatment is M. C. Seymour, "The Manuscripts of Hoccleve's *Regiment of Princes*," *Transactions of the Edinburgh Bibliographical Society* 4 (1974): 255–97, supplemented by A. S. G. Edwards, Hoccleve's *Regiment of Princes*: A Further Manuscript," *Edinburgh Bibliographical Society Transactions* 5 (1978): 32. See also Charles Blyth, "Editing the Regiment of Princes," in *Essays on Thomas Hoccleve*, ed. Catherine Batt (London: Centre for Medieval and Renaissance Studies, Queen Mary and Westfield College, University of London, 1996), 11–28; Richard Firth Green, "Notes on some MSS of Hoccleve's *Regiment of Princes*," *British Library Journal* 4 (1978): 37–41; D. C. Greetham, "Challenges of Theory and Practice in the Editing of Hoccleve's *Regement of Princes*," in *Manuscripts and Texts*, ed. D. Pearsall (Cambridge: D. S. Brewer, 1987), 60–86; Kate Harris, "The Patron of British Library MS Arundel 38," *Notes and Queries* 31 (1984): 462–63; Marcia Smith Marzec, "The Latin Marginalia of the *Regiment of Princes* as an Aid to Stemmatic Analysis," *Text* 3 (1987): 269–84, and also her "Scribal Emendations in Some Later Manuscripts of Hoccleve's *Regiment of Princes*," *Analytical and Enumerative Bibliography* 1 (1987): 41–51.

3. The *Regement* can be quite precisely dated. A *terminus ad quem* is provided by habitual reference to Henry (who became king in March 1413) as "my lord the prince," and a *terminus a quo* is given by the exemplum of the Lollard John Badby burnt at Smithfield on March 1, 1410. Seymour, *Selections*, 114.

4. Peter McNiven describes the relevant chronicle accounts as "so brief and apparently so selective that much of the material which they include makes little sense until it is collated with the gleanings from other sources," and goes on to suggest that "it may be that one of the reasons for the erratic coverage of the period by the chroniclers, most of whom were favourably disposed towards Prince Henry, is that a full and objective account would have proved difficult to reconcile with his

rians argue that he assumed all but formal control of the government, and the accusation was even heard among his enemies that the prince wanted nothing short of his father's abdication.[5] However, by November 1411, the king had recovered his health and removed the prince and the prince's allies from their positions of power on the king's Council.

The prospect of Prince Henry's accession to the throne was thus one to inspire both great hopes and fears. On the one hand, his brief period of administrative control had produced an emphasis on financial order, which had been generally lacking during his father's reign.[6] G. L. Harriss has connected this sense of optimism to the production of works like Hoccleve's *Regement* and Lydgate's *Troy Book:*

> Lydgate records that the *Troy Book* was commissioned on 31 October 1412. The *Regement,* completed in 1411, was probably commenced two years earlier. These two years were precisely those in which the prince, at the head of a council of his own choosing and virtually without reference to his father, was carrying through a programme of "bone governance" to which he had pledged himself in the parliament of January 1410. . . . Its work, in bringing order into the royal finances and in regaining the confidence of parliament, formed the prelude to Henry V's own reign. The prince's brief period of rule thus furnished a solid expectation of an effective and reinvigorated kingship very different from the pious hope which Gower had expressed in Richard II's youth. As Prince Henry prepared to ascend his father's throne in March 1413 he was to an unusual degree the focus of the hopes and apprehensions of his subjects.[7]

---

unblemished image as king." See his "Prince Henry and the Political Crisis of 1412," *History* 65 (1980): 1.

5. For the events of these years, see K. B. McFarlane, "Father and Son," in *Lancastrian Kings and Lollard Knights* (Oxford: Clarendon Press, 1972), 102–13; Christopher Allmand, *Henry V* (Berkeley and Los Angeles: University of California Press, 1992), 39–58; and, especially, McNiven, "Prince Henry and the Political Crisis of 1412," 9–16, where a strong case is made for attributing Prince Henry's actions to his fear that a conspiracy existed at court to disinherit him in favor of his father's favorite son, Thomas.

6. On the chronically poor state of Henry IV's finances and the continual battles over Parliament's attempt to impose controls, see E. F. Jacob, *The Fifteenth Century* (1961; reprint Oxford: Oxford University Press, 1969), esp. 73–89.

7. G. L. Harriss, *King Henry V: The Practice of Kingship* (Oxford: Oxford University Press, 1985), 9. Nevertheless, Harriss is probably incorrect in his dating of the *Regement;* on which see n. 3, above.

On the other hand, alongside this hope was a concern that the tensions between Henry IV and the prince were so potentially volatile that the prince might resort to an armed rising in support of his aims.[8]

Derek Pearsall has described the *Regement of Princes* as a response to the darker possibilities of these years.[9] He suggests that, after these tense years, Prince Henry badly wanted to represent himself as a sound ruler who would be open to wise counsel. The sponsorship of the *Regement* as the first English "Mirror for Princes" provided the prince with an opportunity to make a public declaration that he was not only willing to listen to such counsel but would actively seek it out, a declaration that he was "content enough to play Alexander to Hoccleve's Aristotle" (389).[10] Pearsall is shrewd in not suggesting that the prince actually "commissioned" the piece (and Hoccleve is equally circumspect in avoiding that implication), but as he explains:

> Henry was in any case a subtle enough politician to recognize the disadvantages of blatant self-advertisement. He knew that spontaneous displays of loyalty and admiration are always much to be preferred. The possibility that Henry V, when he was prince, had a part in encouraging Hoccleve to write the *Regement of Princes* cannot, however, be discounted, and it is supported by evidence of the prince's knowledge and use of books, the circumstances of his relationship with Hoccleve, and the destination of early copies of the *Regement*.[11] (393)

Prince Henry had ability and interest in the use of propaganda; a learned clerk in the Privy Seal was a convenient channel for the importation of a French technique of propaganda; and the luxurious presentation copies of this well-distributed manuscript, which were far too expensive for Hoccleve

---

8. McNiven points out that the letter from the prince which has been preserved in Walsingham's Chronicle admits that very serious allegations had been pressed against him, and suggests further that these allegations were so serious that not only disinheritance, but charges of treason might have been levelled against the prince. McNiven, "Prince Henry and the Political Crisis of 1412," 13.

9. Derek Pearsall, "Hoccleve's *Regement of Princes*: The Poetics of Royal Self-Representation," *Speculum* 69 (1994): 386–410.

10. Pearsall also points out in this connection that the chancellor's text for opening the first parliament of Henry V's reign was "*Ante omnem actem consilium stabile*" (Steadfast counsel before all actions).

11. Furthermore, as Pearsall is also aware, there would have been little need for a direct and formal commission, since Hoccleve's proximity to the court and connections through the Privy Seal would have allowed ample informal channels "through whom the prince's wishes, even his unspoken wishes, might be communicated." Ibid., 394.

to have funded, found their way into the hands of important men who were prospective allies of the prince.[12] In short, it seems quite likely that Hoccleve's *Regement* arose out of the promising and troubled career of the prince in the late years of his father's reign. Thus, a volatile mixture of anxiety and ambition produced an auspicious opportunity for the development of serious English propagandistic verse.

In looking at the formal characteristics of the *Regement of Princes* it should be pointed out, however, that this poem is not just, as it is sometimes labeled, a "mirror for princes." The *Regement,* like "La Male Regle," is best understood as an example of a generic hybrid. The first 2,016 lines of this 5,463-line poem make up a prologue in which Hoccleve laments his poverty, the delay in the payment of his annuity, and his fears that his financial situation will only worsen with advancing age. The prologue is thus an example of one of Hoccleve's most typical compositions, the begging poem. The *Regement* proper, in contrast, contains a book of instructions for a prince, a set of moral and political guidelines drawn from three sources: the pseudo-Aristotelian *Secreta Secretorum;* Egidio Colonna's *De Regimine Principum;* and Jacobus de Cessolis's *Liber de Ludo Scacchorum.*[13] It is this second section, the *Regement* proper, that constitutes the first example found in English of that most popular of medieval genres, the mirror of princes.[14]

12. "The little knowledge we have of the destination of early copies of the *Regement* suggests a concerted attempt on the prince's part to cement relationships with possibly doubtful friends." (These recipients were John of Lancaster, Prince Henry's younger brother, who was not so opposed to the prince as was Thomas, Henry IV's favorite son; John Mowbray, who was being courted after the execution of his older brother for treason in 1405; and Edward, Duke of York, who "had vacillated at the time of the deposition, was imprisoned, degraded, reinstated, and again briefly imprisoned in 1405 after being accused of complicity in the Mortimer conspiracy.") Ibid., 395–96.

13. On the sources for the *Regement,* see William Matthews, "Thomas Hoccleve: Commentary and Bibliography," in *A Manual of Writings in Middle English: 1050–1500,* ed. A. E. Hartung (New Haven: Connecticut Academy of Arts and Sciences, 1972), 3:749–50; Jerome Mitchell, *Thomas Hoccleve: A Study in Early Fifteenth-century Poetic* (Urbana: University of Illinois Press, 1968), 24–27; and Allen H. Gilbert, "Notes on the Influence of the *Secretum Secretorum,*" *Speculum* 3 (1928): 84–98.

14. It is hard to overestimate the importance of this genre in the period. Allen Gilbert has estimated that "between the years 800 and 1700 there were accessible some thousand books and large, easily distinguished sections of books telling the king how to conduct himself so that he might be 'clear in his great office.' " *Machiavelli's Prince and Its Forerunners* (Durham: Duke University Press, 1938), 4. Gilbert's estimate is based on a very loose definition of the advice to princes genre, variously referred to as the *Fürstenspiegel,* or the mirror of princes. For an excellent treatment of questions of genre and taxonomy, see Jean-Philippe Genet's introduction to his edition of *Four English Political Tracts.* Genet suggests that the German tradition of scholarship (which Anglo-American scholars rely on implicitly through their adoption of the category of the *Fürstenspiegel*) has been far too inclusive in its taxonomy, tending to lump together very technical works such as John of Salisbury's

It was not unprecedented to bring together a mirror for princes with autobiographical material: Christine de Pizan had created a similar fusion in her *L'Avision*.[15] The *Regement*, however, seems to have struck readers from a very early date as a problematic combination of these two elements. The rubrication among surviving manuscripts varies, suggesting some confusion about the relation between the prologue and the *Regement* proper. On some occasions scribes have labeled the whole five thousand lines as "De Regimine Principum," but on other occasions this title is applied only to the last three thousand lines.[16] Among modern readers, this division between the autobiographical prologue and the latter half of the poem has become a central interpretive crux. The bifurcation between autobiography and counsel has been read in a number of significant ways: as a representation of the typological relations between ethics and state policy; as a device for meditating on the Foucauldian relation between the body of the subject and that of the prince; as a reflection of the historical crisis in annuities and debt connecting petitioner and ruler; and as a focal point for the paradoxes invoked when the powerless offer counsel to the mighty.[17]

The plot of the *Regement*'s prologue is easily summarized. Hoccleve describes lying awake in a sleepless, thought-filled night and then walking out

---

Policraticus with more narrative and popular works like as Chaucer's *Melibee*. Genet describes the English works in this tradition as an outgrowth of a particular literary tradition that originated among Mendicants attached to the Capetian court. To mark this specific point of origin, Genet replaces the too-eclectic *Fürstenspiegel* with the label *miroir*. I adopt his term later in this chapter (though in disagreement with Genet, who considers Hoccleve's work insufficiently technical to count as a true *miroir*). Genet, *Four English Political Tracts of the Later Middle Ages*, Camden 4th ser., 18 (London: Royal Historical Society, 1977).

15. See Rosalind Brown-Grant, "*L'Avision Christine*: Autobiographical Narrative or Mirror for the Prince?" in *Politics, Gender, and Genre: The Political Thought of Christine de Pizan*, ed. Margaret Brabant and Jean-Bethke Elshtain (Boulder, Colo.: Westview, 1992), 95–111. See also Glynnis Cropp, "Boèce et Christine de Pizan," *Le Moyen Age* 87 (1981): 399–409 for a partial listing of verbal parallel between the *Consolatio* and *L'Avision*, which Cropp refers to as "une nouvelle Consolacion," 409.

16. Greetham, "Self-Referential Artifacts," 245.

17. See Greetham, "Self-Referential Artifacts"; Anna Torti, "Specular Narrative: Hoccleve's *Regement of Princes*," in her *Glass of Form: Mirroring Structures from Chaucer to Skelton* (Cambridge: D. S. Brewer, 1991), 87–106; Judith Ferster, "A Mirror for the Prince of Wales: Hoccleve's *Regement of Princes*," in *Fictions of Advice: The Literature and Politics of Counsel in Late Medieval England* (Philadelphia: University of Pennsylvania Press, 1996), 137–59; Antony Hasler, "Hoccleve's Unregimented Body," *Paragraph* 13 (1990): 164–83; and Larry Scanlon, "The King's Two Voices: Narrative and Power in Hoccleve's *Regement of Princes*," in *Literary Practice and Social Change in Britain, 1380–1530*, ed. Lee Patterson (Berkeley and Los Angeles: University of California Press, 1990), 216–47, material from which is reworked in Scanlon's *Narrative, Authority, and Power* (Cambridge: Cambridge University Press, 1994), 299–322.

into the fields, where he meets an unnamed Old Man. Hoccleve laments his poverty, the delay in the payment of his annuity, and his fears that his financial situation will only worsen with age. The two debate for some time the best course of action, and the Old Man concludes by reminding Hoccleve of the virtues that may follow from poverty but also suggests the more practical remedy of writing some work for Prince Henry, the future Henry V, in order to secure patronage and the regular disbursement of his annuity. After this long prologue comes the *Regement* proper, the compendium of moral and political advice directed toward the prince.

My analysis of the *Regement* concentrates on this prologue and proceeds in two sections. First, I look at the traces of the Privy Seal in the *Regement*. Here the most important sign is the representation of scribal labor found in the prologue to the work. In these descriptions, Hoccleve pursues a connection between the work of the scribe and the vulnerability and mortality of the human body, a connection in which we can read both a claim about the importance of writing as a technology for supplementing the body and also a corresponding fear that writing is made at the cost of the scribe's body, literally wasting the writer as he labors. Second, I turn to the vexed question of Boethius's role in this text. The philosophy of Boethius represents the ultimate horizon of much of the ethical and political thought of the early fifteenth century; Hoccleve's invocation of this Boethian world, however, is marked chiefly by his profound resistance to any consolations that might be offered by either this philosophy or the writing such philosophy might urge.

Scribes and Bodies

In the year 1419 John Carpenter, the town clerk of London, completed a collection of city documents, statutes, and letters assembled together for the guidance of future governments. This compilation, known as the *Liber Albus*, begins by setting out Carpenter's reasons for putting himself and his clerks to such labor:

> Quia labilitas humanae memoriae, brevitasque vitae, de singulis rebus memorandis, licet scriptis—praesertim irregulariter et confuse,—et multo magis de non scriptis, certam habere notitiam non permittunt; cumque, per frequentes pestilentias, subtractis velut insimul cunctis gubernatoribus longaevis magis expertis et discretior-

ibus Civitatis Regalis Londoniarum, juniores eis in civitatis regimine succedentes in variis casibus, pro defectu scripturae nimi- rum, saepius ambigebant; unde super judiciis reddendis contro- versia et perplexitas inter eos pluries causabantur: necessarium videbatur a diu, tam superioribus quam subditis dictae civitatis, quoddam volumen, (quod "Repertorium," a contento in eo civita- tis regimine, diceretur), ex notabilibus memorandis tam in libris, rotulis, quam in chartis dictae civitatis inordinate diffuseque pos- itis, compilari.[18]

(Forasmuch as the fallibility of human memory and the shortness of life do not allow us to gain an accurate knowledge of everything that deserves remembrance, even though the same may have been committed to writing,—more especially, if it has been so commit- ted without order or arrangement,—and still more so, when no such written account exists; seeing too that when, as not unfre- quently happens, all the aged, most experienced, and most discreet rulers of the royal City of London have been carried off at the same instant, as it were, by pestilence, younger persons who have succeeded them in the government of the City, have on various occasions been often at a loss from the very want of such written information; the result of which has repeatedly been disputes and perplexity among them as to the decisions which they should give:—it has been long deemed necessary, as well by the superior authorities of the said city as by those of a subordinate rank, that a volume—from the fact of its containing the regulations of the City, it might be designated a "Repertory"—should be compiled from the more noteworthy memoranda that lie scattered without order or classification throughout the books [and] rolls, as well as the Charters of the said city.)[19]

18. Henry Thomas Riley, *Liber Albus, Compiled* A.D. *1419* (London: Longman, Brown, Green, Longmans, and Roberts, 1859), 2. On Carpenter's career and the dating of different sections of the *Liber Albus*, see William Kellaway, "John Carpenter's *Liber Albus*," *Guildhall Studies in London History* 3 (1978): 67–84; and Wendy Scase, "Reginald Pecock, John Carpenter, and John Colop's 'Common- Profit' Books: Aspects of Book Ownership and Circulation in Fifteenth-Century London," *Medium Aevum* 61 (1992): 261–74. On Hoccleve and Carpenter, see also Hagel, *Thomas Hoccleve*, 58–59.

19. Translation from Henry Thomas Riley, ed., *Liber Albus: The White Book of the City of London, Compiled* A.D. *1419 by John Carpenter, Common Clerk, and Richard Whitington, Mayor*, trans. Henry Thomas Riley (London: Richard Griffin and Company, 1861).

This rationale offers a vision of writing as a supplement to the fragile human body. It is a technology necessitated by a sense of crisis, signified by the pestilence that might result not just in scattered deaths but in a generation and its knowledge being carried off at once. Writing is that which guarantees permanence to the contents of human consciousness despite the fragility of human life. To a certain extent, this idea is a reworking of the traditional topoi surrounding connections between poetry and immortality, the potential of poetry to grant immortality through fame.[20] The emphasis here is, however, not on the power of any aesthetically charged virtue but rather on writing as a bureaucratic technology used to battle the passage of time and memory. It is a powerful statement of the more positive dreams of bureaucratic efficacy, the extension of human agency through the archival text.

The sponsor of this compilation, John Carpenter, led a career that, like that of Hoccleve, would have brought him into substantial contact with the bureaucratic technologies of writing.[21] Carpenter is unique among the holders of the office of clerk of the city in that he was also referred to in the records as the city's "Secretary." According to the early nineteenth-century account of his life by Thomas Brewer, Carpenter gained his office through an unusual arrangement, contracting with the man elected to the position, John Marchaunt, to execute the duties of the office in exchange for a portion of its income.[22] Later in life, Carpenter became an artistic patron and paid for a painting of the "dance of death" with an accompanying series of verses provided by Lydgate.[23] The details of John Carpenter's life thus recapitulate the two chief elements from the opening passage of the *Liber Albus:* writing as a technical matter, divorced from the prestige of office or aesthetics (the "Secretary"); and the omnipresence of death, to be expected at any time and not forgotten.

This association between writing and mortality lurks near the surface of any bureaucratic apparatus. Michael Clanchy has suggested that: "Medieval

20. See the compact discussion of this topos in Ernst Robert Curtius, *European Literature and the Latin Middle Ages*, trans. Willard R. Trask (1953; reprint, London: Routledge and Kegan Paul, 1979), 476–77. The invocation of the frailty of human memory as a spur to the creation of a written record is also frequently found in charters and other written guarantors of property. See also Clanchy, *Memory to Written Record*, 118 and passim.

21. Among other parallel interests, we might note that, like Hoccleve, Carpenter represents a significant moment in the history of the signature, being the first common clerk of the town to endorse public documents with his own name. Carpenter began this innovation in 1417. Kellaway, "John Carpenter's *Liber Albus*," 67, n. 5.

22. Thomas Brewer, *Memoir of John Carpenter, Town Clerk of London in the Reigns of Henry V and Henry VI* (London: Arthur Taylor, 1836), 3.

23. Ibid., *Memoir of John Carpenter*, 23.

writing materials themselves made the scribe conscious of time. Because he was presented with the alternatives of wax or parchment as a medium, he made an initial choice between the ephemeral and the permanent."[24] The tools used by any scribe were thus a constant reminder of temporality, of the ability of writing to signify either the permanence of parchment or the dissolution of the image in wax. Moreover, the idea of the document as a record, independent of any living human witness, stems from the need for testimony to legal arrangements that would be reliably available beyond the physical or temporal boundaries of a single biological person. In England, we find a transition in the techniques of verifying property ownership in the shift from the use of human memory, sometimes reinforced by the exchange of symbolic objects, to an increasing reliance on written records.[25] The sense that writing may be partly defined by its ability to exceed the temporality of human life is also suggested by the persistence of those older legal forms in the metonymic expression "living memory."[26] Hoccleve, too, was well aware of the connections between writing and mortality. He describes his own backbreaking work in the *Regement of Princes*, giving a description of all the physical ills that come from too much time bent over a desk—the bad back, failing eyes, and other ills familiar to scriveners of all eras.[27] These descriptions are all marked by a persistent connection between writing and aging. The *Regement* and the *Series* share a dramatic frame in which Hoccleve is advised to amend his financial troubles through his writing. In both cases he takes the advice, but in both he also indicates a price to be paid for this solution. In the *Series*, as we shall see, the price is a risk of madness; in the *Regement*, it is age itself.

Hoccleve's depictions of writing in the *Regement* have been discussed by both Anthony Hasler and Steven Justice. Justice points out the centrality of "boredom" in descriptions of scribal labor by both Chaucer and Hoccleve, and he puts this boredom into the context of a class-based resentment at the mechanization of clerkly labors.[28] For Hasler, however, writing, and particu-

24. Clanchy, *Memory to Written Record*, 116.
25. Ibid., 3, 203–8.
26. The theme of the tension between memory and writing extends, of course, back to Plato's *Phaedras* (King Thamus's charge that writing will bring the death of memory) and has been revived most notably by Derrida's meditations on this passage.
27. Hoccleve was not alone in these complaints. John Brokholes, clerk of the Signet, left an account in which he resigned in 1444, when he was aged, infirm, and almost blind. See Otway-Ruthven, *The King's Secretary*, 181–82.
28. Steven Justice, "Inquisition, Speech, and Writing: A Case from Norwich," in *Criticism and Dissent in the Middle Ages*, ed. Rita Copeland (Cambridge: Cambridge University Press, 1996), 294–96.

larly the pain of writing, is objectified by Hoccleve and turned into an object of amusing humor, a thing to be offered up in exchange for patronage.[29] Hasler's reading of the suffering in these passages, drawing on Louise Fraden-burg's Lacanian analysis of patronage relations, is astute, particularly in its ability to account for the tricky tonal register of such passages.[30] Neverthe-less, this reading may risk lifting the suffering described in this text out of the dramatic context of the conversation between Hoccleve and the Old Man who advises him in the prologue. The problem is that the well-known stanzas on writing and bodily pain are usually read in isolation, but they are in fact the climax of a longer conversation in this text, much of which, although less directly topical than these stanzas, is a necessary part of Hoc-cleve's consideration of the ills of the writer.

In examining scribal labor in the *Regement*, then, it is necessary to start much earlier in the conversation between Hoccleve and the Old Man. The *Regement* is a deeply dramatic work, both in the conversational structure of Hoccleve's verse—its reliance on direct dialogue and the sometimes argu-mentative interchanges between Hoccleve and the Old Man—and also in its concern with space and physical action. The prologue begins by first establishing the scene of Hoccleve's solitary inactivity in his private cham-ber, as he lies awake tormented by the mental restlessness he names and even allegorizes as "thought" ("As I lay in my bed upon a nyght,/Thoght me byrefte of sleep the force and might" lines 6–7). Hoccleve then rises, deter-mined to throw off this debilitating "thought," and walks out of his chamber and into the fields:

> Passe over; whan this stormy nyght was goon
> And day gan at my wyndowe in to prye,
> I roos me up, for boote fond I noon
> In myn unresty bed lenger to lye.
> Into the feeld I dressid me in hye,
> And in my wo I herte-deep gan wade,
> As he that was bareyne of thoghtes glade.
>   (lines 113–19)[31]

29. Hasler, "Hoccleve's Unregimented Body."
30. Louise O. Fradenburg, "The Manciple's Servant Tongue: Politics and Poetry in the *Canter-bury Tales*," *English Literary History* 52 (1985): 85–118.
31. Blyth, ed., *The Regiment of Princes*. Subsequent references are drawn from this edition and cited by line number within the text.

Hoccleve here makes a double departure, looking to escape thought by leaving the contained spaces of both chamber and city, but at first he finds no distance, no change from the restless obsessions of his solitude. Indeed, the allegorical sense of the descriptions (always a sign in Hoccleve of the hyperactivity of thought) perseveres. Hoccleve represents himself in this passage walking out into space but also wading "herte-depe" in his "wo"—as if it were not grass but thought itself that he had to wade through. He continues walking for some time—"By that I walkid hadde a certeyn tyme,/Were it an hour I not, or more or lesse" (lines 120–21)—but only when the unnamed Old Man approaches him and then forcibly engages him in conversation does he leave the isolated landscape of internal allegorization and enters the world of public discourse. The two continue their walk for some seven hundred lines until the Old Man, in frustration with Hoccleve's recalcitrance, demands that Hoccleve pause for a moment and reveal the source of his adversity:

Hoccleve does so in a telling passage:

> "Sauf first, or thow any ferther proceede,
> O thyng of thee wite wolde I, my sone:
> Wher dwellist thow?" "Fadir, withouten dreede,
> In the office of the Privee Seel I wone
> And wryte—there is my custume and wone
> Unto the Seel, and have twenti yeer
> And foure come Estren, and that is neer."
>
> "Now sikir, sone, that is a fair tyme;
> The tokne is good of thy continuance.
> Come hidir, goode, and sitte adoun heer by me,
> For I moot reste a whyle; it is penance
> To me thus longe walke—it dooth nusance
> Unto my crookid, feeble lymes olde,
> That ben so stif, unnethe I may hem folde."
>
> Whan I was set adoun as he me preide,
> "Telle on," seide he, "how is it with thee, how?"
>   (lines 799–814)

This passage has received little commentary, other than its documentary use in determining dates of Hoccleve's tenure at the Privy Seal. It deserves to be read, however, as also a peculiar moment in the action of the prologue. The passage begins first with the Old Man's injunction to pause before proceeding further, an instruction that, like the wading through thought of the more openly allegorical beginning of the prologue, links the walk taken by the two men to their discursive progress. Hoccleve is meant to pause both in motion and argument. The passage continues thematizing place by its striking cate-gorization of the Privy Seal as a physical home. And, most important, we are not meant to pass over the fact that in the large allegorical schema of motion and stasis it is at the moment when the Privy Seal and the endless writing of this work are invoked that Hoccleve and the Old Man sit to rest. Indeed, it is almost as if the Old Man and Hoccleve, too, are suddenly exhausted by that image of twenty-four years of writing.

The Old Man congratulates Hoccleve on the length of his service "that is a fair tyme" and suggests that it is a good sign for his "continuance" in the work, but despite the explicit intentions of setting Hoccleve's financial wor-ries to rest, this "continuance" is hard to take as an entirely good thing. As many readers have noted, there is throughout the prologue an odd sense of identification between Hoccleve and the Old Man. The Old Man appears in many ways as the exact image of the aged state Hoccleve fears, an image of garrulous, aged penury. In addition, the dialogue form leads them to reflect each other's concerns and at times to transfer qualities back and forth. Hasler nicely characterizes this as a situation in which the two "ascribe their own attributes to each other in a transitivism offset by specular aggressivity."[32] At this moment in the text, this cross-identification functions as Hoccleve, within twenty lines, has adopted the Old Man's language of aging and physi-cal decay and is anticipating his own age and impoverishment. Hoccleve continues to describe his own decline, then the troubles of the forgotten veterans of the French war who are neglected by those still young, then shifts without interruption into the often-quoted lines on the physical effects of writing. Hoccleve's depiction of writing in the prologue is thus not isolated in the few stanzas usually quoted in critical discussion but is a part of a long segmented series of episodes. First, the subject of writing at the Privy Seal causes Hoccleve and the Old Man to pull up short; then, the Old Man complains of his "feeble lymes olde" and the blight of age transfers immedi-ately to Hoccleve's imagination; this leads him to discuss first his own poor future and then to turn back to writing. It is a neat and emphatic chiastic structure, whose function is to link the topic of writing with the inexorable decline of the body in age.

32. Hasler, "Hoccleve's Unregimented Body," 174.

This dramatic point is then driven home by this long description of the woes of writing, a mirror for any scrivener:

"With plow can I nat medlen ne with harwe,
Ne woot nat what lond good is for what corn,
And for to lade a cart or fille a barwe,
To which I never usid was toforn;
My bak unbuxum hath swich thyng forsworn,
At instaunce of wrytynge, his werreyour,
That stowpynge hath him spilt with his labour.

"Many men, fadir, weenen that wrytynge
No travaille is; they holde it but a game;
Aart hath no fo but swich folk unkonnynge.
But whoso list desporte him in that same,
Let him continue and he shal fynde it grame;
It is wel gretter labour than it seemeth;
The blynde man of colours al wrong deemeth.

"A wryter moot thre thynges to him knytte,
And in tho may be no disseverance:
Mynde, ye, and hand—noon may from othir flitte,
But in hem moot be joynt continuance;
The mynde al hool, withouten variance,
On ye and hand awayte moot alway,
And they two eek on him, it is no nay.

"Whoso shal wryte, may nat holde a tale
With him and him, ne synge this ne that;
But al his wittes hoole, grete and smale,
Ther muste appeere and holden hem therat;
And syn he speke may ne synge nat,
Bot bothe two he needes moot forbere,
His labour to him is the elengere.

"Thise artificers see I day by day,
In the hootteste of al hir bysynesse,
Talken and synge and make game and play,
And foorth hir labour passith with gladnesse;
But we laboure in travaillous stilnesse;

We stowpe and stare upon the sheepes skyn,
And keepe moot our song and wordes yn.

"Wrytyng also dooth grete annoyes thre,
Of which ful fewe folkes taken heede
Sauf we ourself, and thise, lo, they be:
Stommak is oon, whom stowpynge out of dreede
Annoyeth sore; and to our bakkes neede
Moot it be grevous; and the thridde oure yen
Upon the whyte mochil sorwe dryen.

"What man that three and twenti yeer and more
In wrytynge hath continued, as have I,
I dar wel seyn, it smertith him ful sore
In every veyne and place of his body;
And yen moost it greeveth treewely,
Of any craft that man can ymagyne.
Fadir, in feith, it spilt hath wel ny myne.

(lines 981–1029)

This passage presents us with a catalogue of the physical complaints caused by writing. Writing is allegorized as the warrior waging war on his back, where his stooping has led to grievous results; his stomach, too, is "annoyed." His eyes suffer the worst: they are quite nearly ruined by twenty-three years, and a bit more, of peering onto so much white parchment (the dizzying blankness of the page). We see in this passage a characteristic form of allegory for Hoccleve, the breakdown of a single subject into a series of fragmented psychic or anatomic categories. Here the stylistic mechanism for this allegorization is the tricolonic structure used to organize both the requirements ("A wryter moot thre thynges to him knytte") and the ills ("Wrytyng also dooth grete annoyes thre") of writing. The anatomical fragmentation of the self is significant here because it precisely mirrors the Old Man's presentation of himself in the earlier scene. The Old Man had not complained of a general aging but rather of his "crookid, feeble lymes olde." In other words, the Old Man's language implicitly describes age as a fragmentation of the unitary body into a collection of anatomical fragments, a perspectival fragmentation caused by the awareness of separate disfunctions. The same fragmentation happens in an instant here to the body of the writer.

Moreover, there is in this passage a tendency to use a broadly penitential set of categories to describe writing, categories that, in the broader context of the *Regement*, are often associated with the opposition between age and youth (via the contrast between the Old Man and foolish younger folk). Writing, for instance, requires the concentration of absolute silence, here represented as a repression of speech and song. Artificers, or craftsmen, sing when they work, but "we laboure in travaillous stilnesse" and "keepe moot our song and wordes yn." Similarly, both the second and fifth stanzas are organized by an opposition between "game" and "travaille," a traditional opposition of penitential literature, here mobilized to stress the bookish re-nunciation of pleasure that is part of the writer's lot.

Finally, we should notice in this passage a very complex play between community and solitude. Both the scrivener and his opposite, the artificers who talk and sing at their work, are represented as groupings, as classes in a sense. This effect is carefully crafted in such a way as to call attention to a paradox in the writer's sense of identification. The writer is first introduced in the abstract singular of "a writer," then turned into the corporate plural of "we" and "our" as a response to the enviably social "artificers." In the last stanza the writer is again solitary but now not an abstraction, rather the "I" of Hoccleve. The writer is thus described both as a member of a communal "we" and as a markedly solitary figure. This indeterminacy is explained by the very strange nature of the writerly "we." Whereas it is clear that the artificers are constituted as a plural entity by their joint communication (speaking and singing), at the very moment the plural is used in reference to the clerks Hoccleve inserts "We stowpe and stare upon the sheepes skyn." The scriveners are thus defined as a community, but a community uniquely marked by the lack of any direct communication: "Whoso shal wryte, may nat holde a tale/With him and him." Among its paradoxes, then, writing seems to promise the formation of some community but demand in its actual practice a renunciation of the verbal links of speech, song, and "tale" that create the broader social world.

Like the *Liber Albus*, writing in the *Regement* holds out the promise of a victory over time and age. The prologue ends with the Old Man having finally convinced Hoccleve to write a treatise for the Prince:

> Recordyng in my mynde the lessoun
> That he me yaf, I hoom to mete wente.
> And on the morwe sette I me adoun,
> And penne and ynke and parchemyn I hente,
> And to parfourme his wil and his entente

I took corage, and whyles it was hoot,
Unto my lord the Prince thus I wroot:
(lines 2010–16)

Hoccleve returns to his home, coming back full circle and seeming to recon-
stitute the self fragmented in his dialogue with the Old Man. This self is
gathered back together within the single intention of writing. Significantly,
we see here the same sort of enumeration of elements that had organized the
anatomical descriptions earlier, but now the objects enumerated are exterior;
they are the instruments of writing, the world perceived as technology avail-
able to a sovereign self. This image, of the writer sitting down in full mastery
before the instruments of his task, is one that would have appealed to the
compiler of the *Liber Albus*. But to take this image as more than an illusory
hope would be to forget what Hoccleve has already said about writing in the
prologue. The magic promised by the *Liber Albus* is the magic of a writing
that could repair the weakness of human mortality and bind up all the docu-
ments of the city into a unified textual representation of the commune; it
would be just the sort of writing expected of workers in the Privy Seal. But
Hoccleve's descriptions of writing dispute just these two possibilities. His
description of the scrivener explores the possibility of a writerly community
yet finds the possibility unlikely, except as a common experience of tedium
and resentment. And far from imagining writing as a tool to banish age,
Hoccleve presents a persistent metaphoric connection between writing and
age. Scribal labor in the *Regement* does not free the writer from age. Writing,
for Hoccleve, is age itself. "Wher dwellist thow? . . . In the office of the
Privee Seel I wone/And wryte . . ." (lines 801–3). To dwell in the Privy Seal
is to dwell in writing itself, which may remain, but only at the cost of the
scribe.[33]

Consolation in the Regement of Princes

The philosophical context for these meditations on writing and mortality is
a Boethian one. As David Lawton has argued, the determining philosophical

33. This dwelling within writing is also a partial explanation of an ambiguity in Hoccleve's
usage of the term *Privy Seal*, which he sometimes uses to describe his home, sometimes his workplace,
and sometimes the institution in the abstract. Hoccleve's sense of immersion in the textual life of
the Privy Seal is so great that the Privy Seal becomes not just a place or office but a condition that
is always with him. For further discussion of his usage of the term, see Burrow, *Thomas Hoccleve*,
7–8.

context for Lancastrian political poetry, and for the culture of early fifteenth-century public verse in general, was the writings of Boethius.[34] Lawton's argument provides a powerful intervention against the received notion that the poetry of the fifteenth century contains nothing but the most conventional repetitions of the philosophical and cultural flowering of the Ricardian period. He takes the common confession of poets in this period that they are "dull" to be both ironically exaggerated self-denigration (in the tradition of the Chaucerian narrative persona) and, at the same time, as the most serious and straightforward of claims. The claim is straightforward: it allowed fifteenth-century poets offering political counsel in dangerous times to claim the license of a sanctioned fool, a "dull" man; and this term activated a precise Boethian language. Within a Boethian universe, the attribute of dullness should not be taken as an admission of particular failing on the part of a particular author; it should be read as the inevitable result of the fundamentally unpredictable nature of Fortune. As Lawton makes the point: "Humans governed by Fortune cannot claim 'connyng.' All in a sublunar world are dull."[35] Dullness thus stands in the early fifteenth century as both a political cover and a conventional invocation of a Boethian stance in relation to Fortune.

Along with the dominance of this authorizing use of Boethius, we also find Boethian themes and tropes used in the period with much more skeptical intent.[36] In the case of Hoccleve's *Regement*, for example, we find a poem that is thoroughly Boethian in its preoccupations and lexicon but quite un-Boethian in its conclusion that philosophical consolation is an interminable and insufficient project. Boethius provides the ultimate philosophical horizon of much of Hoccleve's work, and the widespread penitential stoicism that was grounded in the *Consolation* organizes Hoccleve's many narratives of misfortune and redemption. Hoccleve's attitude toward Boethius, however, is that of a skepticism that has exceeded one philosophical system without moving to another. Although Boethius is inescapable, Hoccleve's use of the tradition is marked by a dynamic of constant resistance. Specifically, he de-

34. Lawton, "Dullness and the Fifteenth Century." One might also construct an alternative narrative of fifteenth-century literary history that would displace both Hoccleve and Lydgate in favor of other literatures, such as the *Piers Plowman* tradition. For an example of this approach, see Helen Barr, *Signes and Sothe: Language in the "Piers Plowman" Tradition*, Piers Plowman Studies, 10 (Cambridge: D. S. Brewer, 1994).

35. Lawton, "Dullness and the Fifteenth Century," 769.

36. Lawton's treatment also recognizes this point, as his reading of "dullness" implicitly suggests that these poets were, by necessity, engaged in complex dialogic games with their Boethian source.

ploys the language and themes of a Boethian culture in such a way as to expose their social and epistemological limitations.[37] The attempt to show Hoccleve's recalcitrance in the face of this Boethian tradition is complicated by the fact that the chief text of the tradition, Boethius's *Consolatio*, is itself an extremely slippery book. Winthrop Wetherbee puts his finger on a central difficulty in reading the *Consolatio* when he comments that it is "a more truly dialogic work than its neo-Platonic models, one which both invokes and deliberately challenges their idealism."[38] This "challenge" is created by the philosophical content of Boethius's text and by his formal mode of presentation. In the content of the work we see a decision, not unlike similar moments in Hoccleve, to balance platonic idealism with a more psychological treatment of despair in the world. In its form, the alternation between prose and verse creates a productive tension between philosophical discourse and exemplary metaphor. Moreover, we should also take note of a technique that Hoccleve borrows in the *Regement*: the uneven progression of the dialogue between Philosophy and the prisoner, a conversation that proceeds through both success and misunderstandings. In this way the work represents communication and the apparent success of classical pedagogy as, at least in part, the product of a series of linguistic misrecognitions. The *Consolatio*, the foundation stone of a tradition so often described as unremittingly conventional and "dull," was itself a text marked by sophisticated dialogic play.[39]

Yet there were also elements of the Boethian tradition, especially as it became identified with a mixture of stoic and penitential theologies, that

37. James Simpson has also argued for a skepticism toward Boethius in the *Regement*. He suggests that Boethian discourse is the backdrop for the dialogue in the prologue but that, in the end, Hoccleve refuses the Old Man's consolations because he recognizes that it is counsel only for those who are wholly destitute, and that "the essence of Hoccleve's position is that he's *not yet* down and out." Simpson, "Nobody's Man: Thomas Hoccleve's *Regement of Princes*," in *London and Europe in the Late Middle Ages*, ed. Julia Boffey and Pamela King (London: Centre for Medieval and Renaissance Studies, Queen Mary and Westfield College, University of London, 1995), 149–80.

38. Winthrop Wetherbee, "Latin Structures and Vernacular Space: Gower, Chaucer, and the Boethian Tradition," in *Chaucer and Gower: Difference, Mutuality, Exchange*, ed. R. F. Yeager (Victoria: University of Victoria, 1991), 11.

39. Indeed, Wetherbee suggests that this very oppositional origin (as a counter-statement to neo-Platonic idealism) makes the *Consolatio* a foundation for the idea of vernacular poetry: "For an ongoing dialogue between poetry in a broad sense and the conventions that determine its role in medieval thought and pedagogy is an important element of the tradition. What begins in Boethius as a challenge to the hermeneutics of late neo-Platonism becomes in the work of Alan of Lille a critique of mythography and the allegorical interpretative tradition. This in turn prepares the way for the increasing assertiveness of writers like Jean de Meun and Dante in claiming something like traditional *auctoritas* for poetry in the vernacular." Ibid., 10.

may seem an ill fit with the skepticism I have been outlining as a persistent strand in Hoccleve's work.[40] First, whatever tensions are contained therein, the general movement of the *Consolatio* is a progression from error to truth, a progression that is figured formally as a transformation of dialogue into monologue.[41] Second, this tradition understood the authorial subject as a variation on the prisoner of the *Consolatio*. A poet wrote in physical and mental isolation with only the shadowy counsel of a Lady Philosophy for society, an image widely recycled by vernacular poets in their own self-representations.[42] And, finally, the stoic posture required of this prisoner was consonant with a broader *contemptus mundi*. Boethius could easily be brought in, with a light seasoning of Job, to reinforce that penitential narrative whereby suffering in this world could be understood as what Hoccleve will call a "visit" from God, an occasion to teach the futility of worldly pleasure.

By re-examining the question of Boethian influence in the *Regement*, I hope to further our understanding of the relation between scribal labor and temporality in this text. Hoccleve typically opens his works by establishing his persona as a man all too aware of his entrapment in a Boethian universe of misfortune. In "La Male Regle," this persona finds himself suddenly bereft of health and prosperity; in the *Regement*, he is a man obsessed with imminent poverty; and in the *Series*, he is suffering the twin blows of madness and social isolation. In other words, his typical opening gambit is the expression of Boethian themes of capricious suffering presented through the generic frame of the complaint. In opening his poems through the complaint,

40. In talking about "Boethius" here, I am not so concerned to give a technically exact reading of the *Consolatio* as to outline the main features of the Boethian culture of the early fifteenth century. This is Boethius not as we might read him now, but Boethius as Hoccleve would have recognized him: a cluster of literary, stoic, and penitential practices, all of which were bound together by their resort to Boethius for language and philosophical authority.

41. See, for example, Seth Lerer: "In the early books of the *Consolation*, the prisoner appears as an orator and dialectician concerned more with the effects of his words than with their philosophical weight. . . . Their dialogue frequently breaks down, and she must exhort the prisoner not to accede to her authority but to sustain discussion. . . . By Book Five . . . the dialogue moves finally to monologue, as Philosophy lectures, using the techniques of philosophical demonstration. The dialogue of the *Consolation* thus chronicles the growth of a debater coming to terms with the limits of his own language and method in the attempt to articulate philosophical [as opposed to dialectical] truths." Lerer, *Boethius and Dialogue: Literary Method in the Consolation of Philosophy* (Princeton: Princeton University Press, 1985), 6.

42. For numerous examples of very literal representations of authors as prisoners (Orléans, Ashby, Usk, James I of Scotland), see Julia Boffey, "Chaucerian Prisoners: The context of *The Kingis Quair*," in *Chaucer and Fifteenth-Century Poetry*, ed. Julia Boffey and Janet Cowen, 84–102. See also Nadia Margolis, "The Human Prison: The Metamorphoses of Misery in the Poetry of Christine de Pizan, Charles d'Orléans, and Francois Villon," *Fifteenth Century Studies* 1 (1978): 185–92.

Hoccleve is in fact following the example of Boethius's *Consolatio* itself, whose first metrum begins with a reworking of many of the elements of Ovid's *Tristia*.[43]

The complaint, from even the very early examples of Ovidian love elegies, has been a genre with a long history of meditations on its own fictive status. Lee Patterson has suggested that this history, what he calls "its capacity to stage questions central to literary culture as a whole," derives from the fact that "what is specific to complaint is that the claim it lays upon the world is virtually always self-cancelling, and that it thus raises questions about writing as a pragmatic activity. Not only does the plaintive voice typically assume the uselessness of its declarations but its uselessness is programmatic."[44] As an example of this paradox, we might look to the progression of generic form within the *Consolatio* itself, especially the complicated sequence through which this work rejects the genre of the complaint on its way to philosophical consolation. Immediately after the prisoner delivers his opening complaint, Lady Philosophy appears and chases away the muses of poetry.[45] By branding the muses as whores and claiming that "they kill the fruitful harvest of reason with the sterile thorns of the passions," Lady Philosophy implies that she believes that the malignancy of elegiac poetry (the literary ancestor of the complaint) derives from the fact that it is inherently unproductive, from the fact that it is useless.[46] But, within the progressive scheme of the *Consolatio* as a whole, there is a certain limited usefulness to this initial complaint. The complaint establishes the experience of suffering that Philosophy needs as raw material for her discourse. It is necessary as the first step in a dialectical process, the bottom rung of a ladder meant to be kicked away

43. Anna Crabbe discusses the relation of the *Consolatio* to the *Tristia* in some detail; see her "Literary Design in the *De Consolatione Philosophiae*," in *Boethius: His Life, Thought, and Influence*, ed. M. T. Gibson (Oxford: Blackwell, 1981), 244–48.

44. Lee Patterson, "Writing Amorous Wrongs: Chaucer and the Order of the Complaint," in *The Idea of Medieval Literature: New Essays on Chaucer and Medieval Culture in Honor of Donald R. Howard*, ed. James M. Dean and Christian K. Zacher (Newark: University of Delaware Press, 1992), 55. See also Robert Deschaux, "La Complainte," in *La Littérature française au XIVe et XVe siècles*, Grundriss der romanischen Literaturen des Mittelalters, ed. D. Poirion, VIII/I (Heidelberg: C. Winter Universitätsverlag, 1988), 77–85.

45. Crabbe traces the action and language of this scene back to one of Propertius's most famous elegies, thus suggesting that Philosophy is hostile to poetry in general, but is especially hostile to *elegiac* poetry. Crabbe, "Literary Design in the *De Consolatione Philosophiae*," 249–50.

46. Boethius, *The Consolation of Philosophy*, trans. Richard Green (New York: Macmillan, 1962), 4. "Hae sunt enim quae infructuosis affectuum spinis uberum fructibus rationis segetem necant." Ludovicus Bieler, *Boethii Philosophiae Consolatio* (Turnhout: Brepols, 1957), 2. Subsequent citations and translations are drawn from these editions.

later. Thus, we are faced with the paradox that in a Boethian frame the complaint is useless but necessary. Hence, perhaps, the infinite echoing of the *contemptus mundi* theme in the later Middle Ages: it is a philosophical stance always already known and insufficient in itself, but it is a necessary preface to serious Boethian discourse.

In opening the prologue to the *Regement* with a complaint, Hoccleve is both claiming the status of a Boethian counselor and also contesting the degrees of "usefulness" allotted to different generic modes in Lady Philosophy's discourse of consolation. Whereas Boethius begins with a complaint only to discard it in the ascent toward abstraction and concentration on the *summum bonum*, Hoccleve begins with the complaint in order to seize the credentials necessary to the Boethian counselor, but he then goes on in the rest of the prologue to indicate the limitations of consolation and the necessity of the voice of complaint. Generically, Boethius's *Consolatio* might be characterized as moving through three modes: first an initial complaint, then dialogue (understood as a violent rejection of complaint), and then the final monologic speech of Lady Philosophy, in which the prisoner disappears and only the voice of pure philosophy remains.[47] Hoccleve follows Boethius in rejecting the monologic lyricism of the complaint, but his dialogue is never allowed to pass into consolation, that higher form of monologue. Instead, Hoccleve creates a form that attempts to be complaint and dialogue at the same time.

Let us clarify this suggestion by turning to two central elements of the *Regement*'s prologue: first, Hoccleve's precocious depiction of "thought," and second, his miming of the dialogue between Boethius and Lady Philosophy through his figure of the Old Man. Each of these examinations will provide us with an example of Hoccleve's basic oppositional technique—the deployment of Boethian complaint with such persistence as to indefinitely defer any moment of consolation.

Hoccleve's prologue begins:

> Musynge upon the restlees bysynesse
> Which that this troubly world hath ay on honde,
> That othir thyng than fruyt of bittirnesse
> Ne yildith naght, as I can undirstonde,
> At Chestres In, right faste by the Stronde,

---

47. For Lerer's emphasis on the "monologic" ending of the *Consolatio*, see n. 41 above.

As I lay in my bed upon a nyght,
Thoght me byrefte of sleep with force and might.

And many a day and nyght that wikkid hyne
Hadde beforn vexed my poore goost
So grevously that of angwissh and pyne
No rycher man was nowhere in no coost.
This dar I seyn, may no wight make his boost
That he with thought was bet than I aqweynted,
For to the deeth he wel ny hath me feynted.

Bysyly in my mynde I gan revolve
The welthe unseur of every creature,
How lightly that Fortune it can dissolve,
Whan that hir list that it no lenger dure;
And of the brotilnesse of hir nature
My tremblynge herte so greet gastnesse hadde
That my spirites were of my lyf sadde.

(lines 1–21)

This passage offers a remarkable image of the Boethian subject, here trapped
in a prison of introspection and anxiety. This sleepless night is, of course, a
revision of the conventional opening of a courtly love vision, altered so that
the poet is overstimulated not by desire but by fear of poverty, "the welthe
unseur of every creature." Similarly, the Boethian dimension of this passage
is presented entirely in fiscal terms. The world is "troubly" because of the
"brotilnesse" of Fortune, but this is so only because of the impact of Fortune
on wealth.

The passage introduces one of Hoccleve's most remarkable inventions,
the partly allegorical, partly clinical element of Thought. The first thing to
note about Hoccleve's presentations of anxiety, of these "thoughty" states,
is that unlike many authors, Boethius among them, who associate anxiety
with a passive, lethargic state, Hoccleve's melancholy is a jittery, hyperactive
thing. Hoccleve's inner life is here presented through no less than four sepa-
rate figures, "thought" most prominently, but also "my poore goost," "My
tremblynge herte," and "my spirites." Each of these elements pursues its
own activity, activities that are not at all coordinated. Thought, part native
participant and part foreign interloper, wrestles with the poor ghost, in a
prolonged bout: "to the deeth he wel ny hath me feynted." Meanwhile,

the trembling heart and spirits look on fearfully. And, in addition to the participants in this scene, there is the speaking "I" who narrates. For a bed-ridden scene, it is a busy one.

If we compare this opening to that of the *Consolatio*, "Carmina qui quon-dam studio florente peregi/flebis, heu, maestos cogor inire modos" (I, who once wrote songs with keen delight am now by sorrow driven to take up melancholy measures), we can see that Hoccleve begins his complaint on very different grounds.[48] Boethius offers no hint of an internally fragmented subjectivity. He was once a happy poet; now he is a melancholy one, and, hence, will turn to elegy. There is in Boethius a stability of genre and of subject, and a clear connection between the two. Since Boethius is in prison now, he will write an elegy; take away the prison, or at least the mental burden of the prison, and he would write something else. It is this clear causality, the fact that his complaint has a single clear grief behind it, that allows the even-tual progression of the prisoner out of his complaints and into consolation. In Hoccleve's work, however, the initial fragmentation of the subject foreshad-ows the difficulty this poet will have in reaching a point of consolation. Dia-logue in the *Regement* is unable to sustain the meditative forward progression of the *Consolatio* for the simple reason that whatever the Old Man may say to fix one problem, there is some part of the Hoccleve persona still left with an unanswered complaint, so the process must begin again.

Along with the complication of the subject of Hoccleve's complaint, there is a matching complication in the implied cause behind his anxiety. C. S. Lewis long ago suggested that part of Hoccleve's revision of the *com-plainte d'amour* lay in just this complication of causality: "He analyzes the state of his emotions during the wakeful night just as the love poets had analyzed the state of the sleepless lover; and Thought personified—as he might be in any erotic allegory—is recognized as the immediate enemy, while the objective circumstances which give rise to Thought are thrust into the background."[49] In effect, there are two levels to this complaint. On the one hand, Hoccleve is complaining about the external and objective causes of his anxiety, namely poverty and the overdue annuity, but on the other hand, the complaint also takes as its object, as Lewis suggests, anxiety itself. It is as though Hoccleve is complaining about being in a mood to write a complaint. In addition, although Lewis's description of these opening stanzas is quite helpful, what becomes most interesting as the prologue proceeds is

48. Boethius, 1.1.1–2.
49. C. S. Lewis, *The Allegory of Love* (Oxford: Oxford University Press, 1936), 238.

the extent to which these "objective circumstances" continue to reassert themselves. The prologue represents the Boethian counsel of the Old Man as a discourse that is not a solution to the problem of Thought but a repression of such a problem, and like anything repressed, the objective circumstances continue to reassert themselves with a vengeance.

This tension between the idealism of a Thought without cause and the materiality of the causes themselves is reflected in another sort of generic ambiguity present throughout this prologue. Earlier, I commented on the hybridity of the generic structure of the work, but numerous readers have also noted a certain ambiguity in the generic presentation of Thought itself. Hoccleve's concept of Thought straddles the line between allegory and psychological realism. C. S. Lewis, again, had characterized this scene as "a description, much infected with allegory but still unallegorical, of a sleepless night."[50] And Stephen Medcalf has more recently described Hoccleve's creation of a textual world of "substantial near-allegory," in which words such as spirit, rest, and trouble: "Though not outright allegories, seem . . . to be more solid than if they were mere abstractions. They suggest a world in which a phrase like Hoccleve's 'substaunce of my memory' means an enduring substance, thoughts are as *thingish* as things, and things easily merge—as according to the Aristotelian doctrine of intelligible species they should merge—with the world of thought."[51] By creating this figure of Thought, half an internal figure and half an intruder, half an allegory and half a piece of psychological realism, Hoccleve greatly complicates his presentation of anxiety and increases the difficulty of consolation. For the Old Man to act the part of Lady Philosophy successfully, he would now have to resolve both the objective causes and the internal, semiautonomous, problem of Thought itself. Let us now turn to Hoccleve's dialogue with the Old Man to judge the success of this endeavor.

After the description of this Thought-filled, sleepless night, Hoccleve wanders out and encounters the Old Man. Hoccleve proves to be a difficult subject, so distant that the Old Man finds it necessary to physically provoke him into a response.

> He stirte unto me and seide, "Sleepstow, man?
> Awake!" and gan me shake wondir faste,
> And with a sigh I answerde atte laste:

50. Ibid., 238.
51. Stephen Medcalf, "Inner and Outer," in his *Later Middle Ages* (New York: Holmes and Meier, 1981), 164, 134. Medcalf suggests that Hoccleve's depictions of psychological processes constitute a rejection of the Lollard separation of interior spirit from external phenomenal world.

"A! who is ther?" "I," quod this olde greye,
"Am heer," and he me tolde the manere
How he spak to me, as yee herde me seye.
"O man," quod I, "for Crystes love deere,
If that thow wilt aght doon at my prayeere,
As go thy way, talke to me no more;
Thy wordes alle annoyen me ful sore.

"Voide fro me, me list no conpaignie.
Encresse nat my greef, I have ynow."

(lines 131–42)

On its surface, moments such as this seem neatly modeled on the relation-
ship between Boethius and Lady Philosophy, so as to anticipate the dialogic
progression and consolatory ethic of Boethius's *Consolatio*. Many readers
have accepted the dialogue between Hoccleve and the Old Man as a fairly
straightforward adaptation of the dialogue in the *Consolatio*, a story in which
an initially resistant Hoccleve is brought around by the Old Man's goodwill
and pious sentiments until he is able to admit that his sufferings are exagger-
ated and liable to be mended through faith and careful appeal to literary
patronage.[52] But the striking point about the relationship between Hoccleve
and the Old Man is the extent to which Hoccleve refuses any of the proffered
consolations. The imperative "Sleepstow, man?/Awake!" in the mouth of
the Old Man, and the description of "this olde greye" are clearly meant to
establish him as a paternal figure of wise counsel, the masculine equivalent
to Lady Philosophy. But where the prisoner in Boethius's *Consolatio* had a
generally willing if initially somewhat petulant attitude, Hoccleve wants
nothing to do with this Old Man. And when the Old Man does finally cajole
Hoccleve into dialogue, his resistance continues through an insistence that
his complaint arises from two separate sources, poverty and thought. Thus,
the self-division that Hoccleve establishes in the opening stanzas reestab-
lishes itself within the Boethian narrative as a doubling of the causes of his
distress.

The Old Man, however, refuses to go away and continues his treatment
by posing a surprising question.

52. Stephen Kohl provides a concise expression of this position. "In the course of this debate,
the old beggar, with his philosophy, succeeds in defeating melancholy Thought and thus saves 'Hoc-
cleve' from the contagion of Despair and spiritual death." Kohl, "More Than Virtues and Vices:
Self-Analysis in Hoccleve's Autobiographies," *Fifteenth-Century Studies* 14 (1988): 119–20. See also
Medcalf, "Inner and Outer," 135–38.

"My sone, hast thow good lust thy sorwe drye
And mayst releeved be? What man art thow?
Wirke aftir me: it shal be for thy prow.
Thow nart but yong and hast but litil seen,
And ful seelde is that yong folk wyse been.

"If that thee lyke to been esid wel,
As suffre me with thee to talke a whyle.
Art thou aght lettred?" "Yee," quod I, "sumdel."
"Blessed be God, than hope I, by Seint Gyle,
That God to thee thy wit shal reconsyle
Which that me thynkith is fer fro thee went
Thurgh the assaut of thy grevous torment.

"Lettered folk han gretter discrecion
And bet conceyve konne a mannes sawe,
And rather wole applie to reson,
And from folie sonner hem withdrawe,
Than he that neithir reson can ne lawe,
Ne lerned hath no maner of letterure.
Plukke up thyn herte—I hope I shal thee cure."
                              (lines 143–61)

"Are you lettered?" This is a question that speaks both to Hoccleve's trou-
bled relationship to his clerkly identity and to an implicit debate about the
efficacy of reason in bringing about the sort of philosophical transformation
represented in the *Consolatio*. In its parallel to the *Consolatio*, this passage
supplies the equivalent of Lady Philosophy's characterization of Boethius as
her star pupil. Though the Old Man asserts that Hoccleve's learning will
enable a cure, Hoccleve is both notably humble about his qualifications to
engage in neo-Platonic dialectic and also skeptical of the idea that reason
and speech can help him.

"Cure, good man? Yee, thow art a fair leeche!
Cure thyself that tremblest as thow goost,
For al thyn aart wole enden in thy speeche.
. . . .

"It muste been a gretter man of might
Than that thow art that sholde me releeve."

> "What, sone myn, thow feelist nat aright;
> To herkne me, what shal it harme or greeve?"
> "Petir, good man, thogh we talke heer til eeve,
> Al is in veyn; thy might may nat atteyne
> To hele me, swich is my woful peyne."

> "What that I may or can ne woost thow noght.
> Hardily, sone, telle on how it is."
> "Man, at a word, it is encombrous thoght
> That causith me thus sorwe and fare amis."
>   (lines 162–64, 176–86)

The problem here, again, is that Hoccleve's melancholy has two sources, and since one is beyond the reach of the Old Man, he cannot really serve as an efficacious figure of counsel. Specifically, we see Hoccleve first reject the Old Man's offer because "al thyn aart wole enden in thy speeche." The Old Man has nothing to offer but words, and since Hoccleve's problem does have its "objective circumstances," the delay of his annuity, words alone are not adequate. "It muste been a gretter man of might / Than that thow art that sholde me releeve." Hoccleve needs a man of means, a potential patron, to stave off the prospect of poverty. Hoccleve's response is a critique of the idealism of the Old Man's solution. As it does not touch on the root cause of his anxiety, reason and speech can do no good.[53]

But, surprisingly, when the Old Man then asks, immediately after this rant about his real financial worries, what the trouble is, Hoccleve replies that "at a word, it is encombrous thoght." Although Hoccleve had rejected the Old Man's promise of philosophical consolation on the grounds that his problem was too practical a one to be resolved through reason and argument, with this line he reverts the ground of his own complaint back to the immaterial level of Thought itself. This exchange establishes the basic rhythm of the dialogue between Hoccleve and the Old Man. Whenever the Old Man offers to turn Hoccleve's complaint concerning his annuity into resolution, Hoccleve responds that his problem really lies in Thought, and whenever the Old Man addresses the problem of Thought, Hoccleve turns again to money. By creating this rupture on the level of causality within the complaint, Hoccleve is able to produce a complaint that endlessly defers consola-

---

53. As Simpson argues, Hoccleve presents himself as "Nobody's man" not only because he has no patron but because speech itself is dangerous to the powerless man, leaving him without even any options for gaining patronage. Simpson, "Nobody's Man," 176.

tion, that circles back recursively through the same twin problems and never allows the consolatory dialogue to resolve itself into the monologic text of counsel.

Therapeutic discourse, whether theological, philosophical, or psychoanalytic, has a long tradition of representing breakthrough and resolution by sudden generic transition. (We might think of Augustine's realization that his life had its own emplotment of sacred epic; Boethius's salvation through dialogic discourse; or Freud's discovery that the unconscious told stories organized around structures of repetition and reiteration.) Hoccleve's *Regement* is notable for refusing such cures. The solution proffered at the end of the prologue to the *Regement*, though it has sometimes been misrecognized as simply a generic shift, is actually much more profound. The final stanza in the prologue is one we have already examined in the context of Hoccleve's representation of writing.

> Recordyng in my mynde the lessoun
> That he me yaf, I hoom to mete wente.
> And on the morwe sette I me adoun,
> And penne and ynke and parchemeyn I hente,
> And to parfourme his wil and his entente
> I took corage, and whyles it was hoot,
> Unto my lord the Prince thus I wroot:
> (lines 2010–16)

The important opposition here is not between complaint and consolation, or between penitential confession and Aristotelian counsel, but simply between speech and writing. At the end of his dialogue with the Old Man Hoccleve pauses, taking the Old Man's advice, and literally transcribes all their discourse into his mind as text: "Recordyng in my mynde the lessoun." By emphasizing the textuality of this moment Hoccleve creates a break not between genres but between two representations of language. The prologue, which had been presented through conventions of direct discourse that render the question of speech vs. text invisible, is suddenly marked as speech that must be recorded. Hoccleve then assembles the tools of writing and prepares to leave the discursive world of speech for that of writing.

The consolation offered here is thus not brought about through a therapeutic shift in genre, nor is it exactly a result of the dialogue between Hoccleve and the Old Man. Indeed, thinking back to the tripartite Boethian structure, the distance between this ending and a properly Boethian moral can be seen in the fact that it is not the Old Man but Hoccleve who takes the reigns of the monologic conclusion. (It is as though the *Consolatio* ended not with Lady Philosophy but Boethius delivering the lecture.) Consolation in this ending is a return to "living in the Privy Seal," a return to "penne and ynke and parchemeyn." But how are we to reconcile this return to writing with the darker connections between scribal labor and death that we saw above? The treatment of writing in the *Regement of Princes* reaches a fine balance of hope and disappointment. Coming from the world of the Privy Seal, with its dependence on patronage and the mediations of the written petition, Hoccleve chooses to represent himself as having found consolation not in philosophy but in the impossible home of textuality. One anonymous fourteenth-century formulary suggested that the good writer should always fit his rhetoric to his purpose as an actor would fit a wax nose to the face.[54] If we recall the place of wax and parchment in a scribe's instrumental repertoire we might take this prescription for rhetoric as an emblem of the scribe's own entanglement in the textuality of his labor. As Hoccleve suggests in the *Regement*, the scribe is embodied in a textuality that aims at the permanence and durability of a vellum *Repertorium* but exhibits more often the fragility of a face of wax.

54. Cheney, *Notaries Public*, 125.

Eulogies and
Usurpations

Father Chaucer
in the
Regement of Princes

Perhaps no ideology is so central to the institution of literary history as that of filial piety. Despite recent debate over the content and function of literary canons, and despite theoretical critiques of organic, continuous historical models, the implicit frame within which we read and teach is still grounded, in the last resort, on notions of sources and influence thoroughly genealogical at their core.[1] It is, indeed, hard to imagine a form of literary history that would not be genealogical. Could we imagine the field of literature other than as a succession of texts arrayed in time, locked together as a category by the influence of the earlier over the later and given meaning by the dynamic interrelations among them? In the assumed parthenogenesis of this tradition, the metaphor of paternity, the relation of fathers and sons, has always been central.[2]

1. The earliest and most influential critique of this model has come through feminist arguments that characterized the idea of literary canons as exclusionary devices. This critique has gained additional momentum from the skepticism toward organic, teleological models of history widespread in poststructuralist thought. Influential examples of these critiques include Michel Foucault's "What Is an Author," in *Language, Counter-Memory, Practice*, ed. and trans. Bouchard and Simon (Ithaca: Cornell University Press, 1977), 113–38; and in the field of medieval studies, Howard Bloch, *Etymologies and Genealogies* (Chicago: University of Chicago Press, 1983), and Louise Fradenburg, " 'Voice, Memorial': Loss and Reparation in Chaucer's Poetry," *Exemplaria* 2 (1990): 169–202.

2. A. C. Spearing emphasizes the ubiquity of this metaphor among poets: "There is ample precedent for seeing the authority of the literary precursor over his successors as analogous to the authority of the father over his sons. Lucretius refers to Epicurus as father; Horace and Propertius both refer to Ennius as father; Cicero calls Isocrates the father of eloquence and Herodotus the father of history;

This metaphor has been nowhere more influential than in representations of early fifteenth-century English verse. The old label for this poetry, "Chaucerian," has always served, to a greater degree than most such nominative constructions, as a dynastic marker, suggesting that poets like Hoccleve and Lydgate were important chiefly for their custodianship as heirs.[3] Consequently, a sense of their poetry as "servile imitation" has always marked the reception of this verse, and its defining characteristics have been read largely as repetitions of or deviations from the models established by Chaucer.[4] It was the authority of the Chaucerian example that established the terms under which Ricardian vernacular experiments were consolidated and formed into a relatively unitary tradition. As A. C. Spearing has suggested, "the fatherhood of Chaucer was in effect the constitutive idea of the English poetic tradition."[5] More recent studies of fifteenth-century verse have returned frequently to this genealogical motif. The most recent, and most ambitious, treatment of this period, Seth Lerer's *Chaucer and His Readers*, has made this genealogical metaphor central to the period's vision of itself, suggesting that paternity was one of the key metaphors to structure both poetic identity and practice in the early fifteenth century.[6]

One difficulty, however, in discussing the impact of this metaphor in the early fifteenth century is the fact that it was actually used by only one poet, Thomas Hoccleve. Although Dryden's influence has made the title commonplace, and although there is certainly some continuity between the

---

and so on. . . . Descent and inheritance from father to son provide a basic explanatory model for literary history, and the model retains its power, for example in Harold Bloom's conception of the tensely Oedipal relation of son to father as characterizing the whole of English poetic history from Milton to the present." Spearing, *Medieval to Renaissance*, 92.

3. As Caroline Spurgeon wrote of Lydgate and Hoccleve: "So great and wholehearted was the admiration and devotion given to Chaucer by these two men, his friends and followers, that we cannot doubt they would have been the first to acknowledge it fitting that the principal value of their writings to us—five centuries later—lies in their references to their 'maister Chaucer.' " Spurgeon, *Five Hundred Years of Chaucer Criticism and Allusion, 1357–1900* (Cambridge: Cambridge University Press, 1925), 1:xiv. Hoccleve's first modern editor, F. J. Furnivall, spoke in similar terms, describing Hoccleve as a "weak, sensitive, look-on-the-worst side kind of man," who made up for his faults chiefly through "his genuine admiration for Chaucer." Furnivall, *Hoccleve's Works*, xxxviii.

4. The phrase *servile imitation* comes from H. S. Bennett, but similar judgements could be drawn from any number of handbooks of literary history. Bennett, *Chaucer and the Fifteenth Century*, 126. Also relevant is David Lawton's challenge to the usual reading of the self-confessed dullness of this age in "Dullness and the Fifteenth Century."

5. Spearing, *Medieval to Renaissance*, 92.

6. "As children to the father, apprentices to the master, or aspirants before the laureate, those who would read and write after the poet share in the shadows of the secondary. It is the purpose of this book to understand the quality of post-Chaucerian writing in these terms." Lerer, *Chaucer and His Readers*, 3.

image of Father Chaucer and the ubiquitous confessions of inadequacy in the poetry of Lydgate and others in the period, the only references to Chaucer as father per se come from three eulogistic passages in Hoccleve's *Regement of Princes*.[7] This chapter thus considers the place of paternity in the fifteenth century by offering a reevaluation of the encomia for Chaucer in Hoccleve's *Regement*. These passages have always been read as one of the earliest appreciations of Chaucer's genius and of Hoccleve's modesty in the face of the Chaucerian example. My argument is that, along with this praise of Chaucer, these passages present a strategy for poetic usurpation. In them we see Hoccleve lay claim to an inherited poetic authority and also interrogate the notions of origins and authority that underwrite the idea of generational succession.

I make this case in three stages. First, I offer an analysis of the operation of "doubling" in the *Regement*, arguing that Hoccleve's verse is marked by a persistent recursivity, a tendency to cycle obsessively through a given set of conceptual terms. Second, I turn to the eulogistic passages in the *Regement* and to the accompanying Chaucer portrait to demonstrate a pattern of instability within Hoccleve's metaphors of generational succession. Last, I turn to the familiar history of Prince Henry's conflict with his father, Henry IV, in 1410–12 and consider this episode as a model for Hoccleve's challenge to Chaucer's prerogative.

"Doubling": Progression and Recursivity

Hoccleve's eulogy of "father Chaucer" is produced in three passages of his *Regement of Princes*. The first two of these passages occur in the prologue to the work and the third comes in the latter section, an interruption to the advice to Prince Henry that makes up the bulk of the poem. I have already commented on the strange hybrid nature of this text, the suture between the introductory prologue and the main body of counsel. In the present context,

---

7. The rhetoric of poets like Lydgate might even be said to avoid suggestions of a specifically parental sponsorship. As Lee Patterson has commented: "Chaucer represents not a clean break from a rejected past but instead a transformation of that which was given: 'Wyth al hys rethorykes swete' he 'amendede our langage.' [Patterson here cites Lydgate, *Pilgrimage of the Life of Man*] He is not source but model, the master who can teach his pupils a technical lesson rather than the father from whom derives an intangible and so all the more indispensable aptitude." Patterson, *Chaucer and the Subject of History* (Madison: University of Wisconsin Press, 1991), 16.

this generic hybridity helps us understand Hoccleve's complex presentation of his debt to Chaucer because it is the first sign of one of Hoccleve's basic techniques in this work, a persistent doubling of key images and concepts. This operation of doubling is crucial to Hoccleve's verse at both narrative and conceptual levels. At the level of narrative structure, both the *Regement of Princes* and the *Series* are shaped by the same shift from an initial solitary complaint into a forced dialogue, with the Old Man in the case of the *Regement* and with the unnamed Friend in the *Series*. James Simpson has commented on this structural similarity, suggesting that it allows Hoccleve's verse to move from private complaint into successively more public forms of address.[8] In addition to this sense of progression there is also, however, a marked recursivity to Hoccleve's verse, a sense that generic shifts such as that from the complaint to the dialogue, which might suggest some progression or resolution of the complaint, actually insist on the nagging presence of the same difficulties through all the changes of generic presentation and form.[9]

As an example, let us return to the most basic of Hoccleve's objects in the *Regement*, his melancholy "thought":

> Musynge upon the restlees bysynesse
> Which that this troubly world hath ay on honde,
> That othir thyng than fruyt of bittirnesse
> Ne yildith naght, as I can undirstonde,
> At Chestres In, right faste by the Stronde,
> As I lay in my bed upon a nyght,
> Thoght me byrefte of sleep with force and might.
>
> And many a day and nyght that wikkid hyne
> Hadde beforn vexed my poore goost
> So grevously that of angwissh and pyne
> No rycher man was nowhere in no coost.
> This dar I seyn, may no wight make his boost
> That he with thought was bet than I aqweynted,
> For to the deeth he wel ny hath me feynted.
>
> Bysyly in my mynde I gan revolve
> The welthe unseur of every creature,
> How lightly that Fortune it can dissolve,

8. Simpson, "Nobody's Man," 167.

9. Paul Strohm has also discussed the Lancastrian interest in recursive structures. Strohm, *England's Empty Throne*, 2.

Whan that hir list that it no lenger dure;
And of the brotilnesse of hir nature
My tremblynge herte so greet gastnesse hadde
That my spirites were of my lyfe sadde.

(lines 1–21)

In analyzing this important passage above (Chapter 3), we took note of the way in which Hoccleve's self-dissection turned the self into a multiplicity of allegorical figures ("thoght" itself; the "my poore goost"; "tremblynge herte"; and "spirites"), in marked contrast to the unified subject of Boethian lament. Considering this same passage within the rubric of narrative technique, we should note than an additional result of this fragmentation is the frustration of progression in favor of recursivity. Hoccleve divides the aspects of consciousness into numerous avatars not in order to resolve his anxiety but rather to stage a self-examination in obsessive detail.[10] The figure he chooses to evoke his cogitation here—"Bysyly in my mynde I gan revolve"—is, after all, the very opposite of any progression.

Thus, the endless deferral of consolation we have seen in the *Regement* is derived both from the specific multiplicity of causes for the complaint and also from a more general technique of doubling in his verse. I will leave behind the difficulties this doubling creates for a Boethian reading and concentrate instead on its impact on notions of paternity, looking at the way paternity in this poem is represented not as a linear transfer of authority but rather as a cyclical and recursive relation.

Tropes of Paternity

It is within the context of deferred consolation that Hoccleve pauses to eulogize Chaucer. These eulogistic passages are usually read either as simply a spontaneous outpouring of Hoccleve's admiration for his predecessor or, especially in relation to the portrait of Chaucer that accompanies the last passage, as part of Hoccleve's bid to establish himself as the heir to a legiti-

10. On "doubleness" see also Batt's insightful introduction to *Essays on Thomas Hoccleve*, 3; and Mills, "The Voices of Thomas Hoccleve."

mate tradition of vernacular *auctoritas*.[11] The three encomia are spaced at wide intervals in the *Regement*, but they are tied together by a consistent metaphoric and functional pattern. Each of the three passages praises Chaucer through the key terms of father and master. Similarly, each passage occurs at a moment in which the invocation of Chaucer and, specifically, the elegiac invocation of his inheritable genius serve to make a claim for Hoccleve's credentials for writing to the prince. Thus, a series of issues are important in determining the strategic use of metaphors of paternity in each of these passages: (1) the stability of these key metaphors; (2) the manipulation of elegy and its associated thematics of inheritance and lineage; and (3) the precise circulation of authority between Hoccleve and the absent figure of Chaucer. In the encomia, Hoccleve uses these terms to construct a figure of vernacular authority from whom to trace his own descent, but he also does so in such a way as to throw the status of fatherhood and mastery into question.

The first of these passages occurs at a moment in the prologue when the Old Man is trying to persuade Hoccleve to write a treatise for Prince Henry. Hoccleve confesses his fear that he is inadequate to such a task and is led to the memory of Chaucer, a master rhetorician, capable of writing even for a prince.[12] This praise of Chaucer as a master of the aureate tradition also serves to suggest the potential dignity of an English vernacular poetry, dignity to which Hoccleve might lay claim as Chaucer's apprentice and immediate successor:

> "With herte as tremblyng as the leef of asp,
> Fadir, syn yee me rede to do so,
> Of my symple conceit wole I the clasp
> Undo and late it at his large go.
> But, weleaway, so is myn herte wo
> That the honour of Englissh tonge is deed,
> Of which I wont was han conseil and reed.
>
> "O maistir deere and fadir reverent,
> My maistir Chaucer, flour of eloquence,
> Mirour of fructuous entendement,

---

11. Alan Gaylord, for example, stresses Hoccleve's construction of Chaucer as an image of wisdom and authority in his "Portrait of a Poet," in *The Ellesmere Chaucer: Essays in Interpretation*, ed. Martin Stevens and Daniel Woodward (San Marino: Huntington Library, 1995), 121–42.

12. Mitchell emphasizes Hoccleve's enthusiasm for Chaucer's aureate rhetoric in his "Hoccleve's Tribute to Chaucer," 275–83.

O universel fadir in science!
Allas that thow thyn excellent prudence
In thy bed mortel mightest nat byqwethe!
What eiled deeth? Allas, why wolde he sle the?
(lines 1954–67)

Reading the eulogistic stanzas alone, as they are usually presented, the passage does indeed seem a straightforward and moving memorialization of Chaucer. However, taken in the context of the prologue, and his relationship with that other father, the Old Man, the elegies to Chaucer must also be understood as a potential disruption of Hoccleve's poetic project. The problem here is one of genre and is reflected in the differing relations between Hoccleve and the two fathers in this passage. Hoccleve's first father is the Old Man, whose counsel encourages him to unlock his "symple conceit" and write something for the prince. But no sooner is this project announced than he thinks of another father, the absent Chaucer. With the thought of Chaucer, the idea of a book for the prince is set aside, and Hoccleve begins again to lament his losses. In other words, the memory of Chaucer functions here just as the threat of poverty had at the poem's outset.[13] It creates a temptation to return endlessly to the complaint, a genre that is always understood in Hoccleve's work to be in conflict with exteriorized public discourse. The presence of two fathers in these stanzas is a refiguration of Hoccleve's chronic trouble, self-division and doubleness. The Old Man gives him fatherly advice, and a solution for his poverty in writing. But just as he is about to avail himself of this advice, another father appears as a source of grief and precipitates him into the elegiac mode or, in essence, back to the complaint with which he began the poem.

The next two stanzas of this passage then go on to find a solution of sorts:

"O deeth, thow didest nat harm singuler
In slaghtre of him, but al this land it smertith.
But nathelees yit hastow no power
His name slee; his hy vertu astertith
Unslayn fro thee, which ay us lyfly hertith
With bookes of his ornat endytyng
That is to al this land enlumynyng.

"Hastow nat eek my maistir Gower slayn,
Whos vertu I am insufficient

13. See Chapter 3.

For to descryve? I woot wel in certayn,
For to sleen al this world thow has yment.
But syn our lord Cryst was obedient
To thee, in feith I can no ferther seye;
His creatures musten thee obeye.
(lines 1968–81)

As these stanzas meditate on the power of death, the magnitude of Hoc-
cleve's loss grows, and so too does the list of fathers. As Charles Blyth has
pointed out, though most readings of these eulogies have focused on Chau-
cer, there is, in fact, a second master, given nearly equal time to Chaucer—
John Gower.[14] But though Hoccleve uses this multiplication to stress the
universal power of death, he also allows it to bring out a potential source of
compensation: the virtue that survives both poets, and the "name" and
works that survive Chaucer and "enlumine" the land. Literary production is
here both a guarantor of immortality and an inheritance. As Hoccleve's
elegy develops here, then, it shifts in its use of Chaucer from a simple elegy
that would threaten the progression of the poem into a use of Chaucer as an
authorizing point of origin for vernacular literature. This moment of reflec-
tion on Chaucer thus functions to reinforce both Hoccleve's legitimacy in
writing for the prince and also the trajectory suggested by the Old Man—
that he should leave behind the lament and turn to writing for the prince
because even death is defeated by the fame of literary works. The two fathers
seem to fall into accord.

However, this accord is disrupted by the stanza immediately following this
eulogy to Chaucer and Gower, a stanza usually not reproduced in discussions
of the eulogies:

"Fadir, yee may lawhe at my lewde speeche,
If that yow list—I am nothyng fourmeel;
My yong konnynge may no hyer reeche;
My wit is also slipir as an eel.
But how I speke, algate I meene weel."
(lines 1982–86)

Laughter is a remarkable conclusion to Hoccleve's elegy. It interrupts the
fictional reverie in which Hoccleve had meditated on the significance of the

14. Blyth, "Thomas Hoccleve's Other Master."

paternal Chaucer, reinserting the alternative, and far less comforting image of the Old Man. In its narrative movement, it is an exact replication of that moment so common in Hoccleve's verse in which he indicates the limitations of monologic genres such as the complaint and the elegy by staging the interruptions of dialogue and the social world. And here the interruption is explicitly connected to a pair of binary conflicts of great importance in the present investigation: youth vs. age and knowledge vs. lewdness. Scanning back over the five stanzas that make up the first eulogy, we can also see that Hoccleve deploys the term fadir with careful symmetry. It is used twice in reference to the Old Man, once at the beginning and once at the conclusion of this reverie, and once in the center for Chaucer. Thus, the appeal to Chaucer's memory is carefully framed by the alternative paternity of this Old Man.

What is the effect of this *emboîtement?* I would suggest that the framing serves to establish the metaphor of paternity as a metaphor linked to a traditional image of counsel, a wise old man, but then corrupts this image by splitting the father into two, one urging a forward movement into writing and the other causing Hoccleve to fall back into the recursive gestures of mourning. Moreover, certain details in the presentation of the Old Man serve to complicate the notion of paternity. Though the Old Man offers himself as a figure of wise counsel, he is also an embodiment of exactly the future Hoccleve tells us he fears in his thoughtful night. He is penniless and seems unable to effectively counsel Hoccleve how to avoid such poverty. And with the final mocking laughter of this passage, Hoccleve suggests a deep conflict between "yong konnynge" whose "wit is also slipir as an eel" and the paternal authority that would "lawhe at my lewde speeche." This passage, then, leaves us with a question: Are we meant to assume here the traditional ascription of wisdom to old age, or is there an alternative claim to be made for "yong konnynge"?

The second eulogy is quite similar and again leans heavily on the key terms of maister and fadir in its invocation of Chaucer:

> Symple is my goost and scars my letterure
> Unto your excellence for to wryte
> Myn inward love, and yit in aventure
> Wole I me putte, thogh I can but lyte.
> My deere maistir, God his soule qwyte,
> And fadir, Chacuer, fayn wolde han me taght,
> But I was dul and lerned lyte or naght.

Allas, my worthy maistir honurable,
This landes verray tresor and richesse,
Deeth by thy deeth hath harm irreparable
Unto us doon; hir vengeable duresse
Despoillid hath this land of the swetnesse
Of rethorik, for unto Tullius
Was nevere man so lyk amonges us.

Also who was heir in philosophie
To Aristotle in our tonge but thow?
The steppes of Virgile in poesie
Thow folwedist eek. Men woot wel ynow
That combreworld that thee, my maistir, slow.
Wolde I slayn were! Deeth was to hastyf
To renne on thee and reve thee thy lyf.
(lines 2073–93)

The opening of the second eulogy is a perfect example of the dullness motif analyzed by David Lawton.[15] This eulogy comes as the second half of a parenthetical address to Prince Henry. Hoccleve uses this passage about Chaucer to shift gracefully from his own obeisance to the prince to a similar humility in the face of Chaucer. This parallel between the prince and Chaucer has the dual effect of emphasizing Hoccleve's humility in front of masters both political and poetical but also of claiming a great dignity for the idea of vernacular poetry by placing Chaucer at a level with the prince as "this landes verray tresor." In its rhetorical function, this passage is very like the first eulogistic sequence. It begins with a confessional doubt about Hoccleve's capacity to write such a commission, then turns to Chaucer as an absent figure of mastery, and then to a meditation on the power of death, and the villainy of death to have taken Chaucer.

There are, however, two significant variations in this second eulogistic passage. The first is that in this passage, Hoccleve's thoughts of death turn to thoughts of self-destruction. To a certain extent, this is just a convention of the pseudo-Boethian language Hoccleve uses in his complaints, but there is also a sense in which this thought of suicide must affect our understanding of these eulogies. In order to represent vernacular poetry and his own efforts with adequate significance to stand before the prince, Hoccleve creates a poetic genealogy through which he might derive poetic virtue from the pa-

15. Lawton, "Dullness and the Fifteenth Century."

ternal figure of Chaucer. And to establish his legitimacy as Chaucer's true heir, Hoccleve presents a highly dramatized display of mourning. This dramatization is reminiscent of Peter Sacks's argument that elegiac lyric develops out of the necessity of heirs to press their claims to inheritance by memorializing their grief. The one who grieves is the one with a right to inherit.[16] When played out fully, however, and in the context of poetic inheritance, the inheritor may be locked into a paradox. If the grief is real, why should the mourner write anything but elegy; and why should they live?

Hoccleve's response to this paradox is to castigate the universal mastery of death:

> Deeth hath but smal consideracioun
> Unto the vertuous, I have espyed;
> No more, as shewith the probacioun,
> Than to a vicious maistir losel tryed
> Among an heep. Every man is maistried
> With here, as wel the poore as is the ryche;
> Leered and lewde eek standen alle ylyche.
>
> Shee mighte han taried hir vengeance a whyle
> Til that sum man had egal to thee be—
> Nay, let be that! Shee kneew wel that this yle
> May nevere man foorth brynge lyk to thee;
> And hir office needes do moot shee.
> God bad hir so, I truste, as for thy beste;
> O maistir, maistir, God thy soule reste!
>
> (lines 2094–107)

The second eulogy is quite similar to the first, so I will make only two points about it here. First, as we saw the key metaphor of fadir destablized in the first passage by the operation of doubling, so we see here the same process affect the term maister. Maister is used first as a description of Chaucer—"my worthy maistir"—then becomes the figure of the "vicious maistir losel," the archtraitor, some figure like Oldcastle, who is tried and condemned and demonstrates death's arbitrary nature by joining Chaucer as another of his victims. This pairing seems to raise no contradictions in the usage, as the "vicious losel" is a master in a sense diametrically opposed to Chaucer and

16. Peter Sacks, *The English Elegy: Studies in the Genre from Spenser to Yeats* (Baltimore: Johns Hopkins University Press, 1985).

so is meant to confirm Chaucer's virtue through the harsh contrast. The "vicious maistir losel" serves as a foil to Chaucer, emphasizing the vital poetic legacy found in Chaucer through a contrast with the illegitimate and corrupting influence of the losel (and, of course, opposing also the viciousness of the losel to Chaucer's implicit benignity). The stability of this neat contrast is lost, however, when we continue on to the third *master* in this passage: "Every man is maistried/With here, as wel the poore as is the ryche." Death, it turns out, is also a master (though, interestingly, a feminine one). The metaphor is troubled here, because death is much more like Chaucer as a master than like the vicious losel. Death, like Chaucer, has power over the whole land equally.

Equally important to the complication of these metaphoric systems is the treatment of Chaucer's foundational status in this passage. After describing Death's universal mastery, Hoccleve concludes the passage by wishing, as he had earlier (lines 2092–93), that Death might have waited before taking Chaucer. But here he adds the surprising qualification that Death might have waited "Til that sum man had egal to thee be." In other words, the virtue of Chaucer, who was so markedly without peer in the opening stanzas of the eulogy (other than Aristotle and Cicero!), has now become contingent and takes its place in a temporal order in which death should properly mean that his successor has arrived. Hoccleve immediately follows this assertion with "Nay, let be that!" This shift in register is, I think, meant to be read as a symptomatic recognition of the scandalous implication of the previous line. The next line and a half then go on to directly contradict the implication that Chaucer is but one in a series by asserting, "this yle/May nevere man foorth brynge lyk to thee." The eulogy concludes with another reference to Chaucer's mastery, "O maistir, maistir, God thy soule reste," but mastery no longer means what it did before, and the stuttering repetition of the term in this line cannot reattach it to Chaucer's virtue after its association with death and the losel.

In these first two eulogies, then, we see fatherhood and mastery put into question through two processes. First, there is a persistent doubling of these metaphoric categories that serves to undermine their simple reference to Chaucer. In addition, especially in this second passage, issues of death, inheritance, and authority begin to collide in such a way as to create a tension between the desire to praise Chaucer as a precedent without equal and the need to assert both his structural role as one in a series and the necessity of his death as necessary preconditions of Hoccleve's inherited authority. The paradox of aggressivity hidden within the elegy is as old as the elegy itself, and is a paradox of which Chaucer had been well aware.[17] I turn now to the third of the three eulogistic passages and to the accompanying portrait, in order to explore further the place of a certain aggression in these eulogies.

The third eulogistic passage has received more critical commentary than the first two, largely because it is accompanied in three of the *Regement* manuscripts by a marginal portrait of Chaucer.[18] The text in the third eulogy refers explicitly to an accompanying image, so Hoccleve most likely meant a portrait to be included in all copies of the poem. (The page containing the eulogistic stanzas—and most likely, the portrait—has been cut out of MS Arundel 38.) The most important of these portraits, which I discuss below, is that found in British Library MS Harley 4866. The image shows Chaucer holding a rosary in his left hand and pointing with his right to the text in which he is described. The portrait is remarkable for its lifelike attention to detail. It is, of course, impossible to determine whether or not the illustration presents the actual image of Chaucer, but its detail gives an impression of verisimilitude, and the language of the eulogy itself suggests an attempt to present the actual likeness:

> The firste fyndere of our fair langage
> Hath seid, in cas semblable, and othir mo,
> So hyly wel that it is my dotage
> For to expresse or touche any of tho.
> Allas, my fadir fro the world is go,
> My worthy maistir Chaucer—him I meene;
> Be thow advocat for him, hevenes queene.
>
> As thow wel knowist, o blessid Virgyne,
> With lovyng herte and hy devocioun,

17. A. C. Spearing makes a similar point, commenting on the relationship between Chaucer's Clerk and Petrarch: " 'He is now deed and nayled in his cheste' (iv 29): the death is much to be regretted and we shall all die in our turn, but how reassuring those nails are that keep Petrarch in his coffin!" Spearing, *Medieval to Renaissance*, 103.

18. British Library MS Harley 4866; British Library MS Royal 17. D. vi; and MS Rosenbach 1083/ 10. For a description and reproduction of these images, see Derek Pearsall, *The Life of Geoffrey Chaucer: A Critical Biography* (Oxford: Blackwell, 1992), 288–90. For additional discussions of this portrait, see Jeanne Krochalis, "Hoccleve's Chaucer Portrait," *Chaucer Review* 21 (1986): 234–45; Jerome Mitchell, *Thomas Hoccleve*, 110–15; David R. Carlson, "Thomas Hoccleve and the Chaucer Portrait," *Huntington Library Quarterly* 54 (1991): 283–300; A. S. G. Edwards, "The Chaucer Portraits in the Harley and Rosenbach Manuscripts," in *English Manuscript Studies, 1100–1700*, ed. Peter Beal and Jeremy Griffiths (London: British Library, 1993), 4:268–71; Alan T. Gaylord, "Portrait of a Poet"; and M. C. Seymour, "Manuscript Portraits of Chaucer and Hoccleve," *Burlington Magazine* 124, no. 955 (October 1982): 618–23.

In thyn honour he wroot ful many a lyne.
O now thyn help and thy promocioun!
To God thy sone make a mocioun,
How he thy servant was, mayden Marie,
And lat his love floure and fructifie.

Althogh his lyf be qweynt, the resemblance
Of him hath in me so fressh lyflynesse
That to putte othir men in remembrance
Of his persone, I have heere his liknesse
Do make, to this ende, in soothfastnesse,
That they that han of him lost thoght and mynde
By this peynture may ageyn him fynde.

(lines 4978–98)

The portrait of Chaucer that accompanies these verses in the Harley MS is one of the earliest we have and is probably based on an exemplar shared with the famous Ellesmere portrait.[19] It is also something of a landmark in the history of illumination, for it claims to present a realistic, mimetic image of Chaucer. Lifelike portraiture, the attempt to model faces not on symbolic or idealized features but on realistic detail, was not a regular feature of manuscript illumination in this period. Such portraiture tended to represent individuality by means not of particular physiognomy but rather through the presence of symbolic objects, clothing, or heraldic devices. For instance, in the illumination found in the Arundel MS showing Hoccleve presenting his book to Prince Henry, the faces of the two men are indistinguishable. The men are distinguished by their clothing and by their relative position (and even physical size) within the frame.[20] But this period also saw the beginnings of major changes in such strategies of representation.

Jeanne Krochalis has singled out the memorial effigy as a likely precedent for Hoccleve's innovative decision to provide a lifelike and not simply icono-

19. Pearsall, *Life of Geoffrey Chaucer*, 288–89.

20. This image is reproduced as the frontispiece to Mitchell's *Thomas Hoccleve* and can be found in Blyth's edition of the *Regement*, 187. Krochalis (237) maintains that the faces are indistinguishable and from my own examination of the reproduction, I would agree. For a differing opinion, see Gervase Mathew's detailed description of the presentation portrait, in which he asserts that it is intended as an individualized picture of the two men. Mathew, *Court of Richard II*, 203–4. For the relative backwardness of English illumination, especially with regard to early Dutch naturalism, see J. J. G. Alexander, "Painting and Manuscript Illumination for Royal Patrons in the Later Middle Ages," in *English Court Culture in the Later Middle Ages*, ed. V. J. Scattergood and J. W. Sherborne (London: Gerald Duckworth, 1983), 141–62.

graphically charged image of Chaucer. This fact, and the fact that the two stanzas which directly follow the portrait and eulogy constitute an attack on Lollard doctrines denying the usefulness of images of the saints, lead her to suggest that in inserting a portrait of Chaucer, Hoccleve seems to be asserting a parallel between the meditation on the images of saints and on the images of poets.[21] We can add to this claim the fact that the memorial passage occurs within a section of the *Regement of Princes* that lays out Hoccleve's claim for the place of poets as necessary counselors to royalty, a section highly reminiscent of one of Hoccleve's sources, the *Secreta Secretorum*. The mythical origins of the *Secreta* were, of course, a series of letters written by Aristotle to his young pupil Alexander the Great while the latter was off on campaign in the East and so unavailable for firsthand edification. In the history of English vernacular poetry, Hoccleve's work is one of the first to assume a position from which it could advise a prince, and in Hoccleve's own life the composition of this text may have been a bid to assume the role of poetic adviser to the court, a figure who would combine the classical virtues of Cicero and Aristotle (as the second eulogy suggested Chaucer had done). The memorial is thus inserted into the *Regement* at this moment both in order to establish a particular interpretation of Chaucer (poet as adviser to princes) and, further, to attach Chaucer's prestige to Hoccleve's own claim on this position. In essence, Hoccleve praises the man but does so in order to establish an office, now vacated by Chaucer's death, which he might claim to inherit.

The language of the eulogy continues to develop these thematic points. The passage opens and closes with what is a very evocative word in this context: fyndere. Fynde contains an important internal contradiction, for it can refer either to the discovery of a pre-existent object, or to the establishment of something that had never before existed (as in the sense "to found a city").[22] This ambiguity is particularly significant to our discussion because

21. "But to put a poet's image in a church is to equate him with saints—which Hoccleve's text comes close to doing—and, by implication, with kings, in dignity and importance, both in this world and the next." Krochalis, "Hoccleve's Chaucer Portrait," 240. James McGregor makes a similar point in "The Iconography of Chaucer in Hoccleve's *De Regimine Principum* and in the Troilus Frontispiece," *Chaucer Review* 11 (1976): 338–50; as does Lawton, in *Chaucer's Narrator's*, 131. The wider origins of the author portrait per se lie in Italy, with commemorations of Dante and Petrarch. See Sylvia Wright, "The Author Portraits in the Bedford Psalter-Hours: Gower, Chaucer, and Hoccleve," *British Library Journal* 18 (1992): 190.

22. Both meanings are attested in Middle English usage. See *Middle English Dictionary*, 3: 568–73. See also Christopher Cannon's comment on this passage. Cannon, *The Making of Chaucer's English: A Study of Words* (Cambridge: Cambridge University Press, 1998), 10–12.

the action of finding is at the root of Chaucer's figurative paternity. In what sense is Chaucer the "finder" of the language? On one level this is a simple reference to Chaucer's creation of a high style—the "fair langage"—out of the raw material of English vernacular. But are we to take him as the founder of something that had never existed, or did he "find" it in the sense of drawing attention to something already there? The modification "first" only increases the suspicion that Chaucer's originary status is not so secure, for it introduces an element of repetition into a rhetoric of foundations. If the founder is only the first in a series of such, how can we consider him to be a source in the strict sense? The use of *find* at the end of the passage (line 4998) is equally problematic. Hoccleve says that he has had an image made to remind his readers of Chaucer's features, to let them "find" his face again. But, as Hoccleve knew well, many of his readers would never have seen Chaucer or any picture of him. So again, the word *find* refers to some operation midway between repetition and original creation. This is a fundamental ambiguity, or an ambiguity in the status of the fundamental.

There may even be a measure of antagonism contained within these ambiguities. This third memorial passage comes as another interruption to the *Regement*, one ostensibly motivated by Hoccleve's recognition that he is wasting labor to write advice to the prince concerning counselors. After all, Chaucer has already written on the subject and done so with far more skill than he could claim. This is, in itself, an example of the highly conventional topos of humility. However, the wording of Hoccleve's self-denigration is, again, functionally ambiguous. He suggests his inferiority to Chaucer through the language of reverence for age (the *maister* here invoking the gravity of an elder counselor or teacher, like Aristotle) and the familial hierarchy of father and son, but the term with which he sums up his inadequacy is *dotage* a word that, then as now, meant foolishness in the context of advanced age.[23] This term reactivates the chain of associations Hoccleve has built through the series of eulogies, raising again the question of whether age is to be associated reflexively with wisdom. He confesses his inadequacy in relation to Chaucer but chooses a word fraught with implications that age brings no wisdom.

The portrait of Chaucer in the *Regement* provides a visual representation of this antigenealogical impulse. Alan Gaylord has described this image in the context of the *Regement*'s thematization of youth and age, of counsel, and of the literature of "prudence," concluding that the presentation of

23. *Middle English Dictionary*, 2: 1244.

Chaucer via "the iconography of wise old men" assists Hoccleve in claiming Chaucer as the "patron and godfather of the book Hoccleve will compile."[24] Much of the iconographical detail does indeed bear out such associations. The portrait represents Chaucer as a bearded and older man, in a costume that might well be associated with the "maister" of the eulogistic descriptions. The left hand holds rosary beads while the right hand points from the right hand margin toward the last stanza of the eulogy, directing the reader's attention toward Hoccleve's text.

But this gesturing hand also suggests another reading, a recontextualization of the wise old man presented in the image. In later portraits Chaucer is uniformly shown pointing to himself, or to a pen-case worn on his chest, as a metonymic sign of his occupation and source of his fame. In the *Regement* portraits, however, the gesturing hand points away from Chaucer's body and towards the text, specifically toward that portion of the text directing the reader to look into the margin at the illustration. The portrait would then direct them back to text and then the text back to the portrait, ad infinitum. In other words, the relation of image to text does not establish Chaucer as an authority underlying Hoccleve's text but rather creates a circuit of authority, one in which Chaucer's authority supports that of the text but is also itself created by the text.[25] Michael Camille's recent work on marginalia in *Images on the Edge* has uncovered numerous examples of such interplay between text and image, both situations in which images reinforce texts and in which marginal illuminations comment satirically.[26] The portrait of Chaucer in the Harley MS should be read as part of this tradition. The text and image do not relate to each other satirically; their mutual dependence suggests, however, that authority is not a legacy to be inherited but a circuit running from the present through the past.

One might be tempted to dismiss this reading with the suggestion that relations between text and margin play mirroring games with such frequency as to make them a commonplace and less than helpful in analyzing the poetic project of any single author. However, we are justified in placing some interpretive pressure on the arrangement of Hoccleve's text and marginalia

24. Alan T. Gaylord, "Portrait of a Poet," 126–29.

25. Tim Machan has also drawn attention to the self-reflexivity created in this arrangement of text and illumination, although I disagree with his suggestion that Hoccleve does not pursue these implications at length. Issues of textual authority are made quite central, though they are consistently mediated by metaphors of genealogical succession. Machan, "Textual Authority and the Works of Hoccleve, Lydgate, and Henryson," *Viator* 23 (1992): 284–85.

26. Michael Camille, *Images on the Edge: The Margins of Medieval Art* (Cambridge, Mass.: Harvard University Press, 1992), esp. 20–22.

for the simple reason that Hoccleve exercised an unusual degree of personal control over the exact appearance of his texts. He was by profession a scribe; he is unique in the number of autograph manuscripts to have survived; and he seems to have taken an active role in the ordering and arrangement of compilations of his own work.[27] If we take seriously the relation between margin and text, we are confronted with a number of paradoxes. First, although Chaucer is still playing the role of the father whose authority Hoccleve wants to attach to his own work, the father is now consigned to a literally marginal position. In addition, this circularity demonstrates the inadequacy of the language of either adoration or Oedipal insurrection in describing Hoccleve's relation to father Chaucer. For neither the text nor the picture may be said to provide a founding authority for the other. Without the picture, the text is incomplete, and without the text, the pointing hand makes no sense.

This portrait provides an ideal metaphor for Hoccleve's relationship to Chaucer. Given the usual accuracy of autobiographical elements in Hoccleve's work, his professed reverence and grief for Chaucer were most likely quite sincere and significant. Equally significant was Chaucer's crucial role as the informal laureate of English vernacular poetry, the predecessor whose prominence might legitimate Hoccleve's own efforts. But at the same time, Hoccleve was well enough aware of the circular nature of such legitimation as to produce a current of resistance to simple expressions of filial devotion. The portrait is thus commissioned but placed in the margin.

Fathers and Sons, 1410–1412

A degree of instability thus appears in the key metaphoric categories that Hoccleve uses to praise Chaucer as father, master, and wise Old Man. The grounds for this instability may be found not simply in the inevitable polyvocality of metaphor but also in the particular historical context in which this poem was composed. As we observed in Chapter 3, the period in which the *Regement* was written were the same years as those in which the ailing Henry IV, still trying to consolidate the rule gained by the usurpation of Richard II's throne, was faced by a strong challenge for power from his eldest son, the

27. Bowers, "Hoccleve's Huntington Holographs."

future Henry V.[28] The prince is a constant presence in the *Regement*, appearing as both patron of the work and potential guarantor of Hoccleve's future. From his position in the Privy Seal, Hoccleve could not have been unaware of the conflict between prince and king. How, then, might this historical incident color Hoccleve's treatment of the metaphoric constellation of age, wisdom and paternity?

The tension between Henry IV and the prince was an open secret in these years, and it is quite likely (as Derek Pearsall has argued) that the *Regement of Princes* was composed, in part, as a propaganda exercise aimed at presenting the prince as a wise ruler, who could be depended on in succession despite the controversies of these years.[29] I would add that the *Regement* was composed not only to assert the prince's receptivity to good counsel but also his filial devotion. The *Regement of Princes* was only one of several documents sponsored by the prince in the years 1410–13 to assert his loyalty to his father and his worthiness for kingship, and it was not unique in its thematization of filial piety.[30] For another example, we might cite the signet letter that Prince Henry sent to his father in June 1412 and that he claimed to have had circulated widely. This letter is a response to his exclusion from power following his removal from the Council in 1411. It addresses both claims that he had been interfering with his father's policies in Aquitaine and assertions that he was dangerously disloyal.[31] The prince contests these charges, offering a complicated version of his exclusion from the campaigns in Aquitaine and the counter-accusation that his enemies had planted suspicions against him in order to disturb the line of succession. He then concludes the letter by protesting the "great love," "great fidelity," and "filial humility" he

---

28. The *Regement* was completed between 1410 and 1413 (see Chapter 3, n. 3). M. C. Seymour and John Burrow both think the poem may have been finished by late 1411, Seymour because the records of Hoccleve's annuities seem to indicate a dry spell in 1411 that would match the specific complaints of the prologue, and Burrow because the presentation of such a poem might have been especially appropriate while the prince was governing the Council. My argument connects language in the *Regement* to documents from as late as June 1412, but is not meant to reflect a belief that the *Regement* was necessarily completed after 1411, as such language was likely current throughout the years from 1410 onward. Burrow, *Thomas Hoccleve*, 18; and Seymour, *Selections*, 114–15.

29. For the details of this conflict, see the discussion above.

30. Antonia Gransden discusses Henry's lifelong concern for effective propaganda in *Historical Writing in England II, c. 1307 to the Early Sixteenth Century* (Ithaca: Cornell University Press, 1982), 197–219.

31. V. H. Galbraith, *The St. Albans Chronicle, 1406–1420* (Oxford: Clarendon Press, 1937), 66–67. This letter is also discussed in McFarlane, "Father and Son," 109–10; and forms the basis of much of McNiven's argument in "Prince Henry in 1412," 7–8.

felt toward his father.[32] The conflict between the prince and king in the years 1410–12 was understood by both participants and onlookers to be a trial of generational succession, in which a highly competent prince demonstrated little patience in waiting for his aging and ill father to vacate the throne. If one were to draw a history of the concept of paternity, especially in its connections to authority and inheritance, the public discourse of the early fifteenth century would provide one of the most complex chapters.

The representation of paternity in the *Regement* is also part of this history. The eulogies for Chaucer, with their ambiguous representation of the role of paternity and the dynamics of inheritance, make up part of a work dedicated to Prince Henry in the very years in which he publicly encroached on his father's prerogative. As Harriss has suggested, many subjects viewed the prince's careful fiscal governance during 1410–11 as a welcome sign of future competence after the chronic fiscal problems of Henry IV's reign.[33] If there was ever a moment in which we should not assume an idealized connection between age and good counsel, or paternity and wisdom, it was this moment. Moreover, we should not lose sight of the fact that the *Regement* was dedicated to the prince and, quite possibly, written on his direct commission, in the years of his struggle with his father. In writing propaganda for the prince, Hoccleve was not just writing for Lancastrian interests. He was also stepping into a potentially dangerous feud within the Lancastrian house itself, a feud between father and son, at a moment at which notions of paternity, inheritance, and counsel could not be used simply and innocently.

This reading of Hoccleve's eulogies to Chaucer is meant to suggest the function of an important ideological concept in Hoccleve but also to draw an implicit portrait of Hoccleve himself and to suggest a certain way of reading his texts. In leaning very heavily on the metaphoric construction of paternity in these eulogies, I am suggesting a greater level of ironic play, or polyvocality, in Hoccleve's texts than is often assumed. In part, this is justified by the complex traditions surrounding the idea of paternity and, in part, by the crises around authority and paternity in the years of the *Regement*'s composition. But the profound ambivalence I have tried to register here should be more central to our general sense of Hoccleve's poetry. Hoccleve has usually been set in opposition to Chaucer as the less subtle metrist, the less interested in the construction of fictional worlds, and the more prosaic

---

32. The prince's letter reads: "tantus amor, tanta fidelitas et tanta subiectio quantas concipere novit aut valet humilitas filialis." Galbraith, *The St. Albans Chronicle, 1406–1420*, 66–67.

33. See Chapter 3.

and colloquial in his vocabulary.[34] Some of these characterizations are warranted, but along with these distinctions has gone a more questionable judgment about tone and, hence, about appropriate interpretive strategies for the two poets. Chaucer, especially in our post-Donaldson readings, has become a poet of linguistic play and of ironic skepticism. Hoccleve, in contrast, is still often read as a poet destined for illustrative historical footnotes. However, Hoccleve's complex depiction of his debt to Chaucer shows he is a poet better read with an eye toward corrosive irony than towards moral idealism and documentary reportage. The final irony here may be that for all his skepticism and play with the concept of inheritance, what we see in these passages is a Hoccleve whose wariness about authority and paternal figures makes him, in these matters at least, a true son of Chaucerian wit.

34. See Burrow, "Hoccleve and Chaucer," 54–61.

Hoccleve and Heresy

Image, Memory,
and the
Vanishing Mediator

Modern critics usually characterize the religious Hoccleve as a harshly orthodox writer, the author of the "Address to Sir John Oldcastle," and an enthusiastic cultural worker in the Lancastrian campaign against Lollardy. There is certainly much to support such an identification in Hoccleve's poetry. He expresses his vehement opposition to Lollardy in three separate works. In the very public and well-distributed *Regement of Princes* Hoccleve describes the burning of John Badby with absolutely no sympathy, referring to him only as "a wrecche / Nat fern ago, which that of heresie / Convict and brent was unto asshen drie" (lines 285–87). In his "Balades to Henry V and the Knights of the Garter" Hoccleve urges Henry to model himself upon Justinian and Constantine as a secular defender of the faith and to combat the heresy that has "torne" the peace, with the implication that he should treat those responsible with equal violence: "Dampnable fro feith were variance!" (line 60).[1] Most famously, in the "Address to Sir John Oldcastle," he energetically condemns both Oldcastle's wanderings from faith and duty and the scheming Lollards who have seduced him from his spiritual birthright.

1. Furnivall, *Hoccleve's Works*. Subsequent citations are taken from Furnivall's edition and cited by line number within the text.

Alongside these attacks on Lollards and Lollardy, however, we also find a number of moments at which Hoccleve emphasizes not distinctions but similarities between himself and the Lollards he attacks. In particular, Hoccleve frequently represents himself as being tempted toward some of the very excesses, particularly those associated with "thought," with which he charges his opponents. His injunction to Oldcastle not to inquire too closely into the interpretation of Scripture bears a striking resemblance to the Old Man's own warnings in the *Regement* that Hoccleve should beware of his tendency to such excessive reflection:

> Sone, swich thoght lurkynge thee withynne,
> That huntith aftir thy confusioun,
> Hy tyme it is to voide and lat him twynne
> (lines 274–76)

To drive the implication home, the Old Man follows this general warning with the cautionary tale of John Badby, the Lollard burned in 1410. The reference to Badby in this context seems less a confirmation of Hoccleve's unimpeachable orthodoxy (as it is usually taken to be) than an externally reflected autocritique, an admission of the dangers of his own thought. Similarly, in the *Series* Hoccleve's discussion of restless thought produces concern in the unnamed Friend that his engagement in study is excessive, that it has driven him into "errour," and that, in the words of Hoccleve's denial, he is prone to "medle of matires grete" ("Dialogue," lines 460, 498). Among the many parallels between the Friend of the *Series* and the Old Man of the *Regement* is Hoccleve's practice of using them both as mirrors through which to engage in autocritique and plant a suspicion that his orthodoxy may not be unimpeachable.

How is it possible to reconcile Hoccleve's firmly orthodox positions on doctrinal matters with his own self-accusations of certain affinities with his religious opponents? Any reader investigating Hoccleve's work for reference to the doctrinal controversies of the early fifteenth century will find that he makes reference to a long list of such debates: the substance of the Eucharist, the special role of the priesthood, the need for the state to use force in defense of orthodox faith, and the impropriety of layfolks (especially women) engaging in study and preaching. Among all these issues, however, the doctrinal question that exercised Hoccleve more than any other was the proper use of devotional images. We have already encountered Hoccleve's precocious and highly charged use of an illuminated miniature of Chaucer in the

Regement, an image he deployed as a secular object of devotion and the foundation of a poetic lineage.[2] This picture is also accompanied by an explicit defense of such images (in their religious form) against Lollard attacks:

> The ymages that in the chirches been
> Maken folk thynke on God and on his seintes
> Whan the ymages they beholde and seen,
> Where ofte unsighte of hem causith restreyntes
> Of thoghtes goode. Whan a thyng depeynt is
> Or entaillid, if men take of it heede,
> Thoght of the liknesse it wole in hem breede.
>
> Yit sum men holde oppinioun and seye
> That noon ymages sholde ymakid be.
> They erren foule and goon out of the weye;
> Of trouthe have they scant sensibilitee.
>
> (lines 4999–5009)

Hoccleve insists that there is nothing wrong with the fabrication of images in church and that the sight of such images is a powerful stimulus to reflection on God and the saints. He makes a similar point in his "Address to Oldcastle":

> And to holde ageyn ymages makynge,
> Be they maad in entaille or in peynture,
> Is greet errour.
>
> (lines 409–11)[3]

It is clear from these passages that Hoccleve casts himself as an opponent of radical Lollard iconoclasm, but beyond this his position is difficult to specify. Debates about the proper use of images are perhaps the preeminent case in which a stark opposition between orthodoxy and Wycliffite thought is most analytically insufficient. Although orthodox polemicists often cast Lollards as uncompromising iconoclasts (a simplification reinforced by later Protestant commentators), the situation was in fact far more complex, with a long

---

2. See Chapter 4.

3. I cite "Address to Sir John Oldcastle" from Seymour, ed., *Selections from Hoccleve,* though I retain the title by which the poem is most widely known (rather than his "Remonstrance Against Oldcastle").

tradition of orthodox theology calling for vigilance against idolatry in the veneration of images and some heterodox thought, including Wycliffe himself, leaving ample room for a positive use of images not as objects of veneration but as pedagogical tools—books for the unlearned, as they were so often called.[4]

Hoccleve's choice of textual sources may also suggest an interest in theological and philosophical traditions colored by a suspicion of the veneration of images. For example, his choice to translate a section of Heinrich Suso's *Wisdom's Watch upon the Hours* as the fourth section of his *Series* ("How to Learn to Die") may well indicate an interest in the continental *devotio moderna*, a movement that shared with some Lollard positions an emphasis on the inner life and a corresponding distrust of external forms.[5] Even more intriguingly, Hoccleve's use of Robert Holcot's *Super sapientum Salomonis* (c. 1334–36) in his "La Male Regle" testifies to an early interest in a thinker who provided both a classical statement of an orthodox critique of images and an aesthetic experiment in didactic literature based on the fabrication of verbal images. Principally remembered among intellectual historians as an Ockhamist and prominent Oxford skeptic of the 1330s, Holcot also included

---

4. On this complex history, see Margaret Aston, "Lollards and Images," in *Lollards and Reformers: Images and Literacy in Late Medieval Religion* (London: Hambledon Press, 1984), 135–92, repr. and exp. in her *England's Iconoclasts*. Vol. 1: *Laws Against Images* (Oxford: Clarendon Press, 1988), 96–159; and W. R. Jones, "Lollards and Images: The Defense of Religious Art in Later Medieval England," *Journal of the History of Ideas* 34 (1973): 27–50.

5. On the circulation of Suso's works in England, see Roger Lovatt, "Henry Suso and the Medieval Mystical Tradition in England," in *The Medieval Mystical Tradition in England*, ed. Marion Glasscoe (Exeter: Exeter University Press, 1982), 47–62. Hoccleve's local use of Suso is, of course, quite consistent with orthodox use of images for meditation; in fact, Hoccleve's selection emphasizes the imagistic element of Suso's work, as Wisdom enjoins the disciple (and, by extension, the reader) into an act of imagination.

> "Beholde now the liknesse and figure
> Of a man dyynge and talkyng with thee."
> The disciple, of þat speeche took good cure,
> And in his conceit / bysyly soghte he,
> And ther-with-al / considere he gan, & see
> In him self put / the figure & liknesse
> Of a yong man of excellent fairnesse

> Whom deeth so ny ransakid had, & soght,
> þat he withynne a whyle sholde dye.

("How to Learn to Die," lines 85–93)

Cited from Furnivall, *Hoccleve's Minor Poetry*.

in his *Super sapientum* a significant critique of the worship of images.[6] Holcot enunciated a series of propositions that would become deeply problematic once debates over images were polarized in the early fifteenth century: namely, that the worship of images lacked scriptural authority; that Aquinas's argument that *latria* given to the object returned to the divine model could not, in the end, effectively defend many practices against charges of idolatry; and, most strikingly, that a living man was a truer image of god than a carving and so more deserving of worship.[7] Moreover, in a point that is crucial in reading Hoccleve's Marian lyrics, Holcot's ideas about the image are part of a larger epistemological debate, the nominalist attack on the ability of intelligible species (usually imagined via analogies with visual perception) to serve as real elements of mediation in cognition. Finally, as Beryl Smalley has suggested, Holcot's ideas on the image were not all theoretical, as he also made the verbal icon central to his own work in the technical innovation he called his "pictures," or highly focused verbal descriptions of moralized figures (designed to be equivalent in use to images) used as an aid to preaching.[8]

In the strategies of his religious poetry, Hoccleve is very much the heir of Robert Holcot and the tradition, both theological and philosophical, for which the image was a necessary but suspect vehicle of cognition and meditation. Hoccleve's religious poetry is largely based on a technique I refer to here as figural hagiography, an extension of the use of the visual image into the creation of verbal icons representing exemplary devotional figures. Hoccleve's conformity with Lancastrian orthodox polemics was both substantial and formal. He used his poetry to defend the substance of a series of doctrines ranging from the devotional use of images to the cult of the Virgin Mary. Moreover, the method of his poetry, his figural hagiography, is in itself an

6. For an account of Holcot's life and thought, see Beryl Smalley, *English Friars and Antiquity in the Early Fourteenth Century* (Oxford: Basil Blackwell, 1960), 133–202. See also Katherine Tachau's introduction to *Seeing the Future Clearly: Questions on Future Contingents by Robert Holcot*, ed. Paul A. Streveler and Katherine H. Tachau (Toronto: Pontifical Institute of Medieval Studies, 1995), 1–27.

7. Aston, *England's Iconoclasts*, 120–22. This last proposition maintains the same distinction between the live image and the dead one fundamental to much Wycliffite thought—a distinction dramatically maintained by Oldcastle himself at his trial when, in response to interrogation on the subject of veneration for the cross, Oldcastle is said to have raised his own arms and declared, "This is a very cross!" For Oldcastle's trial, see "The Examination of Sir John Oldcastle," in *Fifteenth Century Prose and Verse*, ed. Alfred W. Pollard (Westminster: Archibald Constable, 1903), 187. See also the commentary on this moment in Beckwith, *Christ's Body*, 72–74.

8. Smalley, *English Friars*, esp. 165–83.

implicit defense of the centrality of the image to orthodox thought. Nevertheless, despite its outward conformity with orthodox doctrine, a close examination of Hoccleve's religious poetry shows it to be infected by both theological and scholastic skepticism to such a degree that even as he uses such figures, his verse stages a persistent critique of the image. Hoccleve is drawn in his religious poetry toward a series of philosophical instabilities that may have been safe in the day of Holcot but which became potentially dangerous indulgences under Lancastrian orthodoxy. The result of this tension is a typically Hocclevean gambit, one in which religious poetry is founded on the iconic presence of exemplary figures but which also consistently undermines the orthodox philosophical foundation of such icons.

In the "Address to Sir John Oldcastle," for example, Hoccleve uses Oldcastle as a figure through whom to stage an ironic reversal of the Lollard dismissal of images, turning Oldcastle into an exemplary antisaint designed to refute Lollard doctrine in both substance and representational strategy. But as Hoccleve puts Oldcastle on display, his poem also launches a sophisticated critique of the ability of the image to instantiate reality, a critique that asserts the essential unreliability of the ocular tropes so central to orthodox polemic. Hoccleve's Marian lyrics raise the specter of a similar instability, in this case not just the image but a mental category often understood scholastically as an extension of the image, namely memory. Hoccleve's Marian lyrics present a profoundly orthodox meditation on Mary as mediatrix but yet express a recurrent concern that such mediators, like the patrons for whom one searched at court, were as likely to be missing as present at the time of need. Hoccleve's religious work is thus built on a dangerous paradox at the heart of identity, as it seeks to establish the iconic presence of a series of mediatory figures but remains haunted by the tendency of such mediators to vanish away. Before turning to these explicitly religious works, however, let me first return briefly to the *Regement of Princes* to flesh out the sense in which Hoccleve uses that poem to suggest his own susceptibility to the lure of heterodox speculations.

Suburbs and Heresy in the *Regement of Princes*

Stephen Medcalf has commented that Hoccleve "seems to take refuge from his troubles in continual movement, physical and spiritual."[9] The image is

9. Medcalf, "Inner and Outer," 132.

an apt one and helps to explain even some of the critical annoyance with Hoccleve, going back to Furnivall, which has often characterized him as suspiciously shifty. This interest in physical mobility is one of many elements in Hoccleve for which his true precursor seems not Chaucer but Langland. Anne Middleton has drawn attention to the importance of legislation regulating labor and mobility as part of the context for Langland's concerns with liminal social identities, particularly those with a hint of the "gyrovagus," or wanderer, to them.[10] Like Langland, Hoccleve's own restless movement in the *Regement* is best read in the context of a similar matter of contemporary controversy, in his case Lollardy and the suspicion of vernacular speculations that followed in its wake. Hoccleve's wandering is symbolically charged in different ways at different moments, but whether he is going to the tavern or out into the street, wandering is represented almost always as an excursion out into a realm of temptation and danger, both physical and mental. In the *Regement of Princes*, in particular, Hoccleve maps his wandering to emphasize a departure from urban into suburban space, depicting a wandering in which ideological divisions between orthodox and heterodox thought are superimposed onto the topography of metropolitan London.

We have already discussed some elements of Hoccleve's wanderings in the *Regement* (see Chapter 3), principally its connection to the travails of scribal labor, but in thinking about this space as a representation of London and its western suburbs, we must notice also an odd vacillation between the strikingly concrete and the unspecified. Hoccleve begins the prologue with cartographic accuracy, giving us the exact building in which he can't sleep—Chester's Inn—and offering even the address—along the Strand. The poem then becomes suddenly obscure, as he departs into nothing more specific than the fields. It then ends with another moment of concrete specificity, giving a location at the Church of the Carmelites and a schedule of mass there. This oscillation from specific to vague has led to some rather tenuous readings. Douglas McMillan, for instance, has suggested that the transition from Chester's Inn to the Church of the White Friars is meant to indicate that Hoccleve has, in fact, not really awakened, and that the whole of the prologue should be read as a dream vision, something like *Pearl*, in which the church of the Whitefriars simply appears as a vision.[11] The actual key,

10. Anne Middleton, "Acts of Vagrancy: The C Version 'Autobiography' and the Statute of 1388," in *Written Work: Langland, Labor, and Authorship*, ed. Stephen Justice and Katherine Kerby-Fulton (Philadelphia: University of Pennsylvania Press, 1997), 208–317.

11. Douglas J. McMillan, "The Single Most Popular of Thomas Hoccleve's Poems," *Neuphilologische Mitteilungen* 89 (1988): 63–71.

however, to the depiction of space here can be found by taking the contrast between concrete urban surroundings and the more vaguely imagined suburbs as itself a significant distinction. Suburban space in medieval London, as in most medieval cities, was a liminal area, playing host to marginalized professions such as prostitution and tanneries.[12] The division between city and suburb reflected a division between social center and margin, a division imagistically represented by the contrast between the fixity of the walls so often used to visually represent a city and the lack of concrete visual images to fix the suburbs themselves.

The liminality of the suburbs also associated them at times with both heterodox thought and the consequence of that thought—public execution at locations such as Smithfield. This association even finds its way, as John Scattergood has noted, into one of Chaucer's few urban moments, the "Canon's Yeoman's Tale." The Yeoman describes their work: " 'In the suburbes of a toun', quod he, / 'Lurkynge in hernes and in lanes blynde.' "[13] Among the imaginary inhabitants of the late medieval suburbs were such inquirers into arcane and excessive knowledge. There is ambiguity in the chronicle record as to whether Oldcastle's adherents assembled at St. Giles or Ficketts Fields, but the accounts agree that such a gathering was to have happened, as usual with such threats, on the immediate borders of the city. Hoccleve's journey into these suburbs is marked also with invocations of heresy. Hoccleve no sooner finishes describing his own excessive "thought" to the Old Man than the Old Man tells him the story of the Lollard John Badby "brent . . . unto asshen drie," as a cautionary tale.

Indeed, although the precise itinerary of Hoccleve and the Old Man's walk is ambiguous, they must have been moving in the general direction of Smithfield. Hoccleve leaves the Bishop of Chester's Inn for fields. Distracted as he is, it is unlikely he headed south into the river. Moving either east or west along the Strand would, within the hour he mentions as the time of his walk, have brought him not into fields but into the built-up areas of Westminster or London. And the hour's walk must have taken him further than simply up the street to the White Friars. Consequently, and I think for all the evocative liminality of the suburbs this progression is meant to be quite clear, Hoccleve must be moving generally northward and then have come

12. On such social and topographical liminality, see Bronislaw Geremek, *The Margins of Society in Late Medieval Paris*, trans. Jean Birrell (Cambridge: Cambridge University Press, 1987).

13. Quoted by John Scattergood, "Chaucer in the Suburbs," in *Medieval Literature and Antiquities: Studies in Honor of Basil Cottle*, ed. Myra Stokes and T. L. Burton (Cambridge: D. S. Brewer, 1987), 155.

back around to the White Friars precincts. Whether or not we imagine that Hoccleve and the Old Man reached Smithfield itself, their walk takes them through a region of suburbs that contained ample reminders of heresy, disobedience and discipline.

Why should Hoccleve represent himself taking such a journey? Hoccleve uses the topography of urban space in the *Regement* to create an analogy between his own restless thought and the reputation of the suburbs as a location of dangerously boundless speculation. It is an inversion of the Boethian model that governs much of the interactions between Hoccleve and the Old Man. Instead of listening to his counselor trapped in prison, Hoccleve's trouble is an excessive capacity for movement. Derek Pearsall has suggested that the Old Man in this prologue might be meant to be taken as a Carmelite himself, a member of an order known for their staunch opposition to Lollardy.[14] The mid-fifteenth century MS of the *Regement* in the Coventry City Record office contains an image of a man in a white garment with a skull cap, an image that may represent one of the academic authorities cited in the *Regement* but may also be intended as a portrait of this Old Man dressed as a Carmelite friar. This suggestion is tempting, as the function of the Old Man in this poem is to accompany Hoccleve on his wanderings, to point out dangers and to bring him back in time for dinner: "Recordyng in my mynde the lessoun / That he me yaf, I hoom to mete wente" (lines 2010–11). This makes a homely conclusiòn, and as an ending always gives sense to a plot, this ending to the *Regement*'s prologue suggests that the plot had been a journey away from home and back, a journey into the dangers of thought and back. Hoccleve's more strictly religious poetry also shows the mark of this thought. Though orthodox in doctrinal content, the focus on images and memory allows ample room for wandering into the margins of orthodoxy.

Image and Ontology in the
"Address to Sir John Oldcastle"

Hoccleve's "Address to Sir John Oldcastle" was written in exciting times. From the point of view of the Lancastrian authorities with whom Hoccleve sided, the period between the abortive rising of 1414 and Oldcastle's recap-

---

14. Pearsall, "Hoccleve's *Regement*," 407.

ture and trial in 1417 was one swarming with dangers. The attempted coup of 1414 was followed with alarming speed by the plot fostered by Cambridge and Grey in the following year. When Henry V set sail for France in 1415, with Oldcastle still at large and the prospects of his immediate capture slim, the realm must have seemed far from stable.[15] The years between 1414 and 1417 were an interval during which the Lancastrian authorities were even more than usually haunted by the difficulties of combating a diffuse and disturbingly faceless movement. Hoccleve's "Address to Oldcastle" is a response, both political and theological, to this particular crisis. It is one of the tasks of Hoccleve's "Address" to fabricate the presence of John Oldcastle, Lord Cobham, in order to create a face for this disembodied threat. His method for doing this, with pointed irony, is to turn the Lollard case against the veneration of images and saints on its head, and to present the iconoclast Oldcastle as a public face for the movement, a sort of antisaint.

The dominant rhetorical device of this poem is the simple subterfuge of adopting the mode of direct address in relation to a figure who was significant at that moment for his troublesome elusiveness. In adopting this device, the "Address to Oldcastle" shows a close kinship with the King's Bench manuscript containing the original charges against Oldcastle. In his analysis of this document, Paul Strohm has suggested that the Rising of 1414, led by Sir John Oldcastle and intending to unseat both government and church hierarchy, was very probably an event as much tailored after the fact for propagandistic purposes as it was a real and threatening action. Whatever actually happened on that day, the later reconstructions of the event focus tightly on the figure of Oldcastle. Oldcastle seems not to have been present on the morning of the conflict itself, but he is nevertheless central to Lancastrian representations of the event because the revolt needed to have a leader to be turned into effective political narrative (particularly as colored by the providential history of the chroniclers). As Strohm puts the point: "The motive here . . . seems characteristically Lancastrian: the objectification of opposition in a sufficiently vivid form to permit a reciprocal stabilization of the Lancastrian king as the guarantor of civil order and ecclesiastical orthodoxy."[16] In both political and textual responses to this rebellion, the Lancastrian authorities were obsessed with questions of Oldcastle's presence and absence: the danger of Lollard rebellion was distilled into the question

15. The best narrative account of these events remains K. B. McFarlane, *John Wycliffe and the Beginnings of English Nonconformity* (London: English Universities Press, 1952).

16. Strohm, *England's Empty Throne*, 82. An earlier version of this argument may also be found in Strohm's *Sir John Oldcastle: Another Ill-framed Knight* (London: Birkbeck College, 1997).

of a single figure who could be captured or at least made the outlandish villain of the narrative favored by sympathetic chroniclers. Speaking historically, this obsession with individual actors and their visibility most likely derives in part from a Lancastrian sense of encirclement by spies and conspiracy. The knowledge that the Lancastrian throne had been founded on an act of usurpation—grounds of conquest that always invited repetition—produced a constant suspicion of secret plots.[17] Moreover, the wider importance of military espionage throughout the fourteenth and fifteenth centuries kept English authorities on the alert for both French spies and domestic agents of rebellion.[18] The "Address to Oldcastle" places itself squarely in the service of Lancastrian interests and religious orthodoxy by participating in the struggle to summon up absent enemies and make them present in textual form.

In addition to this, however, Hoccleve's "Address to Oldcastle" offers a unique twist to this project as it connects this textual pursuit of the absent enemy to a theologically inspired discussion of the power of the image, yoking the techniques of Lancastrian propaganda to the orthodox polemic in favor of devotional images. Although the "Address" is not usually taken to be a poem centrally concerned with the doctrine of images, it is in fact suffused with a series of ocular metaphors. The central ideological division in the poem, the distinction between orthodoxy and Lollardy, is presented through a contrast between the seen and the unseen, in which the brave visibility of Henry V serves as one of the chief qualities setting him apart from Oldcastle and his allies. Hoccleve's greatest disdain is exercised over the fact that Oldcastle "hydest . . ./And darst nat come and shewe thy visage" (lines 501–2). The Lollards themselves, the faceless mass whose anonymity Oldcastle has adopted, are described in a telling metaphor as "lanterns of darkness" ("of dirknesse the lanternes," line 384), suggesting, through the pedagogically based notion of illumination, that one of the Lollards' worst sins is to lead others into the dark, into not just error but hiding. Even Oldcastle's fall into heresy is imagined in explicitly visual terms, as Hoccleve comments, "Oldcastel, how hath the feend thee blent!" (line 97), and attributes Oldcastle's doctrinal errors to the fact that "Thow lookist mis, thy sighte is nothyng cleer" (line 83).

These ocular metaphors proliferate throughout the poem, creating a pat-

17. See Strohm, *England's Empty Throne*, 63–65.
18. J. R. Alban and C. T. Allmand, "Spies and Spying in the Fourteenth Century," in *War, Literature, and Politics in the Late Middle Ages: Essays in Honor of G. W. Coopland*, ed. C. T. Allmand (Liverpool: Liverpool University Press, 1976), 73–101.

tern of association between Lollardy and both concealment and blindness. Strategically, these metaphors have two functions. On the one hand, they are an excellent example of the way in which the paranoia over Lollardy's very murky outlines led Lancastrian propagandists to project the difficulty of surveillance into an ethical charge that Lollards were duplicitous. In other words, they took the difficult problem of exposing Lollards to the juridical process and turned it around into a diagnosis that in their disobedience Lollards were drawn to duplicity and stealth. On the other hand, these metaphors contest the Lollard attacks on images by suggesting that the well-lit, the unconcealed, the visible, in effect the image itself, is the friend of God and the enemy only of deception.

Hoccleve's most pointed defense of the importance of the image comes toward the end of the poem, where he takes up doctrinal debate about the status of the image very directly, using a metaphor based on eyeglasses.

> And to holde ageyn ymages makynge,
> Be they maad in entaille or in peynture,
> Is greet errour. For they yeuen stirynge
> Of thoghtes goode and causen men honure
> The seint after whom maad is that figure,
> And nat worsshipe it, how gay it be wroght.
> For this knowith wel euery creature
> Þat reson hath, þat a seint is it noght.

> Right as a spectacle helpith feeble sighte
> Whan a man on the book redith or writ
> And causith him to see bet than he mighte,
> In which spectacle his sighte nat abit
> But gooth thurgh and on the book restith it;
> The same may men of ymages seye.
> Thogh the ymage nat the seint be, yit
> The sighte vs myngith to the seint to preye.
> (lines 409–24)

Hoccleve here collapses discussion of the veneration of saints and images into the same category and offers two arguments against the Wycliffite attack. First, he suggests that no rational creature could really believe that the image was equivalent to the saint and that any reasonable judge must therefore conclude that the devotional image serves to incite only virtuous

thoughts, not idolatry. Second, through the figure of the spectacles, Hoc-
cleve offers something approaching what we might call an ontological cri-
tique of the Wycliffite position against images. The metaphor constructs a
homologous relation between an agent looking through spectacles and look-
ing at a devotional image and argues that it would be an error to imagine
that the mind rests on the image or that sight rests at the point of the
spectacles' lens. In effect, Hoccleve's argument is that spectacles (and, by
analogy, the devotional image) function by offering a level of apparent per-
ception that is actually not a thing-in-itself but a level of pure mediation.
This metaphor should call to mind a diagram out of the optical studies of
Grosseteste or Roger Bacon, in which the line of sight is represented as a ray
bisecting the optical lens. The confusion of Lollard writing about images,
Hoccleve implies, is of a more fundamental nature than imagining that the
image could be mistaken for the saint. It is a category error to consider the
image a thing in the first place; like the spectacles, the essence of the devo-
tional image lies in its function as a tool of consciousness, a point of transit
between perception and the object.

I call this an ontological critique to underline the sense in which Hoc-
cleve's description is, in fact, strikingly consonant with a modern language
of ontological critique most familiar to us through deconstructive analyses
and Heideggerian categories.[19] The essential point of Hoccleve's metaphor,
and of his argument about the image, derives from a hidden structure of
temporality that governs the image as an object of perception. Hoccleve
describes sight through the following micronarrative: "In which spectacle his
sighte nat abit / But gooth thurgh and on the book restith it." Both the verb
"abit" and the structure of action here suggest that sight is not to be under-
stood as an instantaneous operation. Sight proceeds to the spectacles and
then does not "abide" but passes through the lens. Hoccleve's insistence on
the temporality of the image is crucial both because it serves as a means for
disputing the claim that the image could ever replace divinity and also be-
cause it helps explain why Hoccleve, elsewhere so skeptical about the rela-
tion between visual representation and truth, can here present himself as a
defender of the devotional use of images. In the Series, for example, he insists
that "Vpon a looke / is hard men them to grownde / What a man is . . ."
("Complaint," lines 211–12). By placing the image in time, however, Hoc-

19. For a discussion of such categories as mediation, presence, and absence in the context of late
medieval optical philosophies, see Katherine H. Tachau, Vision and Certitude in the Age of Ockham:
Optics, Epistemology, and the Foundations of Semantics, 1250–1345 (Leiden: E. J. Brill, 1988).

cleve maintains a sense of the ineluctable difference between image and object while also retaining a structural role for the image as a moment in the sequential chain of perception, a moment not of presence but mediation. The temporal dimension of vision can be found as an explicit concern in both theological and scholastic discussions. It would be difficult to overestimate the diffusion of optical thought in the later Middle Ages. Even Wycliffe himself, later so hostile to much of his early training, confessed in his sermons to a youthful fascination with optical science: "When I was younger and a wanderer among delights, I assiduously and extensively collected from manuals of optics the properties of light and other truths of mathematics which, upon consideration of the allegorical end of Scripture, I conceived to be contained in it."[20] And the temporality of vision, as conceived both in optics and in the theology of illumination, was a frequent crux of debate. Roger Bacon, for example, advanced an argument against Aristotle and his followers to demonstrate that the motion of light is not instantaneous but must be temporally divisible.[21] Hoccleve's emphasis on the temporal dimension of the image allows him to focus on ontological questions of presence and absence and thus to create an unstable figure in the pseudo-hagiography that drives this poem. His treatment of the image emphasizes that the saint is never fully present but available only through the mediatory force of the image. As Oldcastle comes under closer examination, Hoccleve suggests that the figure of this antisaint is revealed to be a conjuring trick, an unstable moment that projects itself as though it were very presence.

The figure of Oldcastle is central to the unabashed propagandistic aims of Hoccleve's poem. As Jeremy Catto has suggested, anxiety about the potential heresy of the gentry was at the forefront of the concerns of Arundel and other Lancastrian leaders at the beginning of the century.[22] Hoccleve's poem is thus meant as a preemptive warning about the fate awaiting any, like Oldcastle, who might stray away from religious orthodoxy and secular obedience. In fact, the poem insists on the connections between Oldcastle's reli-

20. Cited by Heather Phillips, "John Wyclif and the Optics of the Eucharist," in *From Ockham to Wyclif*, ed. Anne Hudson and Michael Wilks (Oxford: Basil Blackwell, for the Ecclesiastical History Society, 1987), 245.

21. Roger Bacon, *Opus Majus*, trans. Robert Burke, 2 vols. (Philadelphia: University of Philadelphia Press, 1928), 1:486–89. See also David C. Lindberg's "Medieval Latin Theories of the Speed of Light," in his *Studies in the History of Medieval Optics* (1978; reprint, London: Variorum Reprints, 1983); and his *Theories of Vision from Al-Kindi to Kepler* (Chicago: University of Chicago Press, 1976).

22. Jeremy Catto, "Religious Change Under Henry V," in *King Henry V: The Practice of Kingship*, ed. G. L. Harris (Oxford: Oxford University Press, 1985), 101.

gious and political rebellions to the point of establishing a none-too-subtle parallel between Henry and God himself. Just as Henry had famously delayed Oldcastle's execution even after Oldcastle had been judged a heretic, giving him time in which to recant, so Hoccleve suggests repeatedly that Oldcastle should repent while he has time, because God, like Henry, can be counted on only for a brief hesitation in justice. The *de casibus* narrative spun around the figure of Oldcastle, the story of his fall from orthodoxy and courtly service, thus offers an ideal propagandistic narrative for an unstable moment. This narrative allows Hoccleve to cast Henry as the divinely sanctioned protector of the church, while making Oldcastle an exemplary figure for the consequences of disobedience to God and Henry.

This exemplary use of Oldcastle provides the first level at which we might think of him as an anti-saint. Orthodox religious texts, including the "Letter to Oldcastle," might call on the saints as exemplars of orthodox behavior to emulate, whereas this text uses Oldcastle as an exemplar of all that should be avoided. The particular moral failings Hoccleve ascribes to Oldcastle are, in fact, inversions of ethical strengths and attributes drawn from the hagiographical tradition. The saints are brave and willingly seek martyrdom; Oldcastle has been offered an easy chance at martyrdom (even if for the wrong cause) and has declined the opportunity. The saints seek out any opportunity to confess their faith; Oldcastle remains mute, and the Lollards with whom he is associated simply "clappe and muse." Oldcastle's destiny was to have been a *miles Christiani*, but he has fallen away from both knighthood and Christ and become the mirror image of what he might have been.[23]

Moreover, the structure of the poem reinforces the sense that Oldcastle is meant to be read with the heightened exemplary function that often distinguishes the rhetorical invocation of saints. As has been noticed at least since Lucy Toulmin Smith's late nineteenth-century edition of the poem, the "Address to Oldcastle" is marked by a strong structural break, indicated in the Huntington manuscript by a large capital initial. This break separates the poem into two halves, the first a direct speech to Oldcastle, urging him to recant, and the second a much harsher address to the collective body of Lollards.[24] The first point we should notice about this division is that it is

---

23. This mirror topos is also activated as part of the ocular constellation in this poem by an implicit contrast between Oldcastle's newfangled faith in his own reason and the traditional wisdom of past generations, who are said to provide an accurate mirror for the present: "Our fadres medled no thyng of swich gere:/ Þat oghte been a good mirour to vs" (lines 159–60).

24. Seymour, *Selections from Hoccleve*, 131.

exactly parallel to the structural divisions in two of Hoccleve's other works, the *Regement of Princes*, with its break between the autobiographical prologue and the main section, and the *Series*, with its division between the autobiographical material of the "Complaint" and "Dialogue with a Friend" and the narratives that follow. In these longer works, as a number of critics have pointed out, Hoccleve uses this bifurcated structure to focus on questions of the relationship between exemplary figures and larger communities. Judith Ferster, Anthony Hasler, and D. C. Greetham have demonstrated numerous ways in which the apparently personal complaints of the *Regement*'s prologue actually anticipate the advice that appears later, couched in the impersonal voice of counsel.[25] The structural division in the "Address to Oldcastle" has a very similar function. By breaking the poem into two different forms of address, Hoccleve is able to emphasize both the anonymity of the Lollard mass and the contrasting notoriety of Oldcastle. As an exemplar, the portrait of Oldcastle anticipates and gives substance to many of the charges Hoccleve will lay against the faceless Lollards in the second half.

To make a more complicated point, this split structure also allows Hoccleve to situate the portrait of Oldcastle in systems of both time and desire. In terms of desire, this two-part structure casts Oldcastle as one term in a romantic triangle. On the one side we find Henry, waiting for Oldcastle's senses to return and, as is made clear in the first section, still willing to take him back ("Do by my reed / it shal be for thy prow: / Flee fro the Feend / folwe tho Princes two!" lines 239–40). On the other side are the Lollards, who, as Hoccleve reminds us again and again in the second section, have "seduced" Oldcastle from his duty and his prince ("Yee þat peruerted him"; "Yee, with your sly coloured argumentes" lines 273, 281). Hoccleve here plays the role of a go-between, trying to restore the appropriate connection between Henry and Oldcastle. The personalization of desire implied by this structure is, of course, a fiction, as the actual motives of the participants were far more political than personal. Nevertheless, this language insists on an aura of desire that both reinforces the significance of his temporary absence and also suggests a similarity between the longing for the saint we see in the devotional exercises of affective piety and the longing for Oldcastle. In a way, this position as go-between is an ideal emblem for Hoccleve's role here. Caught between the mission of a good Lancastrian propagandist determined to make Oldcastle *appear* and the typical fascination of his work with absence and

25. For a discussion of this division and these commentaries on the *Regement*, see Chapter 3.

the fragmentation of identity, Hoccleve coyly plays a philosophical version of the *fort-da* game with Oldcastle—now Henry can see him; now he can't. As part of this game, Hoccleve produces a very strange temporal structure for this poem. To explain this properly, it is necessary to turn briefly to the often oversimplified question of the dating of this poem. The rubric in the Huntington MS gives us testimony for an unusually precise date of composition, suggesting that the poem was "written at the time when King Henry V went to Southampton for his first voyage to Harfleur," which would mean July or early August of 1415.[26] However, as M. C. Seymour has pointed out, the concluding stanzas of the poem, which describe the king already in the field, sound as though they would have had to have been written later in that year, when Henry had already reached France.[27] It is tempting to make a simple conclusion here and attribute this ambiguity to an oversight. However, the temporal disjunction introduced by these two dates can be read as an integral part of the representation of Oldcastle in this poem. What I have so far been describing as the two halves of the poem can also be described as three sections. After the first section addressed to Oldcastle and then the second containing the chastisement of the unnamed Lollards, Hoccleve turns again in the final three stanzas to an appeal to Oldcastle to rejoin his sovereign, now fighting in France. It is not at all coincidental that it is at the moment at which Hoccleve readdresses Oldcastle that the apparently firm time-frame of the rubric slips away and we are suddenly projected some months into the future.[28] This slippage offers a metonymical sign of Oldcastle's absence. The poem begins with a direct address to Oldcastle ("Allas, þat thow . . ."; "O Oldcastel! Allas, what eilid thee" lines 9, 25), speaking to him as though he were present as a compensatory response to his historical absence. It then turns to the faceless mass of Lollards ("Yee þat peruerted him" line 273), admitting implicitly Oldcastle's historical success at disappearing into the countryside. The return to Oldcastle in the final stanzas ("Yit, Oldcastel . . ." line 489), and the temporal dislocation accompanying that return, must be read as a willful projection into the future to the moment at which Oldcastle will again be present and be either reconciled with the king or done away with.

The peculiar structure of this poem, in both its bifurcation and temporal

---

26. See Furnivall, *Hoccleve's Works*, 8.

27. Seymour, *Selections from Hoccleve*, 129.

28. Note also the similarity of this temporal slip to the way in which we find, at the end of the *Series*' "Complaint," that the unnamed Friend has actually been standing outside Hoccleve's door for some time.

instability, is a sign of the textual energy expended to create a face for Lol-lardy out of the absent Oldcastle. In constructing Oldcastle as an antisaint, Hoccleve draws on a very particular form of Lancastrian propaganda: the creation, in defiance of the Lollard attack on the image, of a specific set of spiritual and secular images designed for either reverence or vilification.[29] Oldcastle himself, the arch-Lollard, is thus used, with cutting irony, as if he were the subject of a cathedral window. There is, importantly however, a difficulty in making this suggestion in that there is no image in the manu-script nor even an ekphrastic moment at which any visual depiction is of-fered. Hoccleve's poem is founded on the trope of prosopopeia, the trope in which the conjuring of an absent person is meant, literally, to draw a face where there was none. It is an apostrophe, but a specific form of apostrophe meant to simulate a visual apparition. Because this evocation is based on the substitution of a figure for the thing itself, it is also an apostrophe, as Paul De Man reminds us, most often associated with epitaphs and other generic structures that serve more to admit absence than to affirm presence.[30] Read as an example of Hoccleve's "figural hagiography," the "Address to Oldcastle" testifies to a surprising willingness to incorporate a radical critique of the hagiographical image into even a dedicated piece of anti-Lollard propaganda. Hoccleve conjures up the absent Oldcastle, but through his exploration of these problems of temporality and ontological presence Hoccleve maintains a skeptical distance between himself and the iconic methods of Lancastrian propaganda he is so often taken to exemplify.

Mary as Vanishing Mediator

These questions of presence and absence are equally central to Hoccleve's religious verse even in his most orthodox work, his devotional lyrics. These short poems have received only scant attention. The majority of them are devoted to the Virgin Mary, and many are contained in Huntington MSS 111 and 744, the holograph manuscripts that Doyle and Parkes have argued were originally a single manuscript and that Bowers has suggested were put to-

29. Simon Walker has also described the explicit political use of images of sainthood; see his "Political Saints in Late Medieval England," in *The McFarlane Legacy: Studies in Late Medieval Politics and Society*, ed. R. H. Britnell and A. J. Pollard (New York: St. Martin's Press, 1995), 77–106.

30. Paul De Man, "Autobiography as De-Facement," *Modern Language Notes* 94 (1979): 913–30.

gether by Hoccleve as a compilation of his collected works.[31] One of them has achieved some notoriety for its spurious attribution to Chaucer as "The Ploughman's Tale."[32] Another, "The Complaint of the Virgin," is a translation from Guillaume de Deguileville's *Pelerinage de l'âme*. A. I. Doyle has suggested that Hoccleve may be responsible for a complete translation from Deguileville, but only "The Complaint of the Virgin" is included in the Huntington manuscripts, and there is no pressing evidence to accept the others as Hoccleve's composition.[33] With the exception of "The Complaint of the Virgin," the Marian lyrics are all undatable. They are often assumed to be early works, but this assumption is made only because of a questionable association between lyric poetry and poetic juvenilia and from an even less dependable sense that poetic maturation should proceed properly from private religious devotion into public poetry and civic duty.

Although these lyrics are consistent with orthodox forms of Marian piety and with a Lancastrian emphasis on the veneration of the saints and the Virgin Mary, they also betray a fundamental anxiety about the reliability of Mary as an intercessor that is closely analogous to the emphasis on Oldcastle's absence in the "Address to Oldcastle." In these devotional lyrics, this concern is most often represented through invocations of memory. Hoccleve's devotional lyrics are thoroughly suffused with anxious pleas for remembrance. Among the ten short religious lyrics that may be confidently attributed to him, seven of them included prominent references to memory and "remembrance." Among the six poems found in Huntington MS 744, five mention memory: the "Invocacio ad Patrem" asks that pity arise out of God's memory of his son ("That thow haue of thy sone swich memorie, / That thy pitee / be no thyng for to seeche" lines 24–25); the "Ad spiritum sanctum" ends by asking the Trinity to "have vs in remembrance" (line 70); the "Ad beatam virginem" asks Mary to "haue vs in thy mynde!" (line 4); the "Item de beata virgine" both opens and closes with pleas for memory (to which we will return); and, finally, the spurious Ploughman's Tale—"The Story of the Monk who clad the Virgin by singing Ave Maria"—is a poem both founded on an act of memory, as the monk (like Chaucer's clergeon) must learn the proper way to sing the Ave Maria, and also given the internal

31. Doyle and Parkes, "Production of Copies of the *Canterbury Tales* and the *Confessio Amantis*, 182, n. 38; Bowers, "Hoccleve's Huntington Holographs," 45–46.

32. See the edition and notes by Beverly Boyd, *The Middle English Miracles of the Virgin* (San Marino: Huntington Library, 1964).

33. On this question, see Burrow's argument, *Thomas Hoccleve*, 24–25. Burrow also supplies a characteristically illuminating account of the confused corpus of Hoccleve's religious works.

pseudogeneric title of itself being "a remembraunce" (line 35).[34] Among the four additional lyrics in Huntington MS 111, two mention memory prominently: "The Mother of God" asks Mary to "Ficche" her role as mediatrix "in thy remembrance" (line 45) and to "remembre on the wo and peyne / þat thow souffridist in his passioun" (line 57); in the strange, dream vision / memento mori made for Robert Chichele, the narrator pleads with Mary, "Let me nat slippe out of thy remembrance" (line 46).[35] Even those three poems that do not mention memory specifically are all marked by closely related metaphorical patterns, expressing grief at figurative "departures" and concern over the "preservation" of the sinner.

Like the invocation of images in the "Address to Oldcastle," the references to remembrance here are, of course, part of a conventional Marian piety. Mary is the figure of mercy, an intermediary between the stern justice of the Father and human frailty. The category of remembrance is thus crucial to much Marian piety, as the supplicant must engage the Virgin's knowledge as part of soliciting her advocacy. But these Marian lyrics display a surprising instability around the issue of memory. Memory is linked to the image in that memory is often described, as by Aquinas, as the persistence of mental images in the mind.[36] But even more so than in other uses of the image, the viability of memory is determined by the endurance of the image within time. Hoccleve's Marian lyrics give us a Mary whose powers of remembrance are continually invoked but who herself is represented as vanishing away before the supplicant. This process is clearest in the lyric entitled "The Complaint of the Virgin."

The "Complaint of the Virgin" was circulated widely and occurs in all

34. The neglect of Hoccleve's religious verse requires the use of several editions. With the exception of "The Story of the Monk who clad the Virgin by singing Ave Maria" and the "Complaint of the Virgin" and "Mother of God" from HM 111, the religious lyrics cited above are drawn from Furnivall, Hoccleve's Works. They are edited and entitled by Israel Gollancz and printed in pt. 2 of this edition, "The Minor Poems in the Ashburnham MS Additional 133 (now Huntington Library MS HM 744)" as items no. 1, "Invocacio ad Patrem," 275–79; no. 3, "Ad spiritum sanctum," 281–83; no. 4, "Ad beatam virginem," 283–85; and no. 5, "Item de beata virgine," 285–89.

"The Story of the Monk Who Clad the Virgin by Singing Ave Maria" is cited from the pseudo-Ploughman's Tale in John M. Bowers, ed., The Canterbury Tales: Fifteenth-Century Continuations and Additions (Kalamazoo, TEAMS/Medieval Institute Publications, Western Michigan University, 1992). The "Complaint of the Virgin" and "Mother of God" are cited from the editions in Seymour, ed., Selections from Hoccleve.

35. The balade for Chichele is cited from Furnivall, Hoccleve's Works, as item no. 18, 67–72.

36. On the representation of memory as a persistence of images, see Mary Carruthers, The Book of Memory: A Study of Memory in Medieval Culture (Cambridge: Cambridge University Press, 1990), esp. 54–60, 221–42.

ten complete manuscripts of the Middle English translation of Deguileville's *Pèlerinage de l'âme*. (The poem is also found in Huntington MS 111, where it is missing the six opening stanzas.) It must be a relatively early composition, as the Deguileville translation has been dated to 1413.[37] Generically, this poem is very like several of Hoccleve's other Marian works in that it is structured as a complaint and is meant to inspire the ecstatic visions of Biblical scenes that we see in Margery Kempe's *Book* and in other meditational practices of lay piety.[38] As complaints, the poems offer a structuring subjectivity, either that of the speaker or a persona within the poem, which enables a process of identification allowing the reader to participate in moments of pathos. "The Complaint of the Virgin" depicts scenes of the Passion with an emphasis on Mary's affective response and with sufficient visual cues to invite the reader to participate in that response. The initial description of Christ reads as follows:

> O blessid sone, on thee wole I out throwe
> My salte teeres, for oonly on thee
> My look is set. O thynke, how many a throwe
> Thow in myn armes lay and on my knee
> Thow sat and haddist many a kus of me.
> Eek, thee to sowke, on my brestes yaf Y
> Thee norisshyng faire and tendrely.

> Now thee fro me withdrawith bitter deeth
> And makith a wrongful disseuerance.
> Thynke nat, sone, in me þat any breeth
> Endure may þat feele al this greuance.
> My martirdom me hath at the outrance.
> I needes sterue moot syn I thee see
> Shamely nakid, strecchid on a tree.
> (lines 71–84)

The reader here is invited to participate via both Mary's immediate visual descriptions and also her memory of the young child who is now suffering as an adult. Just as the absent figure of Oldcastle was central to the energies of

---

37. Burrow, *Thomas Hoccleve*, 24.

38. On this devotional current, see Aers and Staley, *The Powers of the Holy*; Beckwith, *Christ's Body*; Catto, "Religious Change Under Henry V"; and, especially on Marian devotion in this period, Eamon Duffy, *The Stripping of the Altars: Traditional Religion in England, 1400–1580* (New Haven: Yale University Press, 1992), 256–65.

the "Address to Oldcastle," so the figure of Mary anchors these lyrics. She is the subject who speaks the complaint, but also, and much more important, she provides a subjective frame for the affective responses meant to be evoked here. In serving in this role, Mary performs an aestheticized version of her traditional theological role. She acts here as a figure of intercession, not between divine justice and the sinner but between an image and the affective potential of the audience. By anchoring the complaint in Mary's emotion, Hoccleve guides the reader/worshipper into a mimetic repetition of Mary's affective responses.

This use of Mary as a ground for affective response was an entirely orthodox and widespread technique in late medieval English poetry.[39] Indeed, this lyric drama was a subgenre that received the approving stamp of Lancastrian patronage. Lydgate wrote his *Life of Our Lady* during the reign of Henry V, and several of the manuscripts have colophons claiming that the work was written at Henry's urging.[40] More broadly, Derek Pearsall has suggested that Lydgate's Marian exercise derived "from the king's desire to encourage quasi-liturgical English composition in the high style, and [from] his understanding that such writing struck at the claims of the Lollards to own the religious vernacular."[41] It is quite likely that Hoccleve's work was part of the same effort to combat Lollardy by the promulgation of vernacular materials centered on Marian devotion.

There is, however, a complication in Hoccleve's presentation of Mary in "The Complaint of the Virgin." The poem begins with Mary establishing a very strong communal framework for her grief. The first eleven stanzas include no less than seven direct apostrophes to figures from her family, either spiritual or earthly, the apostrophes being placed at the beginning of each stanza for emphasis and linked also through anaphora ("O fadir God . . ."; "O holy goost . . ."; "O Gaubriel . . ."; "O thow Elizabeth . . ."; "O Simeon . . ."; "O Ioachim, O deere fadir myn . . ."; "O blessid sone . . ." lines 1, 15, 29, 36, 50, 57, 71) Before encountering the vision of Jesus cited above, Mary established around herself a community of grief, a circle of intimates with whom to share this vision. This community, however, does not last. The opening lines of the poem, even as they build up this circle around

---

39. On such Marian poetry, see Douglas Gray, *Themes and Images in the Medieval English Religious Lyric* (London: Routledge and Kegan Paul, 1972), 75–94; and Rosemary Woolf, *The English Religious Lyric in the Middle Ages* (Oxford: Clarendon Press, 1968), 239–73. For a closely related subgenre, see also the texts collected in Boyd, *The Middle English Miracles of the Virgin*.

40. Derek Pearsall, *John Lydgate, 1371–1449: A Bio-Bibliography* (Victoria, B.C.: English Literary Studies, 1997), 19.

41. Ibid., 19.

Mary, emphasize her sense that she is suffering the wheel's downward spiral: "But now hath sorwe caught me with his trappe./My ioye hath made a permutacioun" (lines 12–13). The accumulation of companions lasts up until the moment at which the Passion is invoked. From this moment, Mary emphasizes her growing isolation. She complains that there is no earthly father present to join her in her grief and surrounds herself, via a new set of apostrophes, with the celestial objects of the natural world, a substitution for the earlier companions that serves only to underline her abandonment by the human world. Then, alone with St. John, she chides her son through a striking version of the Mary/Mara pun, one configured around a play with the letter I.

> And namely syn thow me "womman" callist,
> As I to thee straunge were and vnknowe.
> Therthurgh, my sone, thow my ioie appallist.
> Wel feel I þat deeth his vengeable bowe
> Hath bent & me purposith doun to throwe.
> Of sorwe talke may I nat ynow,
> Syn fro my name "I" doon away is now.
>
> Wel may men clepe and calle me Mara
> From hennesforward, so may men me call.
> How sholde I lenger clept be Maria,
> Syn "I", which is Ihesus, is fro me fall
> This day al my swetnesse is into gall
> Torned, syn þat "I", which was the beautee
> Of my name this day bynome is me.
>
> (lines 176–89)

Mary's argument here is that by distancing himself from her, Jesus (Iesus) has taken her "I" away and changed her from herself, Maria, to Mara, "the bitter one." Beyond this fairly conventional play on Mary/Mara, however, she is also claiming that she is no longer, in some sense, an "I." Mary returns to this particular complaint throughout the rest of the lyric, lamenting that her "wit is [al] aweye" (line 217) and that "of modir haast thow eek lost the style" (line 225).[42]

42. Roger Ellis also calls attention to this witty pun on "I" in the introduction to his forthcoming edition of selected works from Hoccleve. Ellis helpfully notes that this pun is made quite explicit in material contained in one of Hoccleve's French sources. He notes also that the nonholograph manuscripts of Hoccleve's poem show a wide variety of attempts to simplify these lines, suggesting that "the scribes of the other copies did not get the point." I am grateful to him for sharing this work with me.

The image of Mary in "The Complaint of the Virgin" is thus quite complex. On the one hand, she is meant to function as an anchor, a firm subjectivity guiding the perspectival vision and response of the reader; on the other hand, her self-representation emphasizes her disappearance at the end of the poem, until she is not there in "I," in "wit," or even in her role as "mother." To a certain degree, perhaps, even this vanishing away can be accommodated to Marian theology. Mary's most important devotional function is as an intercessor, a channel from divinity to the world, and this role certainly does not put a premium on representations of her subjective particularity. Nevertheless, particularly in the context of the reiterated premium on *remembrance*, this disappearance is troubling. If Mary's function is to represent both a certain stability (the anchor of affective response) and a reliable promise of intercession for the faithful, her disappearance would seem to throw both guarantees into question.

This troubling possibility is reinforced by a similar dynamic found in two of the other Marian lyrics, the "Item de beata virgine" (HM 744—Gollancz V) and "The Story of the Monk who clad the Virgin by singing Ave Maria" (HM 111). The "Item de beata virgine" is a highly conventional appeal to Mary's mercy. As mentioned above, it is one of those lyrics that highlights issues of remembrance, as it both opens and closes with invocations of memory. There is, however, one peculiar element in the treatment of memory in this poem. The opening stanza reads:

> Syn thow, modir of grace, haast euere in mynde
> Alle tho / þat vp-on thee han memorie,
> Thy remembrance ay oghte oure hertes bynde
> Thee for to honure / blisful qweene of glorie,
> To all cristen folk / it is notorie
> þat thow art shee / in whom þat al man-kynde
> May truste fully / grace and help to fynde.
>
> (lines 1–7)

The verse opens by establishing the centrality of memory, but this figure is more complex than the usual plea to Mary to hold the speaker in remembrance. In these lines, memory is constructed as a bewilderingly reflexive arrangement: Mary is said to hold in her mind (memory) all the faithful who have memory of her; and since she holds these people in mind, the remembrance of that fact should serve to bind the hearts of the faithful to her honor (i.e., to preserving her in honored memory). In other words, this figure presents an impossible causality, in which Mary remembers the faithful because of their memory of her but in which the memory of the faithful is said to be founded on Mary's precedent. It is a temporal paradox, one with high stakes.

This self-reflexive arrangement is elaborated more fully in the "The Story of the Monk who clad the Virgin by singing Ave Maria." This brief Marian lyric is usually taken to exemplify a flawlessly orthodox sensibility. In it a young French monk is given a vision of the Virgin Mary: discovering her at first, oddly, clothed only in a sleeveless garment, he discovers, upon asking about the missing sleeves, that the garment she wears is in fact a direct product of his own devotion. The garment has been produced through his performance of the Ave Maria, and Mary tells him that the missing sleeves will only come into being as he learns to say the prayer properly—in three groups of fifty, punctuated by a Pater Noster at every tenth. The Monk does so and not only weaves her garment but becomes the abbot of his monastery, allowing him to perpetuate the new liturgical practice. In its emphasis on teaching the unmediated Latin form of the prayer, the text can be seen to engage in an orthodox polemic against the practice of vernacular devotion.[43] In its plot, the brief narrative shares with many of the products of affective piety an emphasis on the engagement of the individual life with sacred persons. In addition, however, and this is the point most significant to the place of this poem in Hoccleve's peculiar treatment of Marian piety, the poem goes beyond most orthodox meditative exercises in its suggestion that the deeds of a man like the monk might have a concrete significance in the reality of the Virgin's life.

In other words, we see in "The Story of the Monk who clad the Virgin" a narrative analog to the reflexive mutual reliance of the memories of the faithful and Mary seen above in the "Item de beata virgine." As Mary's capacity to act as mediatrix was made dependent on the memorial act of the supplicant in "Item de beata virgine," so is Mary's physical state made dependent on the action of the monk in "The Story of the Monk who clad the Virgin." In each poem we see the presence of a peculiarly self-reflexive spirituality, one in which the agency of the intercessor and supplicant are curiously mixed. Moreover, this self-reflexivity is a corollary to Hoccleve's image of Mary as a vanishing mediator in the "Complaint of the Virgin." Though Mary's presence is not an issue in the latter poems, their imbrication of the agencies of supplicant and intercessor suggest, remarkably, that Mary's identity is not

43. Bowers, *The Canterbury Tales*, 24

entirely self-sufficient, that it requires the supplemental action of worshippers. Hoccleve's figural hagiography is thus a poetry with a theological paradox at its center: like Holcot, he is drawn to a poetry of verbal images, of central iconic objects of meditation; but also, like Holcot, he is unable to set aside the problems of temporal perception and of mediation that dogged attempts to assert the ontological stability of images in his day. He is consequently left with a poetry that insists on the importance of durable images but which continually represents their vulnerability to dissolution.

This paradox also takes us back to the secular and bureaucratic context of the Privy Seal. The issue of intercession, financial rather than spiritual, is a constant motif in Hoccleve's topical verse. On occasion, these petitions inspire some of Hoccleve's most energetic and positive humor. His "Balades to Sir Henry Somer," for example, pursues an analogy between recipient and season, praising him, and asking for financial aid from "Somer, þat rypest mannes sustenance / With holsum hete of the sonnes warmnesse."[44] Other such verses, though still humorous, are darker in their satire, haunted by a sense that the intermediaries controlling access to patronage are likely to be hostile or, at best, unresponsive. In the presentation poems "Balade to John, Duke of Bedford" and "Balade to Edward, Duke of York," Hoccleve speaks of household agents, "maister Massy" and "maistir Picard," both of whom are presented as formidably learned and likely to dismiss his work. Similarly, we find in his "Three Roundels" a satirical treatment of his failure to gain patronage at the hands of his "ladye moneye." His most colorful treatment of such an intercessor, however, is the figure of Nemo in the *Regement*.[45] When, in the prologue to that work, Hoccleve complains about his troubles securing his annuity, the Old Man, in disbelief, asks whether the clerks don't have some friend, some intercessor to whom they might turn for help. Hoccleve responds that they do indeed:

> "But how been thy felawes lookid to
> At hoom? Been they nat wel ybeneficed?"
> "Yis, fadir, yis. Ther is oon clept Nemo:
> He helpith hem, by him been they chericed;
> Nere he, they weren poorely chevyced;
> He hem avanceth, he fully hir freend is;
> Sauf oonly him, they han but fewe freendes."
> (lines 1485–91)

44. Cited from Seymour, *Selections from Hoccleve*.
45. On this figure of Nemo as patron, see also Simpson, "Nobody's Man."

Hoccleve's false enthusiasm is scathing. Is there no one to look after him and his fellow clerks? Of course there is—their good friend Nemo. And it is lucky that Nemo is there, because all the other powerful men with whom they work cheat them shamelessly, looking to get the clerks to help with their legal business but never fulfilling their promises of rewards. As an example, Hoccleve tells an anecdote (meant to be taken as the routine) of a suitor who persuades a clerk to write out documents for him with the promise that the man's lord will certainly reward this clerk for the favor. When the client takes the letter and goes on his way with no payment, the clerk can't complain for fear of this man's power, and worse, when inquiries are made, the lord has never even heard of the man who traded on his name and certainly cannot himself be approached for payment:

> "And whan the mateere is to ende ybroght
> Of the straunger for whom the suyte hath be,
> Than is he to the lord knowen right noght;
> He is to him as unknowen as we;
> The lord nat woot of al this sotiltee,
> Ne we nat dar lete him of it to knowe,
> Lest our conpleynte ourselven overthrowe."
> (lines 1520–26)

In the end, not only are the clerks powerless to do anything about it, they can't even *talk* about it, lest their complaint "ourselven overthrowe."

The only figure to whom they have recourse is Nemo. Nemo is a stock character in medieval ecclesiastical satire and a remarkable creation.[46] Hoccleve would have encountered this character through lyrics in the tradition of clerical satire begun in the late thirteenth century by the French monk Radulphus, the author of a text entitled the *Historia Neminis*, which purported to tell the history of a miraculous figure named Nemo, for whom all impossible things were possible and for whom all forbidden things were permissible. Radulphus invented the character through a simple grammatical trick. He took proverbial biblical expressions, such as "Nemo potest aperire" (It may be revealed to no man) and willfully misread them, taking Nemo as a proper name and reading such a sentence as: "It may be revealed *to Nemo*." In this way, the character Nemo was read into proverbial and scriptural texts

---

46. On the history of Nemo, see Martha Bayless, *Parody in the Middle Ages: The Latin Tradition* (Ann Arbor: University of Michigan Press, 1996); and Jelle Koopmans and Paul Verhuyck, *Sermon Joyeux et Truanderie* (Amsterdam: Rodopi, 1987).

as a running anarchic pun, a hero potentially present behind every restriction. This figure was common in clerical satire of the later middle ages and eventually became part of the early modern tradition of the *sermons joyeux*.[47] This figure of Nemo provides an ideal example of the pitfalls of the patronage system for the clerks of the Privy Seal and of the parallels between this system and the theological paradoxes Hoccleve describes in his religious verse. The invocation of Nemo as a patron is perfect clerkly humor, a joke derived from the disjunction between syntactical possibility and semantic reference. Nemo marks a grammatical slot in which syntax would lead one to expect an agent but which is in fact vacant. This conundrum is both a witty form for the dilemma of clerks laboring in an unreliable patronage network and also a homologous form to the intricacies of the figural hagiographies we have seen Hoccleve write around Oldcastle and the Virgin Mary. Patrons and intercessors are close analogues. The patron requires service and devotion and promises in return to secure the ear of the powerful for the clerk; such devotion is the way to secure payment from the Exchequer. The saintly intercessor also requires service and devotion and promises a channel of mercy to the sinner; such service brings salvation. The disconcerting feature of Hoccleve's use of this structure is that his exemplary figures—whether Oldcastle, Nemo, or Mary—seem to fade away as quickly as they are invoked.

The politics of the Lancastrian dynasty, as a Privy Seal clerk would appreciate, were a politics of appearance, of spectacle, and of a constant interest in the power of textual propaganda to instantiate the image of a new dynasty. In this reliance on the power of the visible to make authority palpable and present, Lancastrian culture is quite consistent with late medieval orthodox thought concerning the power of the image to exist as a present and self-contained source of devotional power. In the face of the religious and political valorization of a search for presence and wholeness, Hoccleve persisted in writing texts that reveal absences at moments when presence and spectacle seem most to be desired.[48] Let us conclude with the fact that Hoccleve was a man who preferred not to wear spectacles. In his "Balade to

47. In his book on Rabelais, Mikhail Bakhtin takes this medieval Nemo as part of the stock of ecclesiastically based images of carnival. For Bakhtin, too, the significance of the medieval Nemo derives from its grammatical origin. For Bakhtin, however, this grammatical transformation implies a utopian vision. As he puts it, "All the gloomy sentences: 'no one may,' 'no one can,' 'no one knows,' 'no one dares' are transformed into gay words: 'Nemo may,' 'Nemo can,' 'Nemo knows,' 'Nemo must,' 'Nemo dares.' " Bakhtin, *Rabelais and His World*, trans. Helene Iswolsky (Bloomington: Indiana University Press), 414.

48. Paul Strohm has succinctly labeled such works in this period as "anti-Lancastrian" texts. See Strohm, *England's Empty Throne*, 201–14.

the Duke of York," he admits that his vanity keeps him from wearing the spectacles, and so mars his work:

> Thow foul book, vnto my lord seye also
> Þat pryde is vnto me so greet a fo
> Þat the spectacle forbedith he me
> And hath ydoon of tyme yore ago.
> And for my sighte blyue hastith me fro
> And lakkith þat þat sholde his confort be,
> No wondir thogh thow haue no beautee.
>
> (lines 55–61)[49]

One couldn't ask for more candor. Hoccleve's writing sets a skeptical (or perhaps vain) distance between itself and the clarity of spectacles, producing a writing that is foul and marred by a sense that the image is never quite there.

---

49. Cited from Seymour, ed., *Selections from Hoccleve.*

"Ful bukkissh is his
brayn"

Writing,

Madness,

and

Bureaucratic

Culture

in the

Series

There is something uncanny about autobiography. As Sartre put it, the writing of autobiography is essentially a posthumous enterprise, one in which the production of meaning requires the ghostly premonition of an ending, some conclusion to draw the narrative of a life to a close and endow it with meaning. Hoccleve's *Series* tempts us to read it as just such a conclusion. His verse is marked throughout his career by a struggle between speech and silence, a persistent conflict between assertion and reticence, and within the context of these thematics the timing of the *Series* itself carries a measure of pathos. Hoccleve had reached his greatest contemporary success with his *Regement of Princes* (1411) and "Address to Sir John Oldcastle" (1415), but this promising career seems to have been interrupted in 1416 by the onset of what he called his "wylde infirmitee," a period of madness and silence whose aftermath became the subject of his last major poetic work, the posthumously titled *Series* (1419–21).[1] The reception of the *Series* has

1. The title of the *Series* is editorial and comes from Eleanor P. Hammond, *English Verse Between Chaucer and Surrey* (Durham: Duke University Press, 1927), 69.
    Although the *Series* was once thought to have been written in 1422, John Burrow has convincingly set an earlier date for at least the "Complaint" and "Dialogue," on the basis of references to the Duke of Gloucester's brief occupancy of the office of Regent in the years 1419–21. See Burrow, "Thomas Hoccleve: Some Redatings," *Review of English Studies* 46 (1995): 366–72. On the dating of Hoccleve's illness, however, I tentatively follow Seymour's suggestion of 1416, both because Hoc-

been very much conditioned both by the frequency of complaint in Hoc-
cleve's verse—complaints that have led his critics to construct a biographical
trajectory of disappointment and failure for him—and, more specifically, by
the sense that the *Series* was written in order to redeem Hoccleve from the
madness and social alienation that struck him as if the culmination of all
earlier complaints. But this is only one half of the story. To read this poem
as a final triumph, as the recovery of a personal voice after years of silence,
is to grant too much power to the world of poetry and too little to the world
of the Privy Seal. I will argue here that this poem must be read as the text
of a clerk who never stopped writing, and that rather than chronicling the
recovery of a personal voice, the *Series* depicts a paradoxical triumph in the
dispersal of that voice into the textual world of the Privy Seal.

This *Series* is an ambitious text, linking five independent poems together
through an ostensibly autobiographical framework. The opening "Com-
plaint" describes a period of madness, offers a prolonged lament for his social
ostracization, and ends in a mood of solitary resignation.[2] This mood and
this solitude are then shattered by the second section, the "Dialogue with a
Friend," in which Hoccleve and an unnamed Friend debate whether a new
poem is more likely to convince people of Hoccleve's recovery or to arouse
their suspicions that he is still not right in the head. Hoccleve insists that
poetry will help him, and the two consider what Hoccleve might write to
fulfill a commission for Humphrey of Gloucester.[3] The final three poems are
then presented as the composition meant for Humphrey, two translations of
stories out of the *Gesta Romanorum*, entitled "Jereslaus's Wife" and the "Tale
of Jonathas," and set between them a translation of part of Heinrich Suso's
Wisdom's Watch upon the Hours entitled "How to Learn to Die."[4]

---

cleve's Easter annuity for that year was paid out through proxies (Seymour, *Selections*, 133) and
because the discussion in the "Dialogue" of Hoccleve's desire to take up writing again fits best a
scenario in which his infirmity fell after his composition of the "Address to Sir John Oldcastle." This
would not leave a gap larger than that signified by Hoccleve in his reference to the "fiue yeer /
neither more ne lesse" ("Complaint," line 56), as revision of the *Series* continued through at least
1421.

2. Though the "Complaint" is not all lament. As David Mills points out, the initial tone of
lament lapses quickly and repeatedly into "grievance rather than lament." Mills, "Voices of Hoc-
cleve," 89.

3. On Humphrey's literary interests, see K. H. Vickers, *Humphrey, Duke of Gloucester* (London:
Archibald Constable, 1907), 340–82; and Roberto Weiss, *Humanism in England During the Fifteenth
Century* (Oxford: Basil Blackwell, 1967).

4. Much of the criticism of the *Series* has been devoted to studies of the sources for these sec-
tions. Jerome Mitchell has done much to make this material available through his bibliographies, his
treatment of source texts in *Thomas Hoccleve*, 86–96, and his transcription of the *Gesta Romanorum*
sources for the "Tale of Jonathas" and "Jereslaus's Wife" in the first appendix to "Thomas Hoccleve:

This framework offers a near-parallel with the *Regement of Princes*, in that both poems present an introductory dialogue largely concerned with writing which then serves as a foil for a concluding text. In some ways, however, the metafictional introduction to the *Series* is very different from the *Regement*'s prologue. First, although writing might not solve all of Hoccleve's troubles in the *Regement*, it is still proposed by his interlocutor there as an unequivocably good thing. In the *Series*, on the other hand, the Friend is concerned that it was Hoccleve's writing that caused his madness and, moreover, that any attempt to prove his sanity by writing will not only provide an unfortunate reminder of his former madness but also might actually drive him back into insanity. In other words, whereas the prologue to the *Regement* is structured so as to justify the text that it introduces, the opening "Complaint" and "Dialogue" insist that writing the *Series* might be a very bad idea. This impression is reinforced by the structural contrast between the two works. The *Regement* is structured as a neat binary, a textual relation rather like a diptych with two halves presented as discrete sections, whereas the *Series* establishes a much more open form. The multiplicity of tales following the "Dialogue" carries an implication that the *Series* is organized only as a loose anthology with no real conclusion. In addition, the precedent of the resumed dialogue between Hoccleve and the Friend at the end of the first of these tales, that of "Jereslaus's Wife," creates an unfulfilled structural expectation that the other tales, particularly the thematically parallel "Tale of Jonathas," might also be followed by the reappearance of the author, armed with some commentary or moralization. With the exception, however, of a brief envoy (which is unique to the Durham MS and bears no dramatic relation to the larger frame), Hoccleve makes no return to the metafictional framework established by the opening "Complaint" and "Dialogue." The *Series* is thus a poem marked by both a self-referential meditation on writing and a form in which the development of narrative tends to exceed the bounds of the framing device.

His Traditionalism and His Individuality" (Ph.D. diss., Duke University, 1965), 315–32. Also useful for the *Gesta* stories is Sidney J. H. Herrtage, *The Early English Versions of the Gesta Romanorum*, EETS, ES 33 (London: Oxford University Press, 1967). For the penitential treatise, "Learn to Die," see the series of articles published by Benjamin P. Kurtz: "The Source of Occleve's *Learn to Die*," *Modern Language Notes* 38 (1923): 337–40; "The Prose of Occleve's *Learn to Die*," *Modern Language Notes* 39 (1924): 56–57; and "The Relation of Occleve's *Learn to Die* to Its Source," *PMLA* 40 (1925): 252–75. On the references to Isidore's "Book" in the "Complaint," see A. G. Rigg, "Hoccleve's *Complaint* and Isidore of Seville," *Speculum* 45 (1970): 564–74; and John Burrow, "Hoccleve's *Complaint* and Isidore of Seville Again," *Speculum* 73 (1998): 424–28. A convenient translation of Suso's original may be found in Henry Suso, *Wisdom's Watch upon the Hours*, trans. Edmund Colledge (Washington, D.C.: The Catholic University of America Press, 1994).

This self-referential textuality is the element of the work that has received the balance of critical attention. John Burrow, for example, has drawn attention to the metafictional play of the *Series* by comparing the gaps in its frame to those in the *Canterbury Tales*: "In the *Canterbury Tales* the absence of a prologue or epilogue tears a hole in the fabric of the fiction; but the effect here is rather different, since the reader must now understand the double nature of the book he is reading. It not only describes the making of a book, but also *is* that book."[5] D. C. Greetham has similarly described the *Series* as a variation on the *Canterbury Tales*, suggesting that the *Series* is "structurally the *Canterbury Tales* inside out," or, in other words, that the three discrete poems that end the *Series* should be read as "digressions in the portrayal of the poet's psyche," making of the whole poem an intensification of Chaucer's experiment in which several separate narratives are brought together to chart the various psychic moments in the life of a single character.[6] The most nuanced treatment of textuality in this poem, however, is probably that of James Simpson, who suggests that, although the *Series* is a text greatly concerned with depicting its own conditions of composition, it does this not as a metatextual game but in order to create a vivid illusion that certain elements of the *Series* (notably dialogue) are reality itself.[7]

For the purposes of my argument here, these appeals to the textuality of the poem are significant because it is often this sense of textuality that supports a reading of the poem as an exercise in consolation. Burrow and Simpson, for example, both agree that it is in the staging of his own ability to create poetry that Hoccleve demonstrates or even precipitates his recovery of sanity and social position. In Burrow's account, the *Series* gestures insistently toward its own textuality in order to remind its reader that this Hoccleve has recovered and is now a competent poet and sane man again. Not only does his ability to write poetry constitute a claim of recovery, the poem he has written also mimetically depicts this recovery as the progression from the solitary lament of the "Complaint" to the confident paternal adviser who produces the "Tale of Jonathas."[8] For Simpson, Hoccleve's aim is to assert

5. John Burrow, "Hoccleve's *Series*: Experience and Books," in *Fifteenth Century Studies: Recent Essays*, ed. R. F. Yeager (Hamden: Archon Books, 1984), 266.

6. Greetham, "Self-Referential Artifacts," 247.

7. James Simpson, "Madness and Texts: Hoccleve's *Series*," in *Chaucer and Fifteenth-Century Poetry*, ed. Julia Boffey and Janet Cowen (London: Centre for Late Antique and Medieval Studies, King's College London, 1991), 15–29.

8. Burrow, "Hoccleve's *Series*," 267; the point is reiterated in his "Autobiographical Poetry," 404.

his stability and sanity by counterposing the level of textuality depicted in the "Complaint" to the "extratextual effect of dialogue."[In this argument, Hoccleve's great trouble lies in the instability of texts, in the fact that they can always be interpreted amiss and so taken as evidence of his continuing infirmity. In response, Hoccleve produces the sense of extra-textual reality in the "Dialogue" as a foundation upon which to assert his recovery. Thus, in these readings it is Hoccleve's masterful control of alternating levels of textuality that, providentially, creates both an opportunity for and a depiction of his resumption of social position and poetic vocation.

These accounts and others that construe the *Series* as the triumph of poetry over alienation are based on an implicit biographical narrative in which Hoccleve goes mad, recovers, and then writes the *Series* as a device for social regeneration. I want to complicate this narrative with two suggestions: first, that in this poem madness is never truly surmounted; and second, that the plangent isolation forming the backdrop for consolation in this text is moderated from beginning to end by a series of connections to the social world of the Privy Seal. (I am not here suggesting a need to adjudicate between more and less factually accurate autobiographical contexts but rather between different representations of this biographical narrative within the *Series* itself.) What Hoccleve presents in the *Series* is not a narrative of recovery and consolation but a sophisticated meditation upon the irresolvable fragmentation of the self and the intricate connections between his poetic project and the specific cultural milieu of the Privy Seal. Among the remarks Hoccleve reports having overheard in his madness was the accusation that "Ful bukkissh is his brayn" ("Complaint," line 123), a diagnosis that his mind was both *buckish* (one in a series of animal metaphors) and also suspiciously *bookish*.[10] In his depiction of this "bukkissh" mind, Hoccleve ironizes his own claims to recovery and consolation. This stunning poem provides a fitting conclusion for Hoccleve's experiments in vernacular autobiography, as it insists to the end that the self is an elusive thing whether mad or sane and that a triumphant poetry might be made out of the syncretic textuality and urban milieu of the Privy Seal as well as out of the lyric intensity of the individual poetic voice.

9. Simpson, "Madness and Texts," 22.
10. Burrow, *Hoccleve's Complaint and Dialogue*. Subsequent citations from these sections of the *Series* are drawn from this edition and will be cited by subsection and line number within the text. See also Mary Ruth Pryor, "Thomas Hoccleve's *Series*: An Edition of MS Durham Cosin V iii 9," (Ph.D. diss., University of California at Los Angeles, 1968).

Hoccleve's "pilgrym wit"

The *Regement*'s alternation between private bedchamber and public pre-
cincts, between the allegorical ramblings of thought (which take place in
Hoccleve's head) and the concretely realized interaction of Hoccleve and
the Old Man (which takes place in the Suburbs of Hoccleve's London), is
replayed in the opening sections of Hoccleve's *Series*. In the *Series*, we see
that most distinctive element of Hoccleve's verse: his obsessive interest in
the representation of the self. And one of Hoccleve's techniques for fashion-
ing autobiography is the creation of a strong sense of a crowded urban envi-
ronment, what he calls the "press," which surrounds the individual and
forces self-reflection as a response to its (largely hostile) pressure. As in the
Regement, Hoccleve stages scenes of isolation, solitary complaint, and Boe-
thian disenchantment, and he stages these as a prelude to their interruption
by and eruption into an emphatically public and social world, a world marked
by the urban press of the crowd, on the one hand, and the communal nature
of bureaucratic *habitus*, on the other.

Hoccleve's "Complaint" begins with a rewriting of the first lines of Chau-
cer's "General Prologue," a variation transposed into a substantially more
bitter key:

> Aftir þat heruest inned had his sheeues,
> And þat the broun sesoun of Mighelmesse
> Was come / and gan / the trees robbe of hir leeues
> þat greene had been / and in lusty fresshnesse
> And hem into colour / of yelownesse
> Had died / and doun throwen vndir foote,
> þat chaunge sank / into myn herte roote.
>
> For fresshly broghte it / to my remembrance
> þat stablenesse / in this world / is ther noon;
> There is no thyng / but chaunge and variance.
>   ("Complaint," lines 1–10)[11]

11. The lack of a complete modern edition of the *Series* necessitates a reliance on two editions.
Citations from the sections of *Series* known as the "Complaint" and "Dialogue" are drawn from
Burrow's new edition and cited by line number within the text. Citations from later sections of the
Series are taken from Furnivall's edition.

Far from the "Whan that Aprill . . ." of the love poets, Hoccleve's work begins with the decayed autumn of a Boethian lament.[12] Everything here, from the conventional imagery of autumnal corruption to the invasion of the organic decay into his own heart, insists on the fact that this is a poem begun with the narrator already at the end of his rope. Particularly striking here is the bitter irony of "fresshly." The yellowing that evokes the end of life is the only thing fresh to him, and "freshness" itself has slipped into the closed economy of repetition through its association with "remembrance." This seasonal pattern evokes the same recursivity we have seen marking so much of Hoccleve's verse. It is also a powerful assertion that the task of this poem will be a search for consolation.

As the prologue concludes and the "Complaint" proper begins, Hoccleve introduces us to the immediate cause of his Boethian disenchantment. He has had what he rather archly refers to as a "visit" from God:

> Almighty God / as lykith his goodnesse,
> Visiteth folk al day / as men may see,
> With los of good / and bodily seeknesse,
> And among othir / he forgat nat me;
> Witnesse vpon / the wylde infirmitee
> Which þat I hadde / as man a man wel kneew,
> And which me out of myself / cast and threew.
> ("Complaint," lines 36–42)[13]

God has afflicted him with a "wylde infirmitee," cause enough to be re-minded of the Boethian instability of the world. However, two stanzas later we find that although "the substance of my memorie wente to pleye," God has already "made it for to retourne"—made it return, in fact, some five years ago. The cause of his disenchantment is thus not simply his mental collapse but, more important, the social isolation resulting from his friends' refusal to believe in his recovery: "For thogh þat my wit / were hoom come ageyn, / Men wolde it nat so / vndirstonde or take" ("Complaint," lines 64–65). Be-cause his fellows do not believe that Hoccleve has recovered, they refuse to

---

12. This allusion to Chaucer is noted by several recent editors. See Seymour, *Selections*, 134; Wogan-Browne et al., *Idea of the Vernacular*, 41; and Derek Pearsall, ed., *Chaucer to Spenser: An Anthology of Writing in English, 1375–1575* (Oxford: Blackwell Publishers, 1999), 335.

13. *Visit* is Hoccleve's characteristic term for these sudden trials and recurs frequently, as in the *Regement*, line 914: "God as him list visitith folk and smit."

recognize him in the street or to hear his claims to reason as anything but further proof of insanity. The narrative structure that Thomas spins out here is a potent and familiar one, with roots in both complaint literature and the psalmic *vox clamantis* tradition; the reader is here made a confidant and is offered a privileged glimpse into an isolated and misunderstood subject.[14]

This is, however, precisely the framework (and understanding of this Thomas) we are meant to distrust by the end of the *Series*. Although this generic framework tempts us to privilege Thomas's insistence on his recovery, what Hoccleve actually depicts in the *Series* are a set of descriptions of madness that are almost indistinguishable from sanity, accompanied by a series of proofs of sanity that are ironized and undercut as soon as they are presented. Hoccleve's descriptions of his "wylde infirmitee" in the "Complaint" represent this malady through a series of micronarratives of fragmentation in which the self is dispersed, wandering away only to return later. As Hoccleve describes the incident, in a set of very similar passages: "me out of myself / caste and threew" (line 42); "the substance / of my memorie / Wente to pleye / as for a certein space" until God "made it for to retourne" (lines 50–54); and, perhaps most evocatively, "Right so / thogh Þat my wit / were a pilgrym / And wente fer from hoom / he cam agayn" (lines 232–33). In each of these instances, Hoccleve represents his passage into madness through a fundamentally Augustinian language of procession and return; his madness is figured as an pathetically reversed pilgrimage, in which his true self vanishes into exile but is vouchsafed a return by God's grace. Furthermore, this pattern of procession and return is reinforced by its metaphoric linkage to a number of a central concerns in Hoccleve's thinking, which all circulate around an anxiety he calls "mutabilite," such as the struggle against Boethian instability, the terrifying unpredictability of God's "visits," and the psalmic pattern in which he describes himself in his troubles as "a lost vessel" ("Complaint," line 82) wandering on the sea. Madness is thus governed by what seems to be one of Hoccleve's primary imaginative structures, the unpredictable ebb and flow that patterns both fortune in the world and also, even more threateningly, the cohesion of a sane self.

Once we begin to take note of the larger presence of these patterns of loss and recurrence, however, a very strange thing begins to happen to Hoccleve's arguments about his own recovery. When Hoccleve overhears people in the street suggesting that his recovery is only temporary, we must note that their arguments eerily mirror his own description of his return to sanity:

14. Models for this dramatic technique range from the French *dits* to earlier English devotional texts, most prominently those of Richard Rolle and his followers.

Thus spak many oon / and seide by me:
"Althogh from him / his seeknesse sauage
Withdrawe and past / as for a tyme be,
Resorte it wole / namly in swich age
As he is of"
("Complaint," lines 85–89)

Whereas the patterning of madness as an improper pilgrimage had implicitly asserted the permanence of the true, sane, self and the temporariness of madness, these gossips reverse his argument and suggest that it is the recurrence of sanity that is only temporary. Hoccleve never attempts to dispute the suggestion that recovery from madness is often a temporary thing, and this leads us to a logical difficulty in Hoccleve's argument, a perspectival problem: If the true self is to be represented as that which proceeds and returns, and both "memorie" and "seeknesse" obey this pattern, how is one to know which self is in fact authentic? This difficulty forces Hoccleve to argue inconsistently both for and against "mutabilite." On the one hand, he asserts that his cure is dependent on the fungibility of the self ("If a man ones / falle in dronkenesse / Shal he continue / therin euere mo?" "Complaint," lines 225–26), while at other moments he suggests that his recovery is secured by the presence of something authentic and steadfast, a self that waits as the home to which the pilgrim wit might return.

This breakdown of the distinction between madness and sanity is encouraged by the fact that Hoccleve's attempts to demonstrate his sanity demonstrate nothing so much as the difficulty of either shaping or recognizing a coherent self. In the narrative of the "Complaint," the doubts and suspicions of passersby drive Hoccleve into convoluted and futile attempts to find a foolproof way to represent himself as a sane man. He soon realizes a first difficulty: it is dangerous for a madman to defend himself, because anything he says may be taken as proof of madness:

I leide an ere ay to / as I by wente
And herde al / and thus in myn herte I caste:
"Of long abydynge heere / I may repente;
Lest þat of hastinesse / I at the laste
Answere amis / best is / hens hie faste,
For if I in this prees / amis me gye
To harm wole it me torne / and to folie."
And this I deemed wel / and kneew wel eek,

Whatso þat euere / I sholde answere or seye
They wolden nat / han holde it worth a leek;
Forwhy / as I had lost my tonges keye
Kepte I me cloos / and trussid me my weye
Droupynge and heuy / and al wo bistad;
Smal cause hadde I / me thoghte, to be glad.
                    ("Complaint," lines 134–47)

Passing through the streets, Hoccleve overhears people speaking of his mad-
ness and decides that the best course is not to respond, not even to linger
nearby lest he be tempted to respond, but rather to pretend that he had "lost
my tonges keye" and remain secluded and silent. Silence, too, is thus added
to the complex of anxieties swirling around "mutabilite," as his fear is figur-
ally represented by the possibility that he will "amis me gye," a possibility
that is countered by placing his speech under close guard: "Kepte I me cloos /
and trussid me my weye." The threat here is again a dispersal of the self, and
the response, in a return to his central metaphor, is to bind the self to the
self by locking away his voice and losing the key.
    His experience is also marked as the specifically urban experience of the
"press" of the crowd. In a vivid passage, he berates himself for being such a
fool as to ever venture into the street after his recovery:

For thogh þat my wit / were hoom come ageyn,
Men wolde it nat so / vndirstonde or take.
With me to delen / hadde they desdeyn;
A riotous persone I was / and forsake;
Myn old frendshipe / was al ouershake;
No wight with me / list make daliance.
The world me made / a straunge contenance,

Which þat myn herte / sore gan tormente;
For ofte whan I / in Westmynstre halle
And eek in Londoun / among the prees wente,
I sy the cheere / abaten and apalle
Of hem þat weren wont / me for to calle
To conpaignie / Hire heed they caste awry
Whan I hem mette / as they nat me sy.
                    ("Complaint," lines 64–77)

The camaraderie Hoccleve celebrates in poems such as "La Male Regle" has
now disappeared, leaving in its place only the "prees." The coding of public

space as an urban street here allows Hoccleve to emphasize a sense of simultaneous isolation and claustrophobia. He returns to his usual haunts but finds them now bereft of the friendships he used to enjoy. In their place is a crowd that appears to him as at once a plural gathering of former friends ("hem Þat weren wont/me for to calle/To conpaignie") and, at the same time, a single face confronting him as a stranger—a world represented by a face that regards him with "a straunge contenance."

Faced with this mutual surveillance, watching and listening to this crowd to determine how he is being seen and heard, Hoccleve's response is to return home to the protected and private space of his chamber. What follows then is his justly well-known "mirror scene."

> And in my chambre at hoom/whan Þat I was
> Myself allone/I in this wyse wroghte:
> I streighte vnto my mirour/and my glas
> To looke how Þat me/of my cheere thoghte,
> If any othir were it/than it oghte;
> For fayn wolde I/if it had nat been right,
> Amendid it/to my konnynge and might.
>
> Many a saut made I/to this mirour
> Thynkynge/"If Þat I looke/in this maneere
> Among folk/as I now do/noon errour
> Of suspect look/may in my face appeere.
> This contenance/I am seur/and this cheere
> If I foorth vse/is no thyng repreeuable
> To hem Þat han/conceites resonable."
>
> And therwithal/I thoghte thus anoon:
> "Men in hire owne cas/been blynde alday,
> As I haue herd seyn/many a day agoon,
> And in Þat same plyt/I stonde may.
> How shal I do/which is the beste way
> My troublid spirir/for to brynge in reste?
> If I wiste how/hayn wolde I do the beste."
>
> ("Complaint," lines 155–75)

Here in front of the mirror, the mutual surveillance that Hoccleve had earlier experienced in the press is now transformed into an internal fragmentation, into bits of consciousness determined to spy on each other. The attempt to spy out his own madness leads Hoccleve to inspect himself in the mirror, and he is concerned enough about the possibility of self-deception to check himself by making "a saut," jumping in front of the mirror, in order to try to catch any possible taint. This scene is a remarkable thing to find in a fifteenth-century poem. It is, first, an immediate challenge to any who would still maintain that one cannot expect to find complex, interiorized representations of subjectivity in medieval poetry.[15] Hoccleve presents himself here as both the self looking into the mirror and the self he is trying to surprise by looking at that mirror. It is a moment at which Hoccleve quite intentionally evokes that sense of the uncanny that is particularly associated (by Lacan and others) with the mirror, a simultaneous presence of two images of the self and the consequent fragmentation of that self into both subject and object of perception.

Moreover, in an imagistic trail that should remind us of Hoccleve's scribal labors, this self is emphatically marked as being essentially malleable, a self that is modeled on the materials of a craftsman or scribe.[16] In the stanza that immediately precedes this mirror scene, Hoccleve describes his willingness to make of himself anything that might be taken for a sane man through the language of visual art, saying that "My spirites / laboured bisily // To peynte contenance / cheere and look" ("Complaint," lines 148–49). In this mirror scene itself, he similarly draws on the language of artistic representation, using terminology most applicable to a scribe's correction of a faulty text: "For fayn wolde I / if it had nat been right, / Amendid it . . ." ("Complaint," lines 160–61). Hoccleve's project of demonstrating a sane self is thus entangled and confused with the attempt to craft such a self, a project Hoccleve imagines as being analogous to mimetic forms of artistic representation.[17]

However, these images of mimesis suggest two unbridgeable problems in the attempt to craft a new self for public consumption. There is, first of all, a temporal problem, in that texts and images are crafted and then remain,

15. For a broader argument about subjectivity in the medieval period, see David Aers, "A Whisper in the Ear of Early Modernists; or, Reflections on Literary Critics Writing the History of the Subject," in Culture and History, 1350–1600: Essays on English Communities, Identities and Writings, ed. D. Aers (New York: Harvester Wheatsheaf, 1992), 177–202.

16. Although I disagree with David Boyd as to the ultimate balance between fragmentation and control in this text, these metaphors of self-formation are consistent with his Althusserian reading of this text as a narrative about the interpellation of the transgressive subject into "the complex discursive web" of social order. David Lorenzo Boyd, "Reading Through the Regiment of Princes: Hoccleve's Series and Lydgate's Dance of Death in Yale MS 493," Fifteenth Century Studies 20 (1993): 15–34.

17. See also Albrecht Classen on the importance of self-reflexive images of the artist in Hoccleve's version of autobiography. Classen, "The Autobiographical Voice of Thomas Hoccleve," Archiv für das Studium der neueren Sprachen und Literaturen 228 (1991): 299–310.

but the subject exists in time. This problem, which we encountered earlier in Hoccleve's fragmented portrayal of Oldcastle, is here present as the philosophical point of the mirror scene's comedic pratfalls. Hoccleve doesn't gaze earnestly into the mirror like a Keatsian gallant; he hops, trying to achieve the benefit of surprise and a moment of sudden self-clarity.[18] In part, the point is that although he may counterfeit a face of sanity, he cannot keep track of it. In unguarded moments, he fears, his face may react to overheard slanders in some way that others would read as madness. But even when completely alone, there can be no guarantee that the face he "amends" will remain. Thus he needs to make, as he says, *many* a jump to his mirror, to keep checking for any stray signs of madness.[19] Moving even beyond this temporal difficulty, there is also a basic epistemological problem in Hoccleve's attempt to fabricate an acceptable self: "Men in hire owne cas/been blynde alday" ("Complaint," line 170).[20] Even as he looks at his face in the mirror, Hoccleve doubts his ability to distinguish madness from sanity. After all, if he were mad he might look into the mirror, see his own mad face, and think it reflected only the most serene reason. In other words, the temporal and epistemological problems here undermine the hopes that the self might be treated like the material of the craftsman or artist, some substance to mold and form into a shape adequate to allay the suspicions of those who speak against him.

The fragmentation of the subject is further reinforced by a generic complication very similar to Hoccleve's play with the category of the complaint in the *Regement*. In the *Regement*, the depiction of his troubles was broken into two alternating sources, a doubling of causes that served to create an inconsolable complaint. In the *Series*, his account at times focuses on the malady sent by God, at other times on the mundane consequences of that malady, and at times it conflates the two. Although it is tempting to sort out the relation between these two maladies through a simple chronological distinction—that Hoccleve's heaven-sent madness causes and predates his

18. It is also worth noting that his term *saut* comes from the lexicon of the hunt, and so both furthers his applications of animal metaphors to himself and reiterates the fragmentation of the subject, now making him both the hunter and the prey.

19. See George MacLennan, *Lucid Intervals: Subjective Writing and Madness in history* (Rutherford: Fairleigh Dickinson University Press, 1992), 19–23, for an alternative reading of this mirror scene, one insisting that "this is not an act of introspection."

20. A. C. Spearing also calls attention to this difficulty. Spearing, "The Poetic Subject from Chaucer to Spenser," in *Subjects on the World's Stage: Essays on British Literature of the Middle Ages and the Renaissance*, ed. David C. Allen and Robert A. White (Newark: University of Delaware Press, 1995), 23.

social isolation—this will, in fact, not do. Although the two are linked during the interlude of Hoccleve's madness, the resolution of this complaint deals only with the divinely ordained portion of the lament, not the earthly repercussions. This final separation is made quite clear in the penitential benediction with which Hoccleve concludes his "Complaint":

> He yaf me wit / and he took it away
> Whan þat he sy / þat I it mis despente,
> And yaf ageyn / whan it was to his pay.
> He grauntid me / my giltes to repente
> And hens forward / to sette myn entente
> Vnto his deitee / to do plesance
> And tamende / my synful gouernance.
>
> Laude and honour / and thank vnto thee be,
> Lord God / þat salue art / to al heuynesse:
> Thank of my welthe / and myn aduersitee,
> Thank of myn elde / and of my seeknesse;
> And thank be / to thyn infynyt goodnesse
> For thy yiftes / and benefices alle;
> And vnto thy mercy / and grace I calle.
>
> (lines 400–413)

Hoccleve likens God to a good doctor who has cured him, but significantly the praise for the cure can speak only of God's transformative agency inside Hoccleve. This cure has removed only the "wylde infirmitee"; the social consequences of that madness are left a silent and problematic remainder.

This partial cure is particularly poignant because it allows us to forget for a moment that Hoccleve's melancholy is not simply an epiphenomenon produced by the spell of madness. These two infirmities should be distinguished not as cause and effect but as two parallel sicknesses with divergent literary genealogies and respectively different characteristics. The "wylde infirmitee" is a refugee from the ecclesiastical traditions of penitence and consolation. It descends on Hoccleve as an instant and discrete calamity and then is just as suddenly cured. Its cause is unsure and irrelevant because the lesson of Boethian resignation stems precisely from the arbitrary nature of the misfortune.[21] The "thoghtful maladie" ("Complaint," line 21), in con-

---

21. Penelope Doob argues that madness in this poem is understood to be a conventional presentation of divine retribution visited upon sinners, in the pattern of the punishment of King Nebuchadnezzar. However, even if we accept the possibility that the madness is to be taken as a

trast, is derived in part from the allegorical anatomies of the human psyche drawn in the courtly poetry of *fin amor* and, in part, from Galenic humoral doctrines concerning the melancholic temperament.[22] As a characterological description, Thought is no calamity but an enduring part of Thomas. It predates the specific blows of madness and social isolation, as Hoccleve so nicely indicates by his use of the near-paradox "freshly reminded" in the prologue to the "Complaint." As Thought has no precise origin and is not susceptible to cure, its presence renders the strict logic of penitential discourse untenable. As to its cause, it is wholly overdetermined, being an innate predilection that may be activated by fears of poverty, erotic shortcomings, the onset of madness, or any of a number of other elements throughout Hoccleve's works. And, most important, although the causes of Thought are multiple they are all understood to be social misfortunes. Thought exists in the "Complaint" as a double to the "wylde infirmitee," a malady always represented in relation to the social causes and consequences that penitential discourse erases from madness proper. The presence of this doppelgänger is perhaps the real reason for the insufficiency of the "Complaint's" penitential resolution. God might heal the madness and Hoccleve's fellows might even return, but the deepest wound, Thought, was there first and will outlast the rest.

Like the *Regement*, Hoccleve's "Complaint" is structured by movement through urban space, by another journey, not recursive as in the *Regement* but linear—the movement from the public to the private chamber and then deeper into the individual subject. In depicting this flight from the crowd, however, Hoccleve emphasizes both the permeability of apparently private space and the fragmentation of identity that is the result of such flight. At times, Hoccleve projects a tone of weary tragedy in his depiction of this fragmentation, as in the agonizing introversion of lines such as

> This troubly lyf/hath al to longe endurid;
> Nat haue I wist/how in my skyn to tourne.
> But now myself/to myself have ensurid
> ("Complaint," lines 302–4)

---

punishment for sin, as Doob would have it, the stroke is still arbitrary as not every sinner is so punished. Doob, *Nebuchadnezzar's Children: Conventions of Madness in Middle English Literature* (New Haven: Yale University Press, 1974).

22. For background on Galenic theories of cause and treatment of melancholy, see the pair of articles by Stanley W. Jackson: "Galen—On Mental Disorders," *Journal of the History of the Behavioral Sciences* 5 (1969): 365–84; and "Unusual Mental States in Medieval Europe. I. Medical Symptoms of Mental Disorder: 400–1100 A.D.," *Journal of the History of Medicine* 27 (1972): 262–97; and his book *Melancholia and Depression: From Hippocratic Times to Modern Times* (New Haven: Yale University Press, 1986).

in which Hoccleve twists, grotesquely, in his own skin, looking for some point of vantage. At other times, however, Hoccleve alludes to his troubles with a very different tone:

> But algate how so be / my contenance,
> Debat is now noon / twixt me and my wit,
> Althogh þat ther were / a disseuerance
> As for a tyme / betwixt me and it.
> ("Complaint," lines 246–49)

In this second passage, Hoccleve wryly suggests that he and his wit don't argue as much as they used to. There is none of the pathos his Boethian language evokes elsewhere. What we see is rather a broad self-mockery in which Hoccleve pokes fun at his own sometimes melodramatic lamentations. It is toward this second Hoccleve that we will turn in considering his "Dialogue With a Friend." As this poem proceeds, the ironized portion of the portrait becomes more and more dominant, and as Hoccleve begins to suggest that his isolation stemmed as much from pique as ostracization we begin also to see an increasing emphasis on the thematics of community, friendship, and collaboration.

Friendship and Collaboration
"Communynge" in the *Series*

The opening two sections of the *Series* are poems of solitary complaint punctuated by "visits." God came to visit Hoccleve; his wits then took a trip of their own, as his memory went away to play until God called it back, or as Hoccleve puts it in a later description, "my wit were hoom come ageyn" ("Complaint," line 64). The transition between complaint and dialogue is then marked by another visit, as the arrival of Hoccleve's unnamed Friend breaks the peace of the high-toned stoic resignation with which the "Complaint" had concluded:

> And, endid my conpleynte / in this maneere,
> Oon knokkid / at my chambre dore sore
> And cryde alowde / 'How, Hoccleue, art thow heere?
> Opne thy dore / Me thynkith ful yore

Syn I thee sy/What, man, for Goddes ore
Come out/for this quarter/I nat thee sy
By aght I woot'/and out to him cam I.

This man was my good freend/of fern agoon
þat I speek of/and thus he to me seide:
'Thomas/as thow me louest/telle anoon,
What didest thow/whan I knokkid and leide
So faste vpon thy dore?'

("Dialogue," lines 1–12)

Hoccleve had closed the frame of the "Complaint" with the highly wrought benediction cited above (page 172), stanzas constructed with great pomp through the anaphoric repetition of thanks and the careful balancing of metaphors of procession and return. The "Dialogue," however, opens into an entirely different discursive universe, one that appears suddenly colloquial and dialogic. Indeed, as the abrupt stylistic transition from the high rhetoric of theological resignation to this raucous banter should make clear, the "Dialogue" serves retroactively to question the adequacy of the previous pose.[23] We are meant to imagine that just as Hoccleve has been penning his high toned lines of stoic resignation and tragic solitude, one of these late lamented friends has actually been pounding away on the door, trying to get his attention. The sudden enlargement of the dramatic focus suggests that the solitary voice of complaint and the genre of consolation it serves to enact can be made coherent only at the cost of a willful suppression of the larger social context. It is a typically Hocclevian moment, very much like the initial interaction between Hoccleve and the Old Man in the *Regement of Princes* when Hoccleve, who has just spent an anxious and sleepless night, wanders out, has to be hailed twice and shaken physically before he will even respond, and then only with the sigh "A, who is there?" (*Regement*, line 134).

This shift from monologue into dialogue creates a crucial transformation on numerous levels. Not only does this interruption and break into dialogue disrupt the genre of consolation, it also serves, as John Burrow has pointed out, to mark all that has preceded as text (a movement opposite to that which we observed in the *Regement* in which dialogue preceded the textual object).[24] Furthermore, this visit also undercuts the previous representation of Hoc-

23. See also Simpson's discussion of this passage in "Madness and Texts," 19–20.
24. Burrow, "Hoccleve's *Series*," 262–63.

cleve's chamber as a private place, isolated from the gaze of the press. As the Friend and his language enter the poem, the "Dialogue" underlines instead the permeability of this space in the urban fabric, and this permeability provides the foundation for both a new representation of madness and a new relation to textual production. In the "Dialogue," Hoccleve continues his discussion of madness, but his malady comes to seem less a matter of penitential drama than of grousing between colleagues. Similarly, in the place of the solitary voice of complaint the "Dialogue" begins to establish a new vision of poetic production founded on the textual routines of the Privy Seal.

Hoccleve's "Complaint" and "Dialogue" are usually read as having achieved some resolution in their movement away from madness and towards integration of the self, both internally and in its relation to society. Hoccleve himself insists that there is an absolute distinction between his former self and his present self, a distinction that underwrites his own claims to sanity. The most significant fact about the dialogue between Hoccleve and the Friend, however, is the extent to which the formal transformation of textual complaint into verbal dialogue fails to make the problems of the earlier "Complaint" any less insoluble.[25] The Thomas character has been longing for a friend to counter the accusations of the anonymous mass he calls the "prees," but when this Friend arrives he and Thomas remain locked in the same exchange of diagnoses and rebuttals which had structured the "Complaint." Indeed, given the centrality of their debate, any reading of the "Dialogue" is determined to a large extent by a tacit choice to vest authority in either Thomas or the Friend. Since it is usually Thomas who gets the benefit of the doubt in these passages, I will be listening a bit more closely to the Friend.

The Friend presents two chief arguments that Hoccleve is not safely recovered, one made very explicitly and one implied by a rigorously controlled conversational dynamic. Hoccleve and the Friend debate, heatedly and at length, whether or not Hoccleve's writing would convince people of his sanity or remind them of his past madness, and, moreover, whether writing itself was the cause of his madness. The Friend begins the exchange by advising Hoccleve to put this "Complaint" away at once, worrying that the poem written to explain and publicize the return of Hoccleve's sanity would actually be a dangerous document to release. Once reassured by Hoccleve that

25. Matthew Boyd Goldie is one of the few to emphasize these continuities and temporal confusions in the poem. See his "Psychosomatic Illness and Identity in London, 1416–1421: Hoccleve's *Complaint* and *Dialogue with a Friend*," *Exemplaria* 11 (1999): 23–52.

the "Complaint" is not yet in circulation, the Friend goes on to argue that not only should the "Complaint" be kept safely at home but that Hoccleve should set aside any ideas of writing further.

> 'Syn þat seeknesse God hath thee byreft,
> The cause eschue/for it is good left;
> Namely thyng of thoghtful studie kaght
> Perillous is/as þat hath me been taght.

> 'Right as a theef þat hath eschapid ones
> The roop/no dreede hath eft his art to vse
> Til þat the trees him weye vp, body and bones,
> So looth is him/his sory craft refuse,
> S[o] farest thow/ioie hastow for to muse
> Vpon thy book/and there in stare & poure
> Til þat it thy wit/consume and deuoure.
> ("Dialogue," lines 396–406)

The Friend speaks here as one who has taken to heart lessons from Hoccleve's own *Regement of Princes*. The dangers of writing depicted there are now extended to the reading and study that are assumed to be preliminary to the intertextual projects of translation and synthesis that make up Hoccleve's public verse. In a figure reminiscent of the controversies so often stirred by translation, the Friend suggests that to be such a writer is to be a thief, lucky to have gotten away with it once and foolish to try again. Moreover, to be in such a business means contact with those most dangerous objects, books, and the danger that too much time stooping and staring over them will cause one to lose one's wits. In other words, as the Friend goes on to emphasize, writing requires "studie" ("The smert of studie/oghte be mirour/To thee/let yit thy studie be forborn" lines 409–10), and with the hard labor of study comes the risk of overexertion and madness.

Hoccleve contradicts this assertion, and he does so in a way that is usually taken to be the last word in this argument, giving the Friend's prior objections no more force than as a rhetorical opportunity for Hoccleve to yet again assert his recovery.[26] He tells the Friend

> Trustith right wel/þat neuere studie in book
> Was cause/why my mynde me forsook

---

26. See, for instance, Simpson, "Madness and Texts," 23.

But i[t] was causid of my long seeknesse,
And othir wyse nat/in soothfastnesse.
("Dialogue," lines 424–27)

This logic is secure in itself. As he has maintained throughout, Hoccleve
asserts that his sickness was an arbitrary visitation, not itself the result of
either sin or hard work. Nevertheless, a mere seven lines later, Hoccleve's
own language begins to reflect just the vision of study the Friend had warned
him of, as he begins to describe the project he has in mind through the
repeated invocations of "labour" ("the labour is in veyn"; "Shal no stirynge
or excitacioun/Lette me of this labour"; "I thoghte in this laboure me/And
al to preeue my self" lines 436, 437–38, 443). As it was labor that had
worried the Friend in the first place, Hoccleve's assertions that he looks
forward to getting back to work are hardly reassuring. Nevertheless, the
Friend willingly gives his assent to Hoccleve's new project when Hoccleve
promises moderation.

By stirtes/whan þat a fressh lust me takith,
Wole I me bisye now and now a lyte,
But what þat my lust dullith and asslakith,
I stynte wole/and no lenger wryte;
("Dialogue," lines 505–8)

On its surface, then, this debate between Hoccleve and the Friend seems to
result in a healthy compromise, an illustration of the ability of dialogue to
produce concord, one in which the Friend is willing to accept Hoccleve's
narrative of previous sickness and present stability.

Beneath this explicit disagreement about the virtues and dangers of writ-
ing, however, there is another sort of conflict dramatized between Hoccleve
and the Friend. Hoccleve and his Friend argue, in the way of such conflicts
between intimates, not only about writing, but also about the way Hoccleve
responds to his Friend's suggestions. The Friend begins his address to Hoc-
cleve very gingerly, asking Hoccleve not to be angry with what he has to say
("Thomas/soffre me speke/and be nat wrooth" line 20). Hoccleve's subse-
quent responses to his Friend suggest that, despite the Friend's preemptive
soothing tone, Hoccleve does indeed become "wrooth." He is given to verbal
repetition in small outbursts (" 'A, nay,' quod I, 'nay, nay!' " line 35); he
accuses his Friend at several moments of paying no attention ("If e toke
hede . . ." line 43; "Right now, whan I yow redde my conpleynte,/Made it

nat mynde . . . ?" lines 317–18); and he interrupts their discussion to treat the Friend to a lengthy disquisition on the nature of real friendship, suggesting that his Friend's behavior could be improved by a little more attention to Cicero (lines 323–64). The Friend, for his part, adopts a consistently conciliatory tone ("Yis, Thomas, yis/thow hast a good entente" line 295); and he continues to urge Hoccleve not to be angry ("Yit Thomas, herkne a word and be souffrable" line 369). The debate between the Friend and Hoccleve thus has a distinctly testy feel to it, as the Friend tries to keep the peace with a Hoccleve who refuses to be "souffrable."

This testiness leads to two important consequences in our understanding of the "Dialogue." First, it is a sign that despite the Friend's apparent acquiescence we are not meant to take Hoccleve's malady as something yet done away with. Earlier discussions in the "Complaint" of triggers for the recurrence of madness had centered on an association between the summer heat as a malign influence and the "hete" of temper. Those who did not believe in Hoccleve's recovery had said that his illness would return "Whan passynge hete is" (line 92), and Hoccleve had troped from this "hete" to a physiological description of alternation between "frosty cold" and "fyry hoot" (line 154), and from there to an assertion that he remained silent for fear that his anger would surface and seem not justified annoyance but irrational madness.

> Syn I recouered was/haue I ful ofte
> Cause had of anger/and inpacience,
> Where I born haue it/esily and softe,
> Suffryng wrong be doon/to me and offense
> And nat answerd ageyn/but kept silence,
> Lest þat men of me/deeme wolde and seyn
> "See how this man/is fallen in ageyn."
>
> ("Complaint," lines 176–82)

In the context of this metaphoric pattern, Hoccleve's testiness in the "Dialogue" serves to remind us of the warnings that it is in the "hete" of anger that his malady might return.

Moreover, and perhaps even more significantly, this careful attention to tone suggests that friendship itself is one of the subjects at issue in the *Series*.[27] His isolation in the press depicted by his "Complaint" is represented

---

27. The importance of friendship is also underlined by the references to philosophical authorities on friendship. On his use of Cicero, see Burrow, *Hoccleve's Dialogue and Complaint*, 97, n. D344. For an illuminating study of philosophical friendship, especially in its links to literary collaboration,

as a result of broken friendships, and his attempts at reconciliation in the
next poem of the *Series* is mediated entirely by the presence of the generi-
cally named, almost allegorically eponymous, Friend. Furthermore, this
friendship is specifically one of urban space and one of the Privy Seal. In
earlier poems such as "La Male Regle," Hoccleve makes teasing references to
the habits and vices of his colleagues, making them integral parts of his
representation of social space. In the "Dialogue with a Friend" this camara-
derie takes on a new role and begins to shape Hoccleve's depiction of the
process of poetic composition itself, presenting an extraordinary vision of
poetic composition as a product of bureaucratic and urban collaboration.

The "Dialogue" presents a dramatized vision of friendship as *communynge*
(line 470), a loaded term in this poem. Earlier, in his "Complaint," Hoccleve
had complained bitterly about those who thought that they could weigh the
state of his mind by sight alone, suggesting in contrast that "By comunynge /
is the best assay" (line 217). At the simplest level, his point had been that
one had to speak to a person to find out their thoughts and the state of their
mind. In addition, however, this term also functions to connect the contrast
between hostile observation and sympathetic dialogue evoked in the "Com-
plaint" to the larger contrast in Hoccleve's work between the silent solitude
of the writer and the singing and conversation of other laborers (*Regement*,
lines 1009–15). Much of the tragedy of his madness lies in the anxious si-
lence it precipitates, and Hoccleve attaches some of the same tragic aura to
the silence and solitude of writing. To attach a final gloss to the crucial shift
from monologue to dialogue in both the *Series* and the *Regement*, we might
also take this moment as a central emblem for the search for the elusive
compound of values Hoccleve indicates under the term *communynge*. In the
Series, Hoccleve attempts something quite extraordinary in relation to this
value: by refocusing his poem on the relation with this Friend, he depicts an
ideal extension of *communynge* into even that most solitary of activities—
literary composition.

As I remarked earlier, the *Series* is shaped by a very peculiar structure, one
in which a framing fiction is introduced but never brought to conclusion and
in which fictions seem to proliferate more like an unbounded anthology than
an organized, sequential set of poems.[28] The most plausible background that

---

see Lisa Jardine, *Erasmus, Man of Letters: The Construction of Charisma in Print* (Princeton: Princeton
University Press, 1993).

28. On the anthology in this period, see Julia Boffey and John J. Thompson, "Anthologies and
Miscellanies: Production and Choice of Texts," in *Book Production and Publishing in Britain, 1375–
1475*, ed. Jeremy Griffiths and Derek Pearsall (Cambridge: Cambridge University Press, 1989), 279–
315.

has yet been suggested for Hoccleve's structure here is that of the French *dits* such as Machaut's *Voir Dit*. Hoccleve is undoubtedly an author who drew directly on French models, and the organization of this series of poems through the representation of an authorial subject shows a clear debt to the *dits*.[29] In addition to this model, however, there is another model of composition provided internally by the conversations between Hoccleve and the Friend that are interspersed throughout the *Series*.

Hoccleve's Friend meddles continually with the composition of the *Series*. When the Friend finally accepts Hoccleve's proposal that he should return to writing, he first rejects several of Hoccleve's ideas for possible poems, and then insists that Hoccleve should make amends for the putative anti-feminism of the *Letter to Cupid* by translating a tale in praise of women's virtue. Hoccleve agrees and produces the "Tale of Jereslaus's Wife," but the Friend, upon reading, is still not happy. He announces that the text is missing the closing moralization and provides Hoccleve with his own copy for transcription. Hoccleve then is able to add the piece he had originally wanted, "How to Learn to Die," but before he is able to end his project the Friend appears again, declaring himself nervous about his wild son and urging Hoccleve to translate a tale warning young men about evil women. Hoccleve comments, again somewhat testily, that this seems to contradict the Friend's earlier insistence that Hoccleve needs to seem more favorable to women in his verse, but the Friend persists, even providing a copy of the original tale from which to translate. The interspersed conversations between Hoccleve and the Friend thus represent Hoccleve's poetic activity in the *Series* as less a matter of raw creation or even compilation by one man than as a product of dialogue and negotiation.

I would suggest that this vision of collaborative labor and textual compilation is in fact a projection of the labor in the Privy Seal into the world of poetic composition. Work in the Privy Seal was marked by a particular way of handling documents, a procedural habitus that was central in the formation of both bureaucratic identity and also the particular form of collaborative compilation we see described in the *Series*.[30] Since clerks in the central

---

29. On Hoccleve's relation to the *dits*, see John Burrow, "Hoccleve and the Middle French Poets," in *The Long Fifteenth Century: Essays for Douglas Gray*, ed. Helen Cooper and Sally Mapstone (Oxford: Clarendon Press, 1997), 35–49; see also Sylvia Huot, *From Song to Book: The Poetics of Writing in Old French Lyric and Lyrical Narrative Poetry* (Ithaca: Cornell University Press, 1987).

30. See Chapter 1. For another consideration of the impact of Privy Seal culture and its "dangerous skill" see Sarah Tolmie's fine and insightful essay, "The *Prive Scilence* of Thomas Hoccleve," *Studies in the Age of Chaucer* 22 (2000): 281–309.

writing offices were paid, in part, on a piecework basis, a system was developed to produce a maximum flow of paper and hence a maximum number of commissions. As discussed in Chapter 1, warrants were frequently required to be replicated on each occasion that they passed from an originating department through an intermediary to a final destination. A grant from the king might not reach the Exchequer until it had passed through various hands and been partially reduplicated as both a signet letter and a letter under the great seal. This system was entirely inefficient and would seem corrupt to modern eyes, but it had the great advantage of producing commissions as a byproduct of each stage of transmission.

This system also created a distinct textual universe. In these bureaucratic offices, no document was an original composition. The process of invention started out only after the consultation of forms and precedents of the sort Hoccleve himself had provided in such abundance in the *Formulary*. Similarly, few documents were taken to be complete in themselves. Each document existed as a collage or palimpsest of all the writs and letters that had preceded it in interdepartmental correspondence, an assemblage in which any one element was only a fragment in itself.[31] And, last, these documents could not be thought of as the products of single authorial figures. A letter might be issued from the chancellor's scribes, then sent to the Privy Seal for confirmation, then passed on, with an affirmatory note attached, to go to the Exchequer. Here a clean copy might be made for the record, but it would incorporate both the original note and the commentary, as well as any addenda deemed necessary by the clerks in the Exchequer.[32]

The extension of such models of composition from the world of bureaucracy into verse would have been facilitated by their close family relations to more classical and prestigious forms of textuality. Given the clerkly background of these scribal communities, this bureaucratic collage must have seemed a subtle (though unignorable) revision of the model of text and gloss that had been a primary form of understanding for so many earlier clerks. In addition, the *dictamenal* theories that provided a contemporary understand-

---

31. The relevance of this whole/fragment distinction may be confirmed by parallel procedures concerning notarial instruments, in which the document was not considered complete until it had received the notary's authenticating clause. Cheney, *Notaries Public*, 106.

32. Similarly, in the world of petitions, a bill might be created simply by adding an endorsement to a petition and then forwarding it under the privy seal. Tout, *Chapters*, 5:113.

This model of composition as a collage is also reminiscent of the production of poetic manuscripts through the coordination of the separate efforts of numerous scribes, a process that Hoccleve himself briefly supervised in the production of the Trinity manuscript of Gower's *Confessio Amantis*. Doyle and Parkes, "Production of Copies," 166–67.

ing of epistolary form would have supported the sense of the fragmentary and anonymous nature of these texts. From the earliest classical commentaries letters had been viewed as a form particularly related to friendship, with the result that, unlike other texts, the letter was perceived as one half of a dialogue, creating an allusion Giles Constable has referred to as "a quasi-presence and quasi-speech," verging on an ideal of collaborative composition: "A letter was a gift to the recipient, who was considered to own the text. This fact had important implications . . . not only for the character of epistolary collections, into which a letter might be inserted, but also for the text of a letter, which might be revised by the recipient."[33] These classical precedents and procedural habits give us a window onto a vision of textual composition radically different from the world of individual lyric utterance and *fin amor* with which medieval poetry is usually associated. Here the text is not the product of solitary labor, but of communal assemblage as a collaborate form.

Hoccleve's *Series* represents itself as a product of this world of London bureaucracy, created through the collation of texts, and produced in close consultation with a circle of literate colleagues. Hoccleve's Friend himself seems to have arrived straight from the writing offices, expert in the composition and arrangement of texts, owning or having easy access to manuscripts of classical Latin culture and familiar with the procedures for assembling a commission for a patron like Humphrey of Gloucester. And these two colleagues put together Hoccleve's *Series* through a process very like that which would have been used in producing correspondence sent out under the Privy Seal. When the Friend checks Hoccleve's work, it is not for delicacy but accuracy: My tale anoon y fette/and he it nam/In-to his hand/and it al ouersy" ("Moral to Jereslaus's Wife," lines 5–6). And when he finds an error, like any good colleague, he supplies an exemplar with the appropriate addition. The *Series* thus presents a portrait of the friend as a good copyeditor, and of poetry as an art of bureaucratic collaboration.

33. Giles Constable, *Letters and Letter-Collections* (Turnhout: Brepols, 1976), 13 and 16. As Constable elaborates further, "Enough has been said about the way in which a letter was written to show that serious questions can be raised about the authorship. If only the outline of a letter was dictated, sometimes in the vernacular, to a scribe or secretary who wrote the letter in his own words and script, or even more if a colleague or secretary wrote a letter entirely in the name of someone else, who can properly be called the author?"

In Paris, nearly all bureaus resemble each other. In whatever ministry you go to, to ask some slight favor or to obtain redress for a trifling wrong, you will find dark corridors, poorly lighted stairways, doors with oval panes of glass like eyes, just like at the theater, through which you will see fantasies worthy of Callot, and on which you find incomprehensible signs.

Afterword

So appeared the bureaucratic offices, and their inhabitants, to Balzac's penetrating eye in 1838.[1] Balzac describes bureaucracy here as a close cousin to the theater. It is a space entered for trifles, a space opposed to the well-lit realm of nature and the external world. It, like Hoccleve's chamber, is a permeable interior, entered here through the dark corridor and through the refractions of self-conscious artifice—doors pierced by oval panes that appear as unpromising doubles to the supplicant's eyes. And if one were to peer through these ovals, the images within have nothing to do with the clarity and precision usually associated with the ideals of bureaucracy but are instead fantastic grotesques of the sort inhabiting the engravings of Callot. In the sum of its theatricality, bureaucracy here is as distant as one might imagine from the force of rationalization that Weber thought it to be. It is the demimonde, a semi-autonomous cultural space marked by artifice and the diffusion of state power into forms incomprehensible to the outsider.

My hope is that this book will have suggested some of the ways in which Hoccleve's

1. Honoré de Balzac, *The Bureaucrats*, ed. Marco Diani, trans. Charles Foulkes (Evanston: Northwestern University Press, 1993), 73. Callot is the engraver Jacques Callot (1592–1635), well known for his treatments of the "miseries of war."

work is refracted through a demimonde not unlike that of these bureaus. Though Hoccleve may not have poetic progeny in the sense that Lydgate had his followers, we would do well to view him as an early chapter in the genealogy of bureaucratic culture. And by a bureaucratic culture we should think not only of the tedium so often associated with that word but also of the hopes for community, the wry self-reflection, and the political dexterity Hoccleve's work demonstrates from beginning to end. It may seem paradoxical that a poet so self-absorbed as Hoccleve would stand as an example of this art, with its hopes for "communyng." But perhaps this paradox should be taken as a sign that this literature, rising from the press of functionaries and the hum of the writing offices, is always tied to its opposite, the confident and self-aggrandizing visions of courtly literature. Courtly art and bureaucratic art are tied to each other as statement and counterstatement. But where the courtly tradition has its history confirmed and reinforced by the canons of literary genealogy, bureaucratic art always risks appearing as the production of scattered and marginal eccentrics. As I hope I have shown, at least in Hoccleve's case, we must hear this voice (and others, perhaps, such as Skelton, Pepys, and even Kafka) not as the sound of personal alienation but as a voice shaped by a shared culture, speaking the "incomprehensible signs" of a bureaucratic muse.

Bibliography

Aers, David. "A Whisper in the Ear of Early Modernists; or, Reflections on Literary Crit-
ics Writing the History of the Subject." In *Culture and History, 1350–1600: Essays
on English Communities, Identities, and Writings*, ed. David Aers, 177–202. New York:
Harvester Wheatsheaf, 1992.
Aers, David, and Lynn Staley. *The Powers of the Holy: Religion, Politics, and Gender in Late
Medieval English Culture*. University Park: Penn State University Press, 1996.
Alexander, J. J. G. "Painting and Manuscript Illumination for Royal Patrons in the Later
Middle Ages." In *English Court Culture in the Later Middle Ages*, ed. V. J. Scattergood
and J. W. Sherborne, 141–62. London: Gerald Duckworth, 1983.
Alban, J. R., and C. T. Allmand. "Spies and Spying in the Fourteenth Century." In *War,
Literature, and Politics in the Late Middle Ages: Essays in Honor of G. W. Coopland*, ed.
C. T. Allmand, 73–101. Liverpool: Liverpool University Press, 1976.
Allmand, Christopher. *Henry V*. English Monarchs Series. Berkeley and Los Angeles:
University of California Press, 1992.
Altman, Barbara K. *The Love Debate Poems of Christine de Pizan*. Gainesville: University
of Florida Press, 1998.
Ambrisco, Alan S., and Paul Strohm. "Succession and Sovereignty in Lydgate's Prologue
to *The Troy Book*." *Chaucer Review* 30 (1995): 40–57.
Aston, Margaret. "Lollards and Images." In *Lollards and Reformers: Images and Literacy in
Late Medieval Religion*, 135–92. London: Hambledon Press, 1984. Revised and ex-
panded in *England's Iconoclasts I: Laws Against Images*, 96–159. Oxford: Clarendon
Press, 1988.
———. "Lollardy and Sedition, 1381–1431." *Past and Present* 17 (1960): 1–44. Reprinted
in *Lollards and Reformers: Images and Literacy in Late Medieval Religion*, 1–47. London:
Hambledon Press, 1984.
———. "Wyclif and the Vernacular." In *From Ockham to Wyclif*, ed. Anne Hudson and
Michael Wilks, 281–330. Oxford: Basil Blackwell, 1987.
Badel, Pierre Yves. *Le Roman de la Rose au XIVe siècle*. Geneva: Librairie Droz, 1980.
Baird, Joseph L. "Pierre Col and the Querelle de la Rose." *Philological Quarterly* 60 (1981):
273–86.
Baird, Joseph L., and John R. Kane, eds. *La Querelle de la Rose: Letters and Documents*.
UNC Studies in the Romance Languages and Literatures, no. 199. Chapel Hill:
University of North Carolina, 1978.
Balzac, Honoré de. *The Bureaucrats*. Edited and with an introduction by Marco Diani.
Translated by Charles Foulkes. Evanston, Ill.: Northwestern University Press, 1993.

Barr, Helen. *Signes and Sothe: Language in the "Piers Plowman" Tradition.* Piers Plowman Studies, vol. 10. Cambridge: D. S. Brewer, 1994.

Batt, Catherine. "Hoccleve and . . . Feminism? Negotiating Meaning in *The Regiment of Princes.*" In *Essays on Thomas Hoccleve*, ed. C. Batt, 55–84. Westfield Publications in Medieval Studies. London: Centre for Medieval and Renaissance Studies, Queen Mary and Westfield College, University of London, 1996.

———. Introduction to *Essays on Thomas Hoccleve.* Westfield Publications in Medieval Studies. London: Centre for Medieval and Renaissance Studies, Queen Mary and Westfield College, University of London, 1996.

———. "Recreation, the Exemplary and the Body in Caxton's *Game and Playe of the Chesse.*" *Ludica* 2 (1996): 27–44.

Bayless, Martha. *Parody in the Middle Ages: The Latin Tradition.* Ann Arbor: University of Michigan Press, 1996.

Beatty, Nancy. *The Craft of Dying: A Study in the Literary Tradition of the Ars moriendi in England.* New Haven: Yale University Press, 1970.

Beckwith, Sarah. *Christ's Body: Identity, Culture, and Society in Late Medieval Writings.* London: Routledge, 1993.

———. "Problems of Authority in Late Medieval English Mysticism: Language, Agency, and Authority in *The Book of Margery Kempe.*" *Exemplaria* 4 (1992): 171–99.

Bennett, H. S. *Chaucer and the Fifteenth Century.* 1947. New York: Oxford University Press, 1954.

———. *Six Medieval Men and Women.* Cambridge: Cambridge University Press, 1955.

Bentley, Elna-Jean Young. "The Formulary of Thomas Hoccleve." Ph.D. diss., Emory University, 1965.

Bieler, Ludovicus, ed. *Boethii Philosophiae Consolatio.* Corpus Christianorum, vol. 94. Turnhaut: Brepols, 1957.

Blamires, Alcuin. *The Case for Women in Medieval Culture.* Oxford: Oxford University Press, 1997.

———. "The Wife of Bath and Lollardy." *Medium Aevum* 58 (1989): 224–42.

Bloch, R. Howard. *Etymologies and Genealogies.* Chicago: University of Chicago Press, 1983.

Blyth, Charles. "Editing the *Regiment of Princes.*" In *Essays on Thomas Hoccleve*, ed. C. Batt, 11–28. Westfield Publications in Medieval Studies. London: Centre for Medieval and Renaissance Studies, Queen Mary and Westfield College, University of London, 1996.

———, ed. *Thomas Hoccleve: The Regiment of Princes.* Kalamazoo, Michigan: Published for TEAMS by Medieval Institute Publications, Western Michigan University, 1999.

———. "Thomas Hoccleve's Other Master." *Mediaevalia* 16 (1993): 349–59.

Boethius. *The Consolation of Philosophy.* Translated by Richard Green. New York: Macmillan, 1962.

Boffey, Julia. "Chaucerian Prisoners: The Context of *The Kingis Quair.*" In *Chaucer and Fifteenth-Century Poetry*, 84–102, ed. Julia Boffey and Janet Cowen. London: Centre for Late Antique and Medieval Studies, Kings College, 1991.

Boffey, Julia, and John J. Thompson. "Anthologies and Miscellanies: Production and Choice of Texts." In *Book Production and Publishing in Britain, 1375–1475*, ed. Jeremy

Bibliography

Griffiths and Derek Pearsall, 279–315. Cambridge: Cambridge University Press, 1989.

Bornstein, Diane. "Anti-Feminism in Thomas Hoccleve's Translation of Christine de Pizan's *Epistre au dieu d'amours*." *English Language Notes* 19 (1981): 7–14.

Bowers, John M. "Hoccleve's Huntington Holographs: The First 'Collected Poems' in English." *Fifteenth-Century Studies* 15 (1989): 27–51.

———. "Hoccleve's Two Copies of 'Lerne to Dye': Implications for Textual Critics." *Papers of the Bibliographical Society of America* 83 (1989): 437–72.

———. "The House of Chaucer & Son: The Business of Lancastrian Canon-Formation." *Medieval Perspectives* 6 (1991): 135–43.

———, ed. *The Canterbury Tales: Fifteenth-Century Continuations and Additions*. Kalamazoo, Michigan: Published for TEAMS by Medieval Institute Publications, Western Michigan University, 1992.

Boyd, Beverly. *The Middle English Miracles of the Virgin*. San Marino: Huntington Library, 1964.

Boyd, David Lorenzo. "Reading Through the *Regiment of Princes*: Hoccleve's *Series* and Lydgate's *Dance of Death* in Yale MS 493." *Fifteenth-Century Studies* 20 (1993): 15–34.

Bragg, Lois. "Chaucer's Monogram and the 'Hoccleve Portrait' Tradition." *Word & Image* 12 (1996): 127–42.

Brewer, Derek. "Images of Chaucer, 1386–1900." In *Chaucer and Chaucerians*, ed. D. Brewer, 240–70. Alabama: University of Alabama Press, 1966.

Brewer, Thomas. *Memoir of John Carpenter, Town Clerk of London in the Reigns of Henry V and Henry VI*. London: Arthur Taylor, 1836.

Briggs, Charles F. *Giles of Rome's De Regimine Principum*. Cambridge: Cambridge University Press, 1999.

Brosnahan, Leger. "The Pendant in the Chaucer Portraits." *Chaucer Review* 26 (1992): 424–31.

Brown, A. L. "The Authorization of Letters Under the Great Seal." *Bulletin of the Institute of Historical Research* 37 (1964): 125–56.

———. *The Governance of Late Medieval England, 1276–1461*. London: Edward Arnold, 1989.

———. "The Privy Seal Clerks in the Early Fifteenth Century." In *The Study of Medieval Records: Essays in Honour of Kathleen Major*, ed. D. A. Bullough and R. L. Storey, 260–81. Oxford: Oxford University Press, 1971.

———. "The Reign of Henry IV: The establishment of the Lancastrian Regime." In *Fifteenth Century England, 1399–1509: Studies in Politics and Society*, ed. S. B. Chrimes, C. D. Ross, and R. A. Griffiths, 1–28. Manchester: Manchester University Press, 1972.

Brown-Grant, Rosalind. "*L'Avision Christine*: Autobiographical Narrative or Mirror for the Prince?" In *Politics, Gender, and Genre: The Political Thought of Christine de Pizan*, ed. Margaret Brabant and Jean-Bethke Elshtain, 95–111. Boulder, Colo.: Westview, 1992.

Brownlee, Kevin. "Discourses of the Self: Christine de Pizan and the *Romance of the Rose*." In *Rethinking the Romance of the Rose*, ed. Kevin Brownlee and Sylvia Huot, 234–61. Philadelphia: University of Pennsylvania Press, 1992.

———. "Literary Genealogy and the Problem of the Father: Christine de Pizan and

Dante." In *Dante Now: Current Trends in Dante Studies*, ed. T. J. Cachey, 205–35. William and Katherine Devers Series in Dante Studies, no. 1. Notre Dame: University of Notre Dame Press, 1995.

———. *Poetic Identity in Guillaume de Machaut*. Madison: University of Wisconsin Press, 1984.

———. "Widowhood, Sexuality, and Gender in Christine de Pizan." *Romanic Review* 86 (1995): 339–53.

Bühler, Curt, ed. *The Epistle of Othea*. EETS, 264. London: Oxford University Press, 1970.

Burnley, J. D. "Christine de Pizan and the So-Called *Style Clergial*." *Modern Language Review* 81 (1986): 1–6.

Burrow, John. "Autobiographical Poetry in the Middle Ages: The Case of Thomas Hoccleve." *Proceedings of the British Academy* 68 (1982): 389–412.

———. "Hoccleve and Chaucer." In *Chaucer Traditions: Studies in Honour of Derek Brewer*, ed. Ruth Morse and Barry Windeatt, 54–61. Cambridge: Cambridge University Press, 1990.

———. "Hoccleve and the Middle French Poets." In *The Long Fifteenth Century: Essays for Douglas Gray*, ed. Helen Cooper and Sally Mapstone, 35–49. Oxford: Clarendon Press, 1997.

———. "Hoccleve's *Complaint* and Isidore of Seville Again." *Speculum* 73 (1998): 424–28.

———. "Hoccleve's *Series*: Experience and Books." In *Fifteenth Century Studies: Recent Essays*, ed. R. F. Yeager, 259–74. Hamden: Archon Books, 1984.

———. "The Poet and the Book." In *Genres, Themes, and Images in English Literature: The J.A.W. Bennet Memorial Lectures, Perugia, 1986*, ed. Piero Boitani and Anna Torti, 230–45. Tübingen: Gunter Narr, 1988.

———. "The Poet as Petitioner." *Studies in the Age of Chaucer* 3 (1981): 61–75.

———. *Thomas Hoccleve*. Authors of the Middle Ages. Aldershot: Variorum, 1994.

———. "Thomas Hoccleve: Some Redatings." *Review of English Studies* 46 (1995): 366–72.

———, ed. *Thomas Hoccleve's Complaint and Dialogue*. EETS, OS, 313. Oxford: Oxford University Press, 1999.

Calin, William. *The French Tradition and the Literature of Medieval England*. Toronto: University of Toronto Press, 1994.

Camargo, Martin. *Ars Dictaminis, Ars Dictandi*. Typologie des sources du Moyen Âge occidental. Turnhout: Brepols, 1991.

———. *The Middle English Verse Love Epistle*. Studien zur englischen Philologie, neue Folge, Bd. 28. Tübingen: Max Niemeyer, 1991.

Camille, Michael. *Images on the Edge: The Margins of Medieval Art*. Cambridge, Mass.: Harvard University Press, 1992.

Campbell, P. G. C. "Christine de Pizan en Angleterre." *Revue de littérature comparée* 5 (1925): 659–70.

Cannon, Christopher. *The Making of Chaucer's English: A Study of Words*. Cambridge: Cambridge University Press, 1998.

Carlson, David R. "Thomas Hoccleve and the Chaucer Portrait." *Huntington Library Quarterly* 54 (1991): 283–300.

Bibliography

Catto, Jeremy. "The King's Servants." In *King Henry V: The Practice of Kingship*, ed. G. L. Harris, 75–96. Oxford: Oxford University Press, 1985.

———. "Religious Change Under Henry V." In *King Henry V: The Practice of Kingship*, ed. G. L. Harris, 97–116. Oxford: Oxford University Press, 1985.

Cerquiglini, Jacqueline. "Le clerc et l'écriture: Le *Voir Dit* de Guillaume de Machaut et la définition du dit." In *Literatur in der Gesellschaft des Spätmittelalters*, ed. Hans Ulrich Gumbrecht, 151–68. Grundriss der romanischen Literaturen des Mittelalters, 1. Heidelberg: Carl Winter Universitätsverlag, 1980.

———. "Trials of Eros." In *A New History of French Literature*, ed. D. Hollier, 114–18. Cambridge, Mass.: Harvard University Press, 1989.

Chance, Jane. "Christine de Pizan as Literary Mother: Women's Authority and Subjectivity in 'The Floure and the Leafe' and 'The Assembly of Ladies.'" In *The City of Scholars: New Approaches to Christine de Pizan*, ed. Margarete Zimmerman and Dina de Rentiis, 245–59. Berlin: Walter de Gruyter, 1994.

———. "Christine's Minerva, the Mother Valorized." In *Letter of Othea to Hector*, ed. Jane Chance. Newburyport, Mass.: Focus Information Group, 1990.

———. "Gender Trouble in the Garden of Deduit: Christine de Pizan Translating the Rose." *Romance Languages Annual* 4 (1992): 20–28.

Chaplais, Pierre. *English Royal Documents: King John-Henry IV, 1199–1461*. Oxford: Clarendon Press, 1971.

Cheney, C. R. *Notaries Public in England in the Thirteenth and Fourteenth Centuries*. Oxford: Clarendon Press, 1972.

Chrimes, S. B. *Introduction to the Administrative History of England*. Oxford: Basil Blackwell, 1966.

Clanchy, Michael T. *From Memory to Written Record, England 1066–1307*. 1979. 2d ed. Cambridge, Mass.: Harvard University Press, 1993.

Classen, Albrecht. "The Autobiographical Voice of Thomas Hoccleve." *Archiv für das Studium der neueren Sprachen und Literaturen* 228 (1991): 299–310.

———. "Hoccleve's Independence from Chaucer: A Study in Poetic Emancipation." *Fifteenth Century Studies* 15 (1990): 59–81.

———. "Love and Marriage in Late Medieval Verse: Oswald von Wolkenstein, Thomas Hoccleve and Michel Beheim." *Studia Neophilologica* 62 (1990): 163–88.

Coleman, Christopher, and David Starkey, eds. *Revolution Reassessed: Revisions in the History of Tudor Government and Administration*. Oxford: Oxford University Press, 1986.

Constable, Giles. *Letters and Letter-Collections*. Typologie des sources du Moyen Âge occidental. Turnhout: Brepols, 1976.

Copeland, Rita. *Rhetoric, Hermeneutics and Translation in the Middle Ages*. Cambridge: Cambridge University Press, 1991.

Cowen, Janet. "Women as Exempla in Fifteenth Century Verse of the Chaucerian Tradition." In *Chaucer and Fifteenth-Century Poetry*, ed. Julia Boffey and Janet Cowen, 51–65. London: King's College London, Centre for Late Antique and Medieval Studies, 1991.

Crabbe, Anna. "Literary Design in the *De Consolatione Philosophiae*." In *Boethius: His Life, Thought, and Influence*, ed. M. T. Gibson, 237–77. Oxford: Blackwell, 1981.

Cropp, Glynnis. "Boèce et Christine de Pizan." *Le Moyen Age* 87 (1981): 387–417.

Curtius, Ernst Robert. *European Literature and the Latin Middle Ages*. Translated by Willard R. Trask. 1953. Reprint, London: Routledge and Kegan Paul, 1979).

Cuttino, G. P. "King's Clerks and the Community of the Realm." *Speculum* 29 (1954): 395–409.

Delany, Sheila. "History, Politics, and Christine Studies: A Polemical Reply." In *Politics, Gender, and Genre: The Political Thought of Christine de Pizan*, ed. Margaret Brabant and Jean-Bethke Elshtain, 193–206. Boulder, Colo.: Westview, 1992.

———. " 'Mothers to Think Back Through': Who Are They? The Ambiguous Example of Christine de Pizan." In *Medieval Literary Politics: Shapes of Ideology*. Manchester: Manchester University Press, 1990.

———. "Rewriting Woman Good: Gender and the Anxiety of Influence in Two Late-Medieval Texts." In *Medieval Literary Politics: Shapes of Ideology*. Manchester: Manchester University Press, 1990.

De Looze, Laurence. *Pseudo-Autobiography in the Fourteenth Century: Juan Ruiz, Guillaume de Machaut, Jean Froissart, and Geoffrey Chaucer*. Gainesville: University of Florida Press, 1997.

Deschaux, Robert. "La Complainte." In *La Littérature française au XIVe et XVe siècles*, ed. D. Poirion, 77–85. Grundriss der romanischen Literaturen des Mittelalters, VIII/I. Heidelberg: C. Winter Universitätsverlag, 1988.

Desmond, Marilyn, ed. *Christine de Pizan and the Categories of Difference*. Minneapolis: University of Minnesota Press, 1998.

Doob, Penelope B. R. *Nebuchadnezzar's Children: Conventions of Madness in Middle English Literature*. New Haven: Yale University Press, 1974.

Doyle, A. I. "English Books In and Out of Court from Edward III to Henry IV." In *English Court Culture in the Later Middle Ages*, ed. V. J. Scattergood and J. W. Sherborne, 163–203. London: Gerald Duckworth, 1983.

Doyle, A. I., and M. B. Parkes. "The Production of Copies of the *Canterbury Tales* and the *Confessio Amantis* in the Early Fifteenth Century." In *Medieval Scribes, Manuscripts, and Libraries: Essays Presented to N. R. Ker*, ed. M. B. Parkes and A. G. Watson, 163–81. London: Scholar Press, 1978.

Dronke, Peter. *The Medieval Lyric*. 1968. 2d ed. Cambridge: D. S. Brewer, 1996.

Duffy, Eamon. *The Stripping of the Altars: Traditional Religion in England, 1400–1580*. New Haven: Yale University Press, 1992.

Eberle, Patricia J. "The Politics of Courtly Style at the Court of Richard II." In *The Spirit of the Court: Selected Proceedings of the Fourth Congress of the International Courtly Literature Society*, ed. Glyn S. Burgess and Robert A. Taylor, 168–78. Cambridge: D. S. Brewer, 1985.

Ebin, Lois. *Illuminator, Makar, Vates: Visions of Poetry in the Fifteenth Century*. Lincoln: University of Nebraska Press, 1988.

Edmond, Mary. "Thomas Hoccleve: Some Redatings." *Review of English Studies* 46 (1995): 366–72.

Edwards, A. S. G. "The Chaucer Portraits in the Harley and Rosenbach Manuscripts." In *English Manuscript Studies, 1100–1700*, vol. 4, ed. Peter Beal and Jeremy Griffiths, 268–71. London: British Library, 1993.

———. "Hoccleve's *Regiment of Princes*: A Further Manuscript." *Edinburgh Bibliographical Society Transactions* 5 (1978): 32.

Edwards, A. S. G., and Derek Pearsall. "The Manuscripts of the Major English Poetical Texts." In *Book Production and Publishing in Britain, 1375–1475*, ed. Jeremy Griffiths and Derek Pearsall, 257–78. Cambridge: Cambridge University Press, 1989.

Ellis, Roger. "Chaucer, Christine de Pizan, and *The Letter of Cupid*." In *Essays on Thomas Hoccleve*, ed. C. Batt, 29–54. Westfield Publications in Medieval Studies. London: Centre for Medieval and Renaissance Studies, Queen Mary and Westfield College, University of London, 1996.

Fenster, Thelma. "Did Christine Have a Sense of Humor? The Evidence of the 'Epistre au dieu d'Amours.' " In *Reinterpreting Christine de Pizan*, ed. E. J. Richards, 23–36. Athens: University of Georgia Press, 1992.

Fenster, Thelma A., and Mary Carpenter Erler, eds. *Poems of Cupid, God of Love*. Leiden: E. J. Brill, 1990.

Ferster, Judith. *Fictions of Advice: The Literature and Politics of Counsel in Late Medieval England*. Philadelphia: University of Pennsylvania Press, 1996.

Fisher, John. "Chancery and the Emergence of Standard Written English in the Fifteenth Century." *Speculum* 52 (1977): 870–99. Reprinted in *The Emergence of Standard English*. Lexington: University of Kentucky Press, 1996.

———. *John Gower: Moral Philosopher and Friend of Chaucer*. New York: New York University Press, 1964.

———. "A Language Policy for Lancastrian England." *PMLA* 107 (1992): 1168–80. Reprinted in *The Emergence of Standard English*. Lexington: University of Kentucky Press, 1996.

Fleming, John. "Hoccleve's 'Letter of Cupid' and the 'Quarrel' over the *Roman de la Rose*." *Medium Aevum* 40 (1971): 21–40.

———. "Jean de Meun and the Ancient Poets." In *Rethinking the Romance of the Rose*, ed. Kevin Brownlee and Sylvia Huot, 81–100. Philadelphia: University of Pennsylvania Press, 1992.

Foucault, Michel. "Nietzche, Genealogy, History." In *Language, Counter-Memory, Practice: Selected Essays and Interviews*, ed. Donald F. Bouchard, 139–64. Ithaca: Cornell University Press, 1977.

———. "What Is an Author?" In *Language, Counter-Memory, Practice: Selected Essays and Interviews*, ed. Donald F. Bouchard, 113–38. Ithaca: Cornell University Press, 1977.

Fowler, David C., Charles F. Briggs, and Paul G. Remley. *The Governance of Kings and Princes: John Trevisa's Middle English Translation of the De Regimine Principum of Aegidius Romanus*. Garland Medieval Texts. New York: Garland, 1997.

Fox, Denton. "Chaucer's Influence on Fifteenth-Century Poetry." In *Companion to Chaucer Studies*, ed. B. Rowland, 385–402. Toronto: Oxford University Press, 1968.

Fradenburg, Louise O. "The Manciple's Servant Tongue: Politics and Poetry in the *Canterbury Tales*." *English Literary History* 52 (1985): 85–118.

———. " 'Voice, Memorial': Loss and Reparation in Chaucer's Poetry." *Exemplaria* 2 (1990): 169–202.

Fraenkel, Béatrice. *La Signature: Genèse d'un signe*. Paris: Gallimard, 1992.

Furnivall, F. J., ed. *Hoccleve's Works, 3: The Regement of Princes, and Fourteen of Hoccleve's Minor Poems from the Egerton MS. 615*. EETS, ES 72. London: Oxford University Press, 1892.

Furnivall, F. J., and I. Gollancz, eds. *Hoccleve's Works: The Minor Poems in the Phillipps MS. 8151, the Durham ms.III.9, and Ashburnham MS. Additional 133*. EETS, ES 61. London: Oxford University Press, 1892. Revised by A. I. Doyle and J. Mitchell, 1970.

Galbraith, V. H. *The St. Albans Chronicle, 1406–1420*. Oxford: Clarendon Press, 1937.

Galloway, Andrew. "Private Selves and the Intellectual Marketplace in Late Fourteenth-Century England: The Case of the Two Usks." *New Literary History* 28 (1997): 291–318.

Gaunt, Simon. *Gender and Genre in Medieval French Literature*. Cambridge: Cambridge University Press, 1995.

Gaylord, Alan T. "Portrait of a Poet." In *The Ellesmere Chaucer: Essays in Interpretation*, ed. Martin Stevens and Daniel Woodward, 121–42. San Marino: Huntington Library, 1995.

Genet, Jean-Philippe. "Ecclesiastics and Political Theory in Late Medieval England: The End of a Monopoly." In *The Church, Politics, and Patronage in the Fifteenth Century*, ed. R. B. Dobson, 23–44. Gloucester: Alan Sutton Publishing, 1984.

———, ed. *Four English Political Tracts of the Later Middle Ages*. Camden Fourth Series, 18. London: Royal Historical Society, 1977.

Geremek, Bronislaw. *The Margins of Society in Late Medieval Paris*. Translated by Jean Birrell. Cambridge: Cambridge University Press, 1987.

Gilbert, Allen H. *Machiavelli's Prince and Its Forerunners*. Durham: Duke University Press, 1938.

———. "Notes on the Influence of the *Secretum Secretorum*." *Speculum* 3 (1928): 84–98.

Goldie, Matthew Boyd. "Psychosomatic Illness and Identity in London, 1416–1421: Hoccleve's *Complaint* and *Dialogue with a Friend*," *Exemplaria* 11 (1999): 23–52.

Gransden, Antonia. *Historical Writing in England, II, c. 1307 to the Early Sixteenth Century*. Ithaca: Cornell University Press, 1982.

Gray, Douglas. *Themes and Images in the Medieval English Religious Lyric*. London: Routledge and Kegan Paul, 1972.

Green, Richard Firth. "Chaucer's Victimized Women." *Studies in the Age of Chaucer* 10 (1988): 3–21.

———. "The *Familia Regis* and the *Familia Cupidinis*." In *English Court Culture in the Later Middle Ages*, ed. V. J. Scattergood and J. W. Sherborne, 87–108. London: Gerald Duckworth, 1983.

———. "Notes on some MSS of Hoccleve's *Regiment of Princes*." *The British Library Journal* 4 (1978): 37–41.

———. *Poets and Princepleasers: Literature and the English Court in the Later Middle Ages*. Toronto: University of Toronto, 1980.

———. "Three Fifteenth-Century Notes." *English Language Notes* 14 (1976–77): 14–17.

Greetham, D. C. "Challenges of Theory and Practice in the Editing of Hoccleve's *Regement of Princes*." In *Manuscripts and Texts: Editorial Problems in Later Middle English Literature*, ed. D. Pearsall, 60–86. Cambridge: D. S. Brewer, 1987.

———. "Self-Referential Artifacts: Hoccleve's Persona as a Literary Device." *Modern Philology* 86 (1989): 242–51.

Griffiths, R. A. "Public and Private Bureaucracies in England and Wales in the Fifteenth Century." *Transactions of the Royal Historical Society*, 5th ser., 30 (1980): 109–30.

Hagel, Günter. *Thomas Hoccleve: Leben und Werk eines Schriftstellers im England des Spätmittelalters*. Frankfurt: Peter Lang, 1984.

Hammond, Eleanor P., ed. *English Verse Between Chaucer and Surrey*. Durham: Duke University Press, 1927.

Hansen, Elaine Tuttle. *Chaucer and the Fictions of Gender*. Berkeley and Los Angeles: University of California Press, 1992.

Harris, Kate. "The Patron of British Library MS Arundel 38." *Notes and Queries* 31 (1984): 462–63.

Harriss, G. L. *King Henry V: The Practice of Kingship*. Oxford: Oxford University Press, 1985.

———. "Medieval Government and Statecraft." *Past and Present* 25 (1963): 8–39.

Hasler, Antony. "Hoccleve's Unregimented Body." *Paragraph* 13 (1990): 164–83.

Herrtage, Sidney J. H., ed. *The Early English Versions of the Gesta Romanorum*. EETS, ES 33. London: Oxford University Press, 1967.

Hicks, Eric, ed. *Le débat sur la "Roman de la Rose."* Paris: Champion, 1977.

Hindman, Sandra. "The Composition of the Manuscript of Christine de Pizan's Collected Works in the British Library: A Reassessment." *British Library Journal* 9 (1983): 93–123.

———. "With Ink and Mortar: Christine de Pizan's *Cité des Dames*: An Art Essay." *Feminist Studies* 10 (1984): 457–84.

Hudson, Anne. *The Premature Reformation: Wycliffite Texts and Lollard History*. Oxford: Clarendon Press, 1988.

Hornsby, Joseph. "Clipped Coins and Heresy: Thomas Hoccleve's Poetics and the Lancastrian Law of Treason." In *Law in Mediaeval Life and Thought*, 217–30. Sewanee Medieval Studies, no. 5. Sewanee: The Press of the University of the South, 1990.

Hulbert, J. R. "An Hoccleve Item." *Modern Language Notes* 36 (1921): 59.

Huot, Sylvia. "Seduction and Sublimation: Christine de Pizan, Jean de Meun, and Dante." *Romance Notes* 25 (1985): 361–73.

———. *From Song to Book: The Poetics of Writing in Old French Lyric and Lyrical Narrative Poetry*. Ithaca: Cornell University Press, 1987.

Ingram, Elizabeth. "Thomas Hoccleve and Guy de Rouclif." *Notes and Queries* 218 (1973): 42–43.

Irvine, Martin. *The Making of Textual Culture: "Grammatica" and Literary Theory, 350–1100*. Cambridge: Cambridge University Press, 1994.

Jackson, Stanley W. "Galen—On Mental Disorders." *Journal of the History of the Behavioral Sciences* 5 (1969): 365–84.

———. "Unusual Mental States in Medieval Europe. I. Medical Symptoms of Mental Disorder, 400–1100 A.D." *Journal of the History of Medicine* 27 (1972): 262–97.

———. *Melancholia and Depression: From Hippocratic Times to Modern Times*. New Haven: Yale University Press, 1986.

Jacob, E. F. *The Fifteenth Century*. Oxford History of England. 1961. Reprint, Oxford: Oxford University Press, 1969.

Jardine, Lisa. *Erasmus, Man of Letters: The Construction of Charisma in Print*. Princeton: Princeton University Press, 1993.

Jefferson, Judith A. "The Hoccleve Holographs and Hoccleve's Metrical Practice." In

Manuscripts and Texts: Editorial Problems in Later Middle English Literature, ed. D. Pearsall, 95–109. Cambridge: D. S. Brewer, 1987.

Jones, W. R. "Lollards and Images: The Defense of Religious Art in Later Medieval England." *Journal of the History of Ideas* 34 (1973): 27–50.

Justice, Steven. "Inquisition, Speech, and Writing: A Case from Late Medieval Norwich." In *Criticism and Dissent in the Middle Ages*, ed. R. Copeland, 289–322. Cambridge: Cambridge University Press, 1996.

———. *Writing and Rebellion: England in 1381*. Berkeley and Los Angeles: University of California Press, 1994.

Keen, Maurice. *English Society in the Later Middle Ages, 1348–1500*. London: Penguin Books, 1990.

Kellaway, William. "John Carpenter's *Liber Albus*." *Guildhall Studies in London History* 3 (1978): 67–84.

Kerby-Fulton, Kathryn. "Langland and the Bibliographical Ego." In *Written Work: Langland, Labor, and Authorship*, ed. Steven Justice and Kathryn Kerby-Fulton, 67–143. Philadephia: University of Pennsylvania Press, 1997.

Kerby-Fulton, Kathryn, and Steven Justice. "Langlandian Reading Circles and the Civil Service in London and Dublin, 1380–1427." *New Medieval Literatures* 1 (1997): 59–83.

———. "Reformist Intellectual Culture in the English and Irish Civil Service: The *Modus Tenendi Parliamentum* and Its Literary Relations." *Traditio* 53 (1998): 149–202.

Kimmelman, Burt. *The Poetics of Authorship in the Later Middle Ages: The Emergence of the Modern Literary Persona*. Studies in the Humanities: Literature, Politics, Society, 21. New York: Peter Lang, 1996.

King, Pamela M. "Chaucer, Chaucerians, and the Theme of Poetry." In *Chaucer and Fifteenth Century Poetry*, ed. Julia Boffey and Janet Cowen, 1–14. Exeter: Short Run Press, 1991.

Kingsford, C. J. "London in the Fifteenth Century." In *Prejudice and Promise in the Fifteenth Century*. 1925. Reprint, Oxford: Oxford University Press, 1962.

Kirby, J. L. "An Account of Robert Southwell, Receiver-General of John Mowbray, Earl Marshall, 1422–23." *Bulletin of the Institute of Historical Research* 27 (1954): 196.

Kohl, Stephen. "More Than Virtues and Vices: Self-Analysis in Hoccleve's Autobiographies." *Fifteenth Century Studies* 14 (1988): 115–27.

Koopmans, Jelle, and Paul Verhuyck. *Sermon Joyeux et Truanderie (Villon–Nemo–Ulespiègle)*. Amsterdam: Rodopi, 1987.

Krochalis, Jeanne E. "Hoccleve's Chaucer Portrait." *Chaucer Review* 21 (1986): 234–45.

Kurath, Hans, Sherman M. Kuhn, John Reidy, and Robert E. Lewis, eds. *Middle English Dictionary*. Ann Arbor: University of Michigan Press, 1952.

Kurtz, Benjamin P. "The Relation of Occleve's *Learn to Die* to Its Source." *PMLA* 40 (1925): 252–75.

———. "The Prose of Occleve's *Learn to Die*." *Modern Language Notes* 39 (1924): 56–57.

———. "The Source of Occleve's *Learn to Die*." *Modern Language Notes* 38 (1923): 337–40.

Laidlaw, J. C. "Christine de Pizan, the Earl of Salisbury and Henry IV." *French Studies* 36 (1982): 129–43.

―――, ed. *The Poetical Works of Alain Chartier*. London: Cambridge University Press, 1974.

Laird, Judith. "Good Women and Bonnes Dames: Virtuous Females in Chaucer and Christine de Pizan." *Chaucer Review* 30 (1995): 58–70.

Lander, J. R. *Conflict and Stability in Fifteenth-Century England*. London: Hutchinson University Library, 1969.

Lawton, David. "Analytical Survey I: Literary History and Cultural Study." *New Medieval Literatures* 1 (1997): 237–69.

―――. *Chaucer's Narrators*. Chaucer Studies, 13. Cambridge: D. S. Brewer, 1985.

―――. "Dullness and the Fifteenth Century." *English Literary History* 54 (1987): 761–99.

Legge, M. Dominica. *Anglo-Norman Letters and Petitions*. Oxford: Basil Blackwell, 1941.

Lerer, Seth. *Boethius and Dialogue: Literary Method in the Consolation of Philosophy*. Princeton: Princeton University Press, 1985.

―――. *Chaucer and His Readers: Imagining the Author in Late-Medieval England*. Princeton: Princeton University Press, 1993.

Lewis, C. S. *The Allegory of Love*. Oxford: Oxford University Press, 1936.

Lindberg, David C. "Medieval Latin Theories of the Speed of Light." In *Studies in the History of Medieval Optics*. 1978. Reprint, London: Variorum Reprints, 1983.

―――. *Theories of Vision from Al-Kindi to Kepler*. Chicago: University of Chicago Press, 1976.

Lindenbaum, Sheila. "London Texts and Literate Practice." In *The Cambridge History of Medieval English Literature*, ed. David Wallace, 284–309. Cambridge: Cambridge University Press, 1999.

Lochrie, Karma. *Covert Operations: The Medieval Uses of Secrecy*. Philadelphia: University of Pennsylvania Press, 1999.

Lovatt, Roger. "Henry Suso and the Medieval Mystical Tradition in England." In *The Medieval Mystical Tradition in England*, ed. M. Glasscoe, 47–62. Exeter: Exeter University Press, 1982.

Machan, Tim William. "Textual Authority and the Works of Hoccleve, Lydgate, and Henryson." *Viator* 23 (1992): 281–99.

MacLennan, George. *Lucid Intervals: Subjective Writing and Madness in History*. Rutherford: Fairleigh Dickinson University Press, 1992.

Manzalaoui, M. A., ed. *Secretum Secretorum: Nine English Versions*. EETS, OS, 276. Oxford: Oxford University Press, 1977.

Margolis, Nadia. "The Human Prison: The Metamorphoses of Misery in the Poetry of Christine de Pizan, Charles d'Orleans, and Francois Villon." *Fifteenth-Century Studies* 1 (1978): 185–92.

Markus, Manfred. "Truth, Fiction and Metafiction in Fifteenth-Century English Literature, Particularly in Lydgate and Hoccleve." *Fifteenth-Century Studies* 8 (1983): 117–39.

Marzec, Marcia Smith. "The Latin Marginalia of the *Regiment of Princes* as an Aid to Stemmatic Analysis." *Text* 3 (1987): 269–84.

―――. "Scribal Emendations in Some Later Manuscripts of Hoccleve's *Regiment of Princes*." *Analytical and Enumerative Bibliography* 1 (1987): 41–51.

Mathew, Gervase. *The Court of Richard II*. London: John Murray, 1968.

Matthews, William. "Thomas Hoccleve: Commentary and Bibliography." In *A Manual of Writings in Middle English: 1050–1500*, ed. A. E. Hartung, 3: 746–56, 903–8. New Haven: Connecticut Academy of Arts and Sciences, 1972.

McFarlane, K. B. "Father and Son." In *Lancastrian Kings and Lollard Knights*. Oxford: Clarendon Press, 1972.

McGregor, James. "The Iconography of Chaucer in Hoccleve's *De Regimine Principum* and in the *Troilus* Frontispiece." *Chaucer Review* 11 (1976): 338–50.

McKinley, Mary. "The Subversive 'Seulette.'" In *Politics, Gender and Genre: The Political Thought of Christine de Pizan*, ed. Margaret Brabant and Jean-Bethke Elshtain, 157–69. Boulder: Westview, 1992.

McLeod, Glenda K. "A Case of *faux semblans:* 'L'Epistre au dieu d'amours' and 'The Letter of Cupid.'" In *The Reception of Christine de Pizan from the Fifteenth Through the Nineteenth Centuries: Visitors to the City*, ed. G. K. McLeod, 11–24. Lewiston, N.Y.: Mellen, 1991.

McMillan, Douglas J. "The Single Most Popular of Thomas Hoccleve's Poems: *The Regement of Princes*." *Neuphilologische Mittelungen* 89 (1988): 63–71.

McNiven, Peter. *Heresy and Politics in the Reign of Henry IV: The Burning of John Badby*. Woodbridge: Boydell and Brewer, 1987.

———. "Prince Henry and the Political Crisis of 1412." *History* 65 (1980): 1–16.

Medcalf, Stephen, ed. *The Later Middle Ages*. New York: Holmes and Meier, 1981.

Middleton, Anne. "Acts of Vagrancy: The C Version 'Autobiography' and the Statute of 1388." In *Written Work: Langland, Labor, and Authorship*, ed. Steven Justice and Kathryn Kerby-Fulton, 208–317. Philadelphia: University of Pennsylvania Press, 1997.

———. "Chaucer's 'New Men' and the Good of Literature in the *Canterbury Tales*." In *Literature and Society*, ed. Edward Said, 15–56. English Institute Essays, 3. Baltimore: Johns Hopkins University Press, 1980.

———. "William Langland's 'Kynd Name': Authorial Signature and Social Identity in Late Fourteenth-Century England." In *Literary Practice and Social Change in Britain, 1300–1500*, ed. L. Patterson, 15–82. New Historicism Studies in Cultural Poetics, 8. Berkeley and Los Angeles: University of California Press, 1990.

Mills, David. "The Voices of Thomas Hoccleve." In *Essays on Thomas Hoccleve*, ed. C. Batt, 85–108. Westfield Publications in Medieval Studies. London: Centre for Medieval and Renaissance Studies, Queen Mary and Westfield College, University of London, 1996.

Minnis, Alastair. "Aspects of the Medieval French and English Traditions of the *De Consolatione Philosophiae*." In *Boethius: His Life, Thought, and Influence*, ed. M. T. Gibson, 312–61. Oxford: Blackwell, 1981.

———. "The Author's Two Bodies? Authority and Fallibility in Late Medieval Textual Theory." In *Of the Making of Books: Medieval Manuscripts, Their Scribes and Readers: Essays Presented to M. B. Parkes*, ed. P. R. Robinson and Rivkah Zim, 259–79. Aldershot: Scolar, 1997.

———. *Medieval Theory of Authorship*. Philadelphia: University of Pennsylvania Press, 1988.

Mitchell, Jerome. "Hoccleve's *Minor Poems*: Addenda and Corrigenda." *Edinburgh Bibliographical Society Transactions* 5 (1983): 9–16.

————. "Hoccleve Studies, 1965–1981." In *Fifteenth-Century Studies: Recent Essays*, ed. R. F. Yeager, 49–64. Hamden: Archon Books, 1984.

————. "Hoccleve's Tribute to Chaucer." In *Chaucer und seine Zeit: Symposium für Walter F. Schirmer*, ed. A. Esch, 275–83. Tübingen: Max Niemeyer, 1968.

————. "Thomas Hoccleve: His Traditionalism and His Individuality." Ph.D. diss., Duke University, 1965.

————. *Thomas Hoccleve: A Study in Early Fifteenth-Century Poetic*. Urbana: University of Illinois Press, 1968.

Otway-Ruthven, J. *The King's Secretary and the Signet Office in the Fifteenth Century*. Cambridge: Cambridge University Press, 1939.

Ouy, Gilbert. "Une énigme codicologique: Les signatures des cahiers dans les manuscrits autographes et originaux de Christine de Pisan." In *Calames et cahiers: Mélanges de codicologie et de paléographie offerts à Léon Gilissen*, ed. J. Lemaire and E. van Balberghe, 119–31. Bruxelles: Centre d'étude des manuscrits, 1985.

Parkes, M. B. "The Influence of the Concepts of *Ordinatio* and *Compilatio* on the Development of the Book." In *Medieval Learning and Literature: Essays Presented to R. W. Hunt*, ed. J. G. Alexander and M. T. Gibson, 115–41. Oxford: Oxford University Press, 1975.

Patch, Howard Rollin. *Tradition of Boethius: A Study of His Importance in Medieval Culture*. New York: Oxford University Press, 1935.

Patterson, Lee. *Chaucer and the Subject of History*. Madison: University of Wisconsin Press, 1991.

————. "Making Identities in Fifteenth-Century England: Henry V and Lydgate." In *New Historical Literary Study*, ed. Jeffrey N. Cox and Larry J. Reynolds, 69–107. Princeton: Princeton University Press, 1993.

————. "On the Margin: Postmodernism, Ironic History, and Medieval Studies." *Speculum* 65 (1990): 87–108.

————. "Writing Amorous Wrongs: Chaucer and the Order of the Complaint." In *The Idea of Medieval Literature: New Essays on Chaucer and Medieval Culture in Honor of Donald R. Howard*, ed. James M. Dean and Christian K. Zacher, 55–71. Newark: University of Delaware Press, 1992.

Paupert, Anne. "Le 'Je' lyrique féminin dans l'oeuvre poétique de Christine de Pizan." In *Et c'est la fin pour quoi sommes ensemble: Hommage à Jean Dufournet: Littérature, historie et langue du Moyen Age*, ed. J. Aubailly, 1057–71. Paris: Champion, 1993.

Payne, Robert O. "Late Medieval Images and Self-Images of the Poet: Chaucer, Gower, Lydgate, Henryson, Dunbar." In *Vernacular Poetics in the Middle Ages*, ed. L. Ebin, 249–61. Kalamazoo: Medieval Institute Publications, 1984.

Pearsall, Derek. "English Chaucerians." In *Chaucer and Chaucerians*, ed. D. S. Brewer, 201–39. Alabama: University of Alabama Press, 1966.

————. "Hoccleve's *Regement of Princes*: The Poetics of Royal Self-Representation." *Speculum* 69 (1994): 386–410.

————. *John Lydgate, 1371–1449: A Bio-Bibliography*. ELS Monograph Series, 71. Victoria, B.C.: English Literary Studies, 1997.

————. *The Life of Geoffrey Chaucer: A Critical Biography*. Oxford: Blackwell, 1992.

————. *Old English and Middle English Poetry*. The Routledge History of English Poetry, 1. London: Routledge and Kegan Paul, 1977.

————., ed. *Chaucer to Spenser: An Anthology of Writing in English, 1375–1575*. Oxford: Blackwell, 1999.

Perroy, Edouard, ed. *The Diplomatic Correspondence of Richard II*. Camden 3d ser., 48. London: Royal Historical Society, 1933.

Petroff, Elizabeth Alvida, ed. *Medieval Women's Visionary Literature*. Oxford: Oxford University Press, 1986.

Petrucci, Armando. *Writers and Readers in Medieval Italy: Studies in the History of Written Culture*. Translated by Charles M. Radding. New Haven: Yale University Press, 1995.

Phillippy, Patricia. "Establishing Authority: Boccaccio's *De Claris Mulieribus* and Christine de Pizan's *Le Livre de la Cité des Dames*." *Romanic Review* 77 (1986): 167–93.

Phillips, Heather. "John Wyclif and the Optics of the Eucharist." In *From Ockham to Wyclif*, ed. Anne Hudson and Michael Wilks, 245–58. Oxford: Basil Blackwell, for the Ecclesiastical History Society, 1987.

Pizan, Christine de. *The Book of the City of Ladies*. Translated by Earl Jeffrey Richards. New York: Persea Books, 1982.

Pollard, Alfred W., ed. *Fifteenth-Century Prose and Verse*. Westminster: Archibald Constable and Co., 1903.

Pritchard, V. *English Medieval Graffiti*. Cambridge: Cambridge University Press, 1967.

Pryor, Mary Ruth. "Thomas Hoccleve's *Series*: An Edition of ms Durham Cosin V iii 9." Ph.D. diss., University of California, Los Angeles, 1968.

Quilligan, Maureen. *The Allegory of Female Authority: Christine de Pizan's Cité des Dames*. Ithaca: Cornell University Press, 1991.

————. "The Name of the Author: Self-Representation in Christine de Pizan's *Livre de la Cité des Dames*." *Exemplaria* 4 (1992): 201–28.

Quinn, William. "Hoccleve's 'Epistle of Cupid.' " *Explicator* 45 (1986): 7–10.

Rambuss, Richard. *Spenser's Secret Career*. Cambridge: Cambridge University Press, 1993.

Reeves, A. Compton. "Thomas Hoccleve, Bureaucrat." *Medievalia et Humanistica* 5 (1974): 201–14.

————. "The World of Thomas Hoccleve." *Fifteenth-Century Studies* 2 (1979): 187–99.

Reno, Christine. "Christine de Pizan: Feminism and Irony." In *Seconda miscellanea di studi e ricerche sul Quattrocento francese*, ed. Jonathan Beck and Gianni Mombello, 125–33. Chambéry: Centre d'études franco-italien, 1981.

Richards, Earl Jeffrey. " 'Seullette a part'—The 'Little Woman on the Sidelines' Takes Up Her Pen." In *Dear Sister: Medieval Women and the Epistolary Genre*, ed. Ulrike Withaus and Karen Cherawatuk, 139–70. Philadelphia: University of Pennsylvania Press, 1993.

Richardson, H. G. "Business Training in Medieval Oxford." *American Historical Review* 46 (1941): 259–80.

————. "Letters of the English Dictatores." In *Formularies Which Bear on the History of Oxford, 1204–1420*, ed. H. E. Salter, W. A. Pantin, and H. G. Richardson, 329–449. Oxford Historical Society, n.s., 5. Oxford: Clarendon Press, 1942.

Richardson, Malcolm. "Henry V, the English Chancery, and Chancery English." *Speculum* 55 (1980): 726–50.

————. "Hoccleve in His Social Context." *Chaucer Review* 20 (1986): 313–22.

Rigg, A. G. "Hoccleve's *Complaint* and Isidore of Seville." *Speculum* 45 (1970): 564–74.

Riley, Henry Thomas, ed. *Liber Albus, Compiled 1419*. London: Longman, Brown, Green, Longmans, and Roberts, 1859.

———, ed. *Liber Albus: The White Book of the City of London, Compiled a.d. 1419 by John Carpenter, Common Clerk, and Richard Whitington, Mayor*. Translated by Henry Thomas Riley. London: Richard Griffin, 1861.

Root, Jerry. *"Space to Speke": The Confessional Subject in Medieval Literature*. Romance Languages and Literatures, 225. New York: Peter Lang, 1997.

Sacks, Peter. *The English Elegy: Studies in the Genre from Spenser to Yeats*. Baltimore: Johns Hopkins University Press, 1985.

Salter, Elizabeth. "Chaucer and Internationalism." *Studies in the Age of Chaucer* 2 (1980): 71–79. Reprinted in *English and International: Studies in the Literature, Art, and Patronage of Medieval England*, ed. Derek Pearsall and Nicolette Zeeman, 239–44. Cambridge: Cambridge University Press, 1988.

Sargent, Michael G. "The Transmission by the English Carthusians of Some Late Mediaeval Spiritual Writings." *Journal of Ecclesiastical History* 27 (1976): 225–40.

Saul, Nigel. *Richard II*. New Haven: Yale University Press, 1997.

Scanlon, Larry. "The King's Two Voices: Narrative and Power in Hoccleve's Regement of Princes." In *Literary Practice and Social Change in Britain, 1380–1530*, ed. L. Patterson, 216–47. Berkeley and Los Angeles: University of California Press, 1990.

———. *Narrative, Authority and Power: The Medieval Exemplum and the Chaucerian Tradition*. Cambridge: Cambridge University Press, 1994.

Scase, Wendy. "Reginald Pecock, John Carpenter, and John Colop's 'Common-Profit' Books: Aspects of Book Ownership and Circulation in Fifteenth-Century London." *Medium Aevum* 61 (1992): 261–74.

Scattergood, John. "Chaucer in the Suburbs." In *Medieval Literature and Antiquities: Studies in Honor of Basil Cottle*, ed. Myra Stokes and T. L. Burton, 145–62. Cambridge: D. S. Brewer, 1987.

———. "Literary Culture in the Court of Richard II." In *English Court Culture in the Middle Ages*, ed. V. J. Scattergood and J. W. Sherborne, 29–43. London: Gerald Duckworth, 1983.

———. *Politics and Poetry in the Fifteenth Century*. London: Blandford Press, 1971.

Schulz, H. C. "Thomas Hoccleve, Scribe." *Speculum* 12 (1937): 71–81.

Seymour, M. C. "Manuscript Portraits of Chaucer and Hoccleve." *Burlington Magazine* 124 (1982): 618–23.

———. "The Manuscripts of Hoccleve's *Regiment of Princes*." *Transactions of the Edinburgh Bibliographical Society* 4 (1974): 255–97.

———, ed. *Selections from Hoccleve*. Oxford: Clarendon Press, 1981.

Simpson, James. "Madness and Texts: Hoccleve's *Series*." In *Chaucer and Fifteenth-Century Poetry*, ed. Julia Boffey and Janet Cowen, 15–29. London: King's College London Centre for Late Antique and Medieval Studies, 1991.

———. "Nobody's Man: Thomas Hoccleve's *Regiment of Princes*." In *London and Europe in the Late Middle Ages*, ed. Julia Boffey and Pamela King, 149–80. London: Centre for Medieval and Renaissance Studies, Queen Mary and Westfield College, University of London, 1995.

Smalley, Beryl. *English Friars and Antiquity in the Early Fourteenth Century*. Oxford: Basil Blackwell, 1960.

Solterer, Helen. "Flaming Words: Verbal Violence and Gender in Premodern Paris." *Romanic Review* 86 (1995): 355–78.

———. *The Master and Minerva: Disputing Women in French Medieval Culture*. Berkeley and Los Angeles: University of California Press, 1995.

Somerset, Fiona. *Clerical Discourse and Lay Audience in Late Medieval England*. Cambridge: Cambridge University Press, 1998.

Spacks, Patricia Meyer. *Gossip*. New York: Knopf, 1985.

Spearing, A. C. *Medieval to Renaissance in English Poetry*. Cambridge: Cambridge University Press, 1985.

———. "The Poetic Subject from Chaucer to Spenser." In *Subjects on the World's Stage: Essays on British Literature of the Middle Ages and the Renaissance*, ed. David C. Allen and Robert A. White, 13–37. Newark: University of Delaware Press, 1995.

Spriggs, Gereth M. "Unnoticed Bodleian Manuscripts, Illuminated by Herman Scheerre and His School." *Bodleian Library Record* 7 (1962): 193–203.

Spurgeon, Caroline. *Five Hundred Years of Chaucer Criticism and Allusion, 1357–1900*. 1. Cambridge: Cambridge University Press, 1925.

Stern, Walter M. "The Company of Watermen and Lightermen of the City of London: The Earliest London Transport Executive." *Guildhall Studies in English History* 5 (1981): 36–41.

Stock, Brian. *The Implications of Literacy: Written Language and Models of Interpretation in the Eleventh and Twelfth Centuries*. Princeton: Princeton University Press, 1983.

———. *Listening for the Text*. Baltimore: The Johns Hopkins University Press, 1990.

Stokes, Charity Scott. "Thomas Hoccleve's *Mother of God* and *Balade to the Virgin and Christ*: Latin and Anglo-Norman Sources." *Medium Aevum* 64 (1995): 74–84.

Storey, Robin L. "Gentleman-Bureaucrats." In *Profession, Vocation, and Culture in Later Medieval England*, ed. C. H. Clough, 90–129. Liverpool: Liverpool University Press, 1982.

Strohm, Paul. "Chaucer's Fifteenth-Century Audience and the Narrowing of the 'Chaucer Tradition.'" *Studies in the Age of Chaucer* 4 (1982): 3–32.

———. *England's Empty Throne: Usurpation and the Language of Legitimation, 1399–1422*. New Haven: Yale University Press, 1998.

———. "Fourteenth- and Fifteenth-Century Writers as Readers of Chaucer." In *Genres, Themes and Images in English Literature from the Fourteenth to the Fifteenth Century: The J. A. W. Bennett Memorial Lectures, Perugia, 1986*, ed. Piero Boitani and Anna Torti, 3–32. Tübingen: Gunter Narr, 1988.

———. *Sir John Oldcastle: Another Ill-framed Knight*. William Matthews Lectures. London: Birkbeck College, 1997.

Sullivan, Karen. "At the Limit of Feminist Theory: An Architectonics of the *Querelle de la Rose*." *Exemplaria* 3 (1991): 435–66.

Summit, Jennifer. *Lost Property: The Woman Writer and English Literary History, 1380–1589*. Chicago: University of Chicago Press, 2000.

Suso, Henry. *Wisdom's Watch upon the Hours*. Translated by Edmund Colledge. The Fathers of the Church: Medieval Continuation. Washington, D.C.: Catholic University of America Press, 1994.

Tachau, Katherine H. *Vision and Certitude in the Age of Ockham: Optics, Epistemology, and the Foundations of Semantics, 1250–1345*. Studien und Texte zur Geistesgeschichte des Mittelalters. Leiden: E. J. Brill, 1988.

Tachau, Katherine H., and Paul A. Streveler, eds. *Seeing the Future Clearly: Questions on Future Contingents by Robert Holcot*. Series and Texts, 119. Toronto: Pontifical Institute of Medieval Studies, 1995.

Thornley, Eva M. "The Middle English Penitential Lyric and Hoccleve's Autobiographical Poetry." *Neuphilologische Mitteilungen* 68 (1967): 295–321.

Tolmie, Sarah. "The *Prive Scilence* of Thomas Hoccleve." *Studies in the Age of Chaucer* 22 (2000): 281–309.

Torti, Anna. "Hoccleve's Attitude Towards Women: 'I shoop me do my peyne and diligence/ To wynne hir loue by obedience.'" In *A Wyf Ther Was: Essays in Honour of Paule Mertens-Fonck*, ed. J. Dor, 264–74. Liège: Université de Liège, 1992.

———. "Specular Narrative: Hoccleve's *Regement of Princes*." In *The Glass of Form: Mirroring Structures from Chaucer to Skelton*, 87–106. Cambridge: D. S. Brewer, 1991.

Tout, T. F. "The Beginnings of the Modern Capital: London and Westminster in the Fourteenth Century." In *Collected Papers*, 3:249–75. Manchester: Manchester University Press, 1934.

———. *Chapters in the Administrative History of England*. 6 vols. University of Manchester Historical Series, 34–35, 48–49, 57, 64. Manchester: Manchester University Press, 1920–33.

———. "The English Civil Service in the Fourteenth Century." In *Collected Papers*, vol. 3, 191–221. Manchester: Manchester University Press, 1934.

———. "Literature and Learning in the English Civil Service in the Fourteenth Century." *Speculum* 4 (1929): 365–89.

Trudgill, Marian, and J. A. Burrow. "A Hoccleve Balade." *Notes and Queries* 45 (1998): 178–80.

Tuck, J. A. "Richard II's System of Patronage." In *The Reign of Richard II: Essays in Honor of May McKisack*, ed. F. R. H. Du Boulay and C. M. Barron, 1–20. London: Athlone Press, 1971.

Van Oostrom, Frits Pieter. *Court and Culture, Dutch Literature, 1350–1450*. Translated by Arnold J. Pomerans. Berkeley and Los Angeles: University of California Press, 1992.

Vickers, K. H. *Humphrey, Duke of Gloucester*. London: Archibald Constable, 1907.

Von Nolcken, Christina. ""O, why ne had y lerned for to dye?": *Lerne for to Dye* and the Author's Death in Thomas Hoccleve's *Series*." In *Essays in Medieval Studies*, vol. 10, ed. A. J. Frantzen, 27–51. Illinois Medieval Association, 1993.

Walker, Greg. *John Skelton and the Politics of the 1520s*. Cambridge: Cambridge University Press, 1988.

Walker, Simon. "Political Saints in Late Medieval England." In *The McFarlane Legacy: Studies in Late Medieval Politics and Society*, ed. R. H. Britnell and A. J. Pollard, 77–106. New York: St. Martin's Press, 1995.

Wallace, David. "Chaucer and the Absent City." In *Chaucer's England: Literature in Social Context*, ed. B. Hanawalt, 59–90. Minneapolis: University of Minnesota Press, 1992.

Walters, Lori. "Fathers and Daughters: Christine de Pizan as Reader of the Male Tradition of *Clergie* in the *Dit de la Rose*." In *Reinterpreting Christine de Pizan*, ed. E. J. Richards, 63–76. Athens: University of Georgia Press, 1992.

———. "The Woman Writer and Literary History: Christine de Pizan's Redefinition of the Poetic *Translatio* in the *Epistre au dieu d'amours.*" *French Literature Series* 16 (1989): 1–16.

Watson, Nicholas. "Censorship and Cultural Change in Late-Medieval England: Vernacular Theology, the Oxford Translation Debate, and Arundel's *Constitutions.*" *Speculum* 70 (1995): 822–64.

Weatherbee, Winthrop. "Latin Structures and Vernacular Space: Gower, Chaucer, and the Boethian Tradition." In *Chaucer and Gower: Difference, Mutuality, Exchange*, ed. R. F. Yeager, 7–35. Victoria: University of Victoria, 1991.

Weiss, Roberto. *Humanism in England during the Fifteenth Century.* Oxford: Basil Blackwell, 1956.

Willard, Charity Cannon. *Christine de Pizan: Her Life and Works.* New York: Persea, 1984.

———. "A New Look at Christine de Pizan's 'Epistre au Dieu d'Amours.' " In *Seconda miscellanea di studi e ricerche sul Quattrocento francese*, ed. Jonathan Beck and Gianni Mombello, 73–92. Chambéry: Centre d'études franco-italien, 1981.

Winstead, Karen. " 'I am al othir to yow than yee weene': Hoccleve, Women, and the Series." *Philological Quarterly* 72 (1993): 143–55.

———. *Virgin Martyrs: Legends of Sainthood in Late Medieval England.* Ithaca: Cornell University Press, 1997.

Wogan-Browne, Jocelyn, Nicholas Watson, Andrew Taylor, and Ruth Evans, eds. *The Idea of the Vernacular: An Anthology of Middle English Literary Theory, 1280–1520.* University Park: Penn State University Press, 1999.

Woolf, Rosemary. *The English Religious Lyric in the Middle Ages.* Oxford: Clarendon Press, 1968.

Wright, Sylvia. "The Author Portraits in the Bedford Psalter-Hours: Gower, Chaucer, and Hoccleve." *British Library Journal* 18 (1992): 190–201.

Yeager, Robert F. *Fifteenth-Century Studies: Recent Essays.* Hamden: Archon Books, 1984.

Zink, Michel. *The Invention of Literary Subjectivity.* Translated by David Sices. Baltimore: The Johns Hopkins University Press, 1999.

Zumthor, Paul. "Autobiography in the Middle Ages." *Genre* 3 (1973): 29–48.

Index

DATE DUE